THE DIVIDING RHINE:
POLITICS AND SOCIETY
IN CONTEMPORARY
FRANCE AND GERMANY

INTERNATIONAL PERSPECTIVES ON EUROPE
Series Editor: *John Trumpbour*

Volume I, The Dividing Rhine: Politics and Society in
Contemporary France and Germany

In preparation:
Volume II, Portugal, Spain, Italy and Greece
Volume III, Central and Eastern Europe
Volume IV, Britain and Ireland
Volume V, Scandinavia, the Benelux countries, Austria
and Switzerland

THE DIVIDING RHINE:
POLITICS AND SOCIETY
IN CONTEMPORARY
FRANCE AND GERMANY

Edited by
John Trumpbour

BERG
Oxford / New York / Munich

*Distributed exclusively in the US and Canada by
St Martin's Press, New York*

First published in 1989 by
Berg Publishers Limited
Editorial offices:
77 Morrell Avenue, Oxford OX4 1NQ, UK
165 Taber Avenue, Providence, RI 02906, USA
Westermühlstraße 26, 8000 München 5, FRG

British Library Cataloguing in Publication Data

Trumpbour, John
  The dividing Rhine : Politics and society in
contemporary France and Germany.
  1. Europe. Political events, 1945–
  I. Title
  940.55   D1058

ISBN 0 85496 589 0

Library of Congress Cataloging-in-Publication Data

The dividing Rhine : politics and society in contemporary
  France and Germany / edited by John Trumpbour
      p.   cm. – (International perspectives on Europe ; v. 1)
    Bibliography: p.
    Includes index.
    ISBN 0-85496–589–0 : $44.00
    1. Germany (West)—Social conditions. 2. Germany (West)—Politics
and government. 3. France—Social conditions—1945– 4. France—
Politics and government—1945– 5. Germany (East)—Social
conditions. 6. Germany (East)—Politics and government.
I. Trumpbour, John. II. Series.
HN445.5.P65   1989
306'.0943—dc20   89–6568

Printed in Great Britain by
Billings of Worcester

CONTENTS

EDITOR'S STATEMENT

International Perspectives on Europe seeks to provide an annual forum for both critical and mainstream scholarship on selected topics concerning Europe East and West. We hope to fulfill this aim through the following:

1. Publishing historical overviews and provocative essays covering modern and contemporary Europe
2. Encouraging an international debate and discourse, overcoming the insularity and provincialism of even many progressive intellectuals
3. Producing a publication open not only to academic specialists, but also to public intellectuals and journalists
4. Providing selected bibliography and a list of scholarly resources for further information on the topics covered in these volumes

The format of this annual offers a unique opportunity for an international exchange of views and, simultaneously, for the inclusion of commentaries written by critics outside the academic community. On the former point, Perry Anderson has earlier warned of the twentieth-century contraction of radical thought "into national compartments, sealed off from each other by comparative indifference or ignorance." In this opening volume the observations of Mark Poster on French and German intellectual currents and the reflections of Diana Johnstone on the meaning of Munich for these respective societies appear to confirm his view.

It is also worth remarking that some of the best commentary on contemporary Europe is produced by independent intellectuals and journalists, who are often unfairly ignored by university academicians. C. Wright Mills once observed that any intellectual capable of writing for broader publics is apt to be dismissed as a "popularizer" or, worse still, "a mere journalist." The opening volume of *International Perspectives on Europe* features commentary by Daniel Singer and Diana Johnstone, both of whom work loosely in the genre of Isaac Deutscher, among the premier historians of the twentieth century and a journalist for much of his own career. Through an engagement with ideas from such circles, it is hoped that the dominant university intelligentsia will broaden their horizons.

In the first "five-year plan", the annual will develop coverage of Europe in steps: France and Germany in volume 1; Portugal, Spain, Italy, and Greece in volume 2; followed by numbers on 3) Central and Eastern Europe, 4) Britain and Ireland, 5) Scandinavia and the smaller countries of Western Europe: the Benelux countries, Austria, Switzerland, etc. The latter should more than likely provide mounting challenges in the face of demands for European integration slated for 1992.

Those interested in contributing to next year's volume on Portugal, Spain, Italy, and Greece are encouraged to write to John Trumpbour, c/o Department of History, Harvard University, Cambridge, MA 02138.

INTRODUCTION

Two themes dominate the historical landscape of Western Europe in the 1980s: 1) the conservative retrenchment in politics, most palpable through the triumph of Thatcherism in Britain, the Kohl regime in Germany, and the deradicalization of the French Left in power and the growth of a ferociously racist Front National; and 2) the crisis of historical memory, receiving its greatest notoriety in the bogus solemnity of Bitburg, the Klaus Barbie trial in France, and the Waldheim affair in Austria. In contrast to the seeming political stasis in the West, Eastern and Central Europe confronts an epoch of reform and renewal through *glasnost* and *perestroika*, none the less frustrated and resisted by entrenched elites through-out the bloc and, perhaps most significantly, by the most dynamic economic power of the Warsaw Pact, the GDR.

The opening volume of *International Perspectives on Europe* at-tempts to grapple with some of these issues by examining the current political and intellectual state of France and Germany. We begin by exploring the contemporary meanings of two central events in modern European history in the aftermath of their re-spective anniversaries: Munich 1938 and May 1968. In a sense, Munich 1938 is a monument to the perils of historical memory, while May 1968, in retrospect, serves as a signpost to the depth of conservative retrenchment in the 1980s. To begin, the "lessons" of Munich, suggests Diana Johnstone, are not only instructive for understanding the use and abuse of history by conservative political forces, but also by the Left, which in France has accepted many of the key right-wing shibboleths concerning this signal episode of

1

betrayal. She adds that the German Left, much maligned by important segments of the radical intelligentsia in France and the U.S., has in fact produced a more sober and realistic analysis of its ultimate meaning. Meanwhile Daniel Singer, taking as his point of departure his earlier study, *Prelude to Revolution*, and his recent trenchant critique of Mitterrand, *Is Socialism Doomed?* (New York: Oxford University Press, 1988), provides perspective on the quixotic outcome of May 1968, an event that had represented the largest single rebellion within the contours of advanced industrial capitalism in the postwar epoch.

Perhaps the most treacherous enterprise of historical revaluation is ongoing in Germany today with the conservative effort at "relativizing" the crimes and barbarities of the Holocaust. Charles S. Maier, author of a new study of this controversy, elaborates the issues at stake in the *Historikerstreit* and its implication for German intellectual and political life. Maier's essay is followed by Mark Poster's probing examination of the gulf between French poststructuralism and German post-Frankfurt currents led by Habermas. At odds with those on the Left so willing to denigrate the progressive political commitment of French poststructuralism, represented most forcefully in his rebuke of Perry Anderson, Poster also warns against analysis that conflates the renegade new philosophers (André Glucksmann, Bernard-Henri Lévy, etc.) with Foucault, Derrida, and Lyotard, the latter trio in his view having retained a commitment to an emancipatory political project.

Jolyon Howorth explains the latest developments in French foreign policy and suggests how the Gorbachev initiatives are leading to a greater rift between the French Right and Left, after much celebration of the achievement of "consensus." He also pinpoints how cooperation between Paris and Bonn fits into this response to the "new thinking" from Moscow.

Turning from capitalist France and West Germany, we explore the deformations of actually existing socialism in the GDR. Günter Minnerup provides a historical overview of the development pattern in the GDR and its travail in the Age of *Perestroika*. He concludes with observations on the status of the German question today. Mary Fulbrook takes an in-depth look at the nature of the GDR's ruling elite and observes that traditional models of its structure as essentially totalitarian (Dahrendorf) or as a form of consultative authoritarianism (Ludz) are limited in their explanatory power. While her own alternative model is tentative, she elaborates the tensions among the political, technical, cultural, and moral elites in GDR society and reflects upon the state's previous success at attaining stability, perhaps under its severest challenge since the East Berlin uprising of 1953.

We close on a somewhat lighter note, looking at the rise of a strange brand of academic *haute vulgarisation* dubbed by Robert Darnton "Pop Foucaultism." Pop Foucaultism may have first contributed to a deeper understanding of the marginalized and oppressed in Western societies, but its latest practitioners have brought on a glorification of the deviant and the bizarre that reduces historiography to a sort of late capitalist carnival show masquerading as a discourse of emancipation. In the final essay Simon Schama follows Darnton's analysis with a critique of one of the cleverer works of Pop Foucaultism, Alain Corbin's *The Foul and the Fragrant*, which he contrasts with the fiction of the Munich-based novelist Patrick Süskind.

Readers are encouraged to pursue these topics further by consulting the brief bibliographies in the concluding pages of the volume.

1 THE DIVIDING RHINE
Notes on the Meaning of Munich

Diana Johnstone

Throughout the eighties the French political class has exhibited a rare consensus in stressing a single theme: the vital need to build "Europe" around a special Franco-German relationship. The image of President François Mitterrand of France and Chancellor Helmut Kohl of West Germany holding hands at memorial ceremonies in Verdun in September 1984 has been offered to public opinion as the proof that France and Germany, the past buried, face the future hand in hand.

What was true in the Verdun image was too true, too banal to be so played up without seeming slightly ridiculous. The pathos was superfluous. Kohl and Mitterrand's public gestures in the cemeteries of World War I have long since ceased to be necessary to point out what is clear—fortunately—to everyone: the Franco-German war of the nineteenth and twentieth centuries is over. It cannot and will not resume. That war, which weakened both, was won by other powers who were drawn into it—the United States and the Soviet Union. The destructive passions of the Franco-Prussian War, 1914–18, and Hitler's Third Reich have evaporated. But they have not necessarily given way to the constructive passions that the Kohl-Mitterrand gestures were meant to inspire.

In the 1980s, those who were born at the very end of the Second World War were in their forties. That postwar generation was marked by the radical movements of the 1960s which seemed to be bringing the youth of the world together. But the illusion of unity was broken by the French reaction to the German peace movement of the early 1980s. The Germans who developed the movement of protest against the deployment of nuclear Pershing II and Cruise missiles fully expected to find understanding and support in France. To the postwar German generation, France was the land of the Resistance, of Sartre, of the intellectuals who protested against colonial wars in Algeria and Vietnam. From the German perspective the peace movement should have advanced the rapprochement between the postwar generations in France and Germany.

Quite the opposite occurred. French media and intellectuals stigmatized the German peace movement as "nationalist." Terms like "Munich," "Yalta," and "pacifism" were used in ways showing that words did not have the same meanings in the two countries. A German writer belonging to that disillusioned Francophile generation, Lothar Baier,[1] observed that the institutionalized understanding between political and economic circles in the two countries is matched by "a growing misunderstanding between persons whose raison d'être is precisely understanding," the intellectuals, especially those who identify themselves with the Left. Attempts of intellectuals to understand have been turning into explanations of why understanding is impossible.[2]

French intellectuals invariably point out that in France the very idea of a "peace movement" was discredited by memories of the Communist-led peace movement of the 1950s. The French anticommunism of the eighties points up the fact that if, twenty years ago, French and German radical youth seemed to meet, they were coming from opposite directions. Both were, in a sense, postcommunist. But the West Germans were radicalizing from a background of conformist Cold War anticommunism, in a country where the Communist party was stigmatized and outlawed, and where the project was to revive a new Left out of practically nothing. The French youth rebels of May 1968, on the other hand, were out to destroy the hegemony of the French Communist party in the French Left. That French generation has been marked by a fixation on communism, either (at first) by going farther left to accuse the orthodox communists of blocking the world revolution or else, starting in the late seventies, by an obsessive identification

---

1. Lothar Baier, *Un Allemand né de la dernière guerre: Essai à l'usage des français* (Brussels: Editions Complexe, 1985).
2. See also *Sehfehler links? Uber die deutsch-französische Miss-Verständigung*, contributions by Christian Alix, Lothar Baier, et al. (Geissen: Focus-Verlag, 1985).

of communism with Solzhenitsyn's *Gulag*. This anticommunism has led to a progressive depoliticization (in harmony with philosophical trends such as postmodernist deconstruction), based on the sentiment that political commitment all turns out to be self-deception.

That sentiment was precisely what the German movement of the sixties was trying to get away from. Lothar Baier recalls that "we graduates of 1961 were not only totally apolitical but also deliberately depoliticized," since the prevailing postwar view blamed Nazism on "an excessive politicization of German society which already afflicted the Weimar republic. The logical conclusion was thus to depoliticize society starting with the new generation." The German repoliticization had by the end of the seventies produced a new political culture of social movements. Thus repoliticization in Germany has run parallel to a certain depoliticization in France.

The result of this political misunderstanding is that the dynamic for Franco–German unity is entirely a matter of "processes," mostly economic. This may prove inadequate if and when the processes begin to produce serious social, economic, and political malfunctions.

WHICH EUROPE?

There is no lack of "European" sentiment. The problem is what is meant by "Europe."

Officially what is meant is the European Economic Community (EEC), scheduled finally to become what it has so long been called, a Common Market, at the end of 1992. The EEC, now up to twelve members (with unwanted Turkey knocking at the door), was founded primarily on a deal between France and Germany that favored French agriculture and German industry. The former needed protection and the latter needed markets. The main justification for the 1992 leap forward goes beyond national interests: it is to favor world-scale economic units theoretically able to hold their own in competition with the United States and Japan. This has no clear political meaning. In the practice of the EEC, the ever more complex and technical problems have been turned over to technocrats whose solutions are necessarily accepted by the political authorities. Economic unification seems to have taken on a momentum that is all the more inexorable in that mere political forces

7

cannot understand the process well enough to foresee its results or even to stop it.

Many French people justifiably suspect that, while economic survival may depend on "Europe," as political leaders and the media keep saying, they are unlikely to be the immediate winners in purely economic terms. Whole sectors of the traditionally pro-tected French economy have reason to fear their more competitive neighbors. Enthusiasm for "Europe" has had to be rather artifi-cially pumped up. On the one hand, there is fear of missing the train to modernity, of remaining small-scale and thus archaic. On the other, there is the promise of a special role for France within Europe, a privileged political-military role. This is what France has to offer: a military-industrial complex complete with a nuclear arsenal. Devalorization of nuclear weapons devalorizes France's importance within Europe.

In the context of the centuries-old tradition of the strong French state, the French political class tends to see European unification as a sort of gradual enlargement of the French nation-state. Since this Europe cannot be expected to revolve around France, inasmuch as France is not the strongest economy, the next best solution is for it to turn on a "Franco-German" axis, one that would associate France closely with Europe's strongest economic power and inci-dentally prevent Germany from dominating Europe by itself.

Obviously the German vision of Europe must be something else. When asked about the "Franco-German axis" and the "special relationship" between Bonn and Paris, Germans often reply yes, indeed, and then recall that Italy is also a very important partner in the European community. Not to mention England, Spain, and the others. The strategic puzzle remains unsolved: so far, no way has been found to combine French independent national nuclear deter-rence with a German defense fully integrated into NATO and forbidden to possess its own nuclear weapons. There is also politi-cal reluctance to strengthen a military integration of Western Europe that later could be an obstacle to the eventual reintegration of Europe as a whole. Germans are increasingly likely to recall that "Europe" is also East Germany and Czechoslovakia and the rest of what is now, once again, being called "Central Europe," not to mention Eastern Europe, that is, Russia.

Many in France would agree that "Europe" is both the Western community and, beyond, a broader economic and cultural world to be revived. However, German interest in its Eastern neighbors has been interpreted to the French public by French intellectuals sometimes in the most dire and dramatic way, on other occasions as a dangerous "drift to the East," a readiness to betray "the West" requiring emergency measures to "anchor Germany to Europe," and sometimes as a perfectly understandable national longing for German reunification which France supports.

Throughout the eighties French interpretations of "the German question" have been aimed at "anchoring Germany to Europe," or more precisely, at strengthening the Franco-German coupling. The most famous of these efforts was François Mitterrand's 20 January 1983 speech to the German Bundestag endorsing NATO's missile buildup and, indirectly, the Christian Democrats over the Social Democratic Party (SPD). Like Mitterrand's speech, of which the French Socialists remain extremely proud, these efforts have alienated more Germans than they have seduced. They have succeeded primarily in bringing to light a profound Franco-German misunderstanding.

The French diagnosis of the German problem as a longing for German reunification is not totally false; worse than that, it is largely false, but likely to favor the revival of nationalist tendencies by its very refusal to take into account the antinationalist tendencies of the postwar generation. In this sense the French interpretation risks being proved right by history to the very extent that it has been totally wrong politically.

The French treated the left peace movement as sublimated nationalism, which could be cured by legitimizing outright nationalism, completely ignoring the very origins of the left peace movement in quite conscious rejection of German nationalist demands for reunification of prewar Germany. French commentators insisted that, consciously or not, what the peace demonstrators really wanted was German reunification. They thereby announced that reunification was a more legitimate desire and goal than nuclear disarmament. It remains to be seen how much this French legitimatization has worked to overcome the taboo on German nationalism inherited from Hitler. It is paradoxical to see French opinion makers trying to encourage a revival of German nationalism.

In the eighties the French eagerness to build "Europe" as a sort of enlarged nation-state has run up against a German generation without notable enthusiasm for such a project. This lack of enthusiasm is sometimes interpreted as incorrigible "Atlanticism" (meaning servility toward the United States), and sometimes as semitreacherous leanings toward the Soviet bloc, and sometimes as both at once.

German intellectuals have attempted to explain that not having lived for centuries in a unified state like France, they adjust more readily than the French realize to the existence of two or more German states. This generation has traveled enormously, has taken an interest in the whole planet, and is particularly well prepared to think in global terms rather than in terms of a German or even a European nation. This outlook could prove to be a great asset.

Certainly the process of worldwide economic integration seems to rule out a return to the old nation-states of Europe and their mutually devastating wars. The destruction of the Third Reich, the division of Germany, has been quite thoroughly accepted by the postwar generation not merely as a historic punishment for the crimes of Nazism, but, more positively, as a leap over the historically time-bound age of the nation-state into the dawning age of an integrated world. There is in Germany a truly modern disinterest in the unit of the nation-state, whether German or European (which does not rule out a revived interest in German history and culture). Whether this disinterest endures must depend in part on developments elsewhere.

The vision of a future Europe is also a vision of the role of this Europe in the larger world. Europe can be seen either as the core of ever broader integration processes that may ultimately be planetary or as a third superpower. How this Europe will relate to the rest of the world—especially to the Third World—should be a major political issue for Europe-wide political debate. This would require a density of communication within the European Left far beyond the perfunctory meetings of leaders of the parties in the Socialist International or articles in specialized reviews. Up to now, political communication is running too far behind the economic process to provide direction.

EUROPEAN EMPIRE BUILDING IN HISTORY

Economic processes, and the technocrats who try to control them, are unifying France and Germany, as they are unifying the European community. The majority of Europeans favor this process. And yet, despite all that, the democratic political base of that union is extremely weak. Democratic politics depends on a common understanding which is still underdeveloped.

For a new European political culture to emerge, new movements are needed to crystallize awareness of new realities and abandon old patterns that no longer fit reality. The ecological and disarmament movements in West Germany have represented broad democratic responses to the new issues created by modern transformations. They have counterparts in other advanced industrial societies. In France such movements are exceptionally underdeveloped, and therefore it has been easy to regard the German movements not as something new, but as a resurgence of traditional German aberrations.

The technocratic process assumes that historical memories will fade, and a new common culture will be built on the basis of material transformation—that economic and scientific developments will provide their own new culture. This represents, incidentally, a break with the widely held thesis[3] that the way unification or integration occurs is of great importance for subsequent political life: for example, the belief that Germany's commitment to democracy was inadequate because the nation was unified from above by Bismarck rather than by a democratic revolution from below.

Since Richelieu, a primary aim of French foreign policy was to keep Germany as divided and thus weakened and also to advance territorially toward the Rhine, considered France's "natural boundary." With Napoleon I this succeeded so well that it inspired a German emulative movement toward construction of a unified, centralized nation-state, a job completed by Bismarck, to the distress of German liberals who had dreamed of a republican rather than imperial model. Imperial rivalry won out over republican cooperation in Europe.

Both empires justified their expansion with rationales elevated by homegrown theorists to the level of universal truth. The France that sought a "national boundary" on the Rhine was an old but multiethnic state, with large regional minorities speaking languages other than French: Bretons, Basques, Alsatians, not to mention the sister Latin languages in the Langue d'Oc and Provence. The most

3. For instance, by André Gorz in his 1982 attack on the German peace movement for its lack of a "spirit of resistance," attributed to countries which, unlike Germany, "accomplished their bourgeois revolution." See below.

self-assured of modern nation-states justified its unity on the basis of the power of the state, the law of the realm, the sovereignty of the monarch, until the Revolution provided a more exciting ideological basis of abstract values, social modernity, "liberty, equality, fraternity," human rights, the Republic. The lyric historian Jules Michelet called France a "glorious mother from which every nation should be born to liberty!" Revolutionary and even plain republican values were in fact put on the back burner for much of the nineteenth century during the various empires and monarchies, but revived with the Republic precisely after the Franco-Prussian War, providing an ideologically universal justification for the great national project, reconquering Alsace-Lorraine.

The Prussian victory over France in 1871 detached Alsace and northern Lorraine from France and destroyed the Second Empire at the same time. It was a national trauma comparable to the collapse of France before the Nazi invasion in 1940. By democratic standards Napoleon the Third was no better than Bismarck, and indeed it was Napoleon who stupidly started the disastrous war. But defeated, France was again a Republic, home of both Joan of Arc and the Revolution. The Third Republic lived for one great purpose: to revenge the humiliation of 1871 and win back Alsace-Lorraine.

Bismarck had taken those territories in furtherance of his project of bringing all the ethnic Germans together in a single empire. Already before the war was over, the French historian Fustel de Coulanges wrote to Berlin historian Theodor Mommsen refuting the argument that Alsace was of German nationality because its population was Germanic and spoke German. "What distinguishes nations," wrote Coulanges, "is neither race, nor language. Men feel in their hearts that they are the same people, when they share a community of ideas, interests, affections, memories, and hopes." *La patrie* "is what one loves." What made Alsace French was not Louis XIV who conquered it but "our Revolution of 1789." Since then Alsace has lived a French life and has nothing in common with Germany. "If Alsace is French, it is uniquely because she wants to be."

For Ernest Renan, in 1882, a nation was "a soul, a spiritual principle." Alsatian rabbi Isaac Levy, explaining why he was leaving Colmar rather than accept German rule, said he "loved France especially because she was greathearted, because she was good and generous, because she took in hand the cause of the weak and oppressed, because she initiated progress, spread civilization, because her soil gave rise to the noble ideas of tolerance and fraternity, spreading over the entire universe."[4]

In Alsace, the French case rested on exalting a nationalism based on "ideals" over a nationalism based on "blood." French "patriotism" was idealistic and progressive, contrasted to a German "nationalism" that was physical and reactionary. The rivalry over those border provinces incited patriotic writers and theorists on each side to transform their country's specific case into an eternal universal verity.

The idealistic definition of French patriotism did not at all prevent French policy from encouraging ethnically based nationalist movements in Central Europe, where they could weaken the German-Austrian sphere of influence.

In the world, the French Empire was second to the British, both competitive and dependent. In Europe, French power was supported by Britain to balance the growing power of imperial Germany. France had another historic ally, the United States, whose definition of patriotism most resembled that of France. Ideologically the United States and France have most in common, both exalting patriotism as the voluntary adherence to a political system with a universal messianic role to play in spreading freedom throughout the world.

This common conception prevailed in the form of "self-determination" of nations as adopted by the victorious allies at the end of World War I. This was France's moment of revenge. Just as Bismarck had forced France to cede Alsace-Lorraine and pay war reparations at Versailles in 1871, France took back Alsace-Lorraine at Versailles and imposed equally huge reparations. But that was not all: the Allies used "self-determination" not merely to advance the great Wilsonian principles, but quite deliberately to weaken the Germanic world. By giving more weight to Slavic ethnic claims than to German ones, the Versailles settlement weakened the moral position of the Western allies in their eventual confrontation with Hitler.

The second Versailles treaty, like the first, was unfair. This was

4. This and other citations are in the anthology by Raoul Girardet, *Le Nationalisme français* (Paris: Seuil, 1983).

recognized in France by some, notably by the internationalist working-class movement. Nationalism and internationalism developed in opposition to each other. In the period between Germany's defeat and the rise of Hitler, the French Communist party stressed solidarity with "the German working class" against the exactions of French chauvinism.

FAMOUS LAST WORDS

On 22 October 1941, in reprisal for the assassination of a German officer two days earlier in Nantes, the Germans took twenty-seven French hostages out to be shot in a sandpit near Chateaubriand, between Nantes and Rennes. The prisoners were all Communists, union leaders, and elected officials who had been imprisoned at the start of the Nazi occupation. One of them was Jean-Pierre Timbaud, secretary of the Paris metalworkers of the General Confederation of Labor (CGT).

As they faced the firing squad, each of the French political prisoners bravely shouted a final slogan, "Vive la France!" or "Long live Stalin!" or even "Long live Soviet France!" It was Timbaud whose last words became famous, legendary: "Long live the German Communist party!"

Those were the famous last words of genuine proletarian internationalism in France. They are legendary in the French working-class movement precisely because they are the last, tragic expression of that internationalism which was already mortally wounded by the war of 1914–18, revived by the Bolshevik revolution, and finished off by World War II.

Through the Resistance the French Communist party (PCF) gained a new national legitimacy as the continuator of left-wing patriotism, in contrast to the right-wing collaboration of Vichy. The PCF's "proletarian internationalism" was essentially reduced to its loyalty to Moscow, dropping the old critique of French chauvinism.

Triumphant anticommunism leaves little space to recognize how much the inspirational force behind the formation of the European Communist parties was an attempt to salvage and continue the socialist internationalism that was the first casualty of the war in 1914. For over a century nationalism in France and Germany opposed two kinds of internationalism: finance capital, which works inexorably on the material level to unify the world; and the more idealistic internationalism of the working-class movement. Racist French nationalism of a century ago, followed by Nazism, identified both those forms of internationalism with "international Jewry." The lie of modern political anti-Semitism conceals an important truth, the parallel international thrust of both working-class socialism and free-market finance capital. Socialism is, in a sense, the conscious participation of propertyless working people in the vast process of unifying the world. When the powerful champions of the free market succeed in suppressing it, they may not enjoy what they get in its place. In any case, at the level of democratic politics, as opposed to economic processes, the socialist ideal has been the greatest force of the past century for overcoming nationalist barriers.

In the West, social progress since the Renaissance has gone beyond mere technical improvements and has been marked by great social movements by which masses of ordinary people have changed their understanding and position in the world. In European history, Protestantism was often a mass movement of self-improvement, raising the literacy and awareness of large populations. This is an achievement of Protestantism regardless of the wars, intolerance, and other negative accompanying features.

Since the industrialization of Europe and America, and notably since the late nineteenth century, the working class or labor movement has been the primary movement of mass social self-advancement. This has been true despite the sharp divisions that have afflicted the movement, despite its errors and weaknesses. Although in contrast to Protestantism, the labor movement has only occasionally seen itself as a "self-improvement" movement, this has been the case, and often all the more so when that was the least how it saw itself: ostensibly revolutionary branches of the working-class movement, while failing to bring about the revolution, often did most to enrich the lives of their militants by bringing them a broad worldview, an inspiration to education, and a sense of purpose.

For over a decade, the labor movement and its political partners in the working-class parties have been declining drastically. The purpose here is not to evaluate that decline, but to take note of it in relation to: (1) the weakening of the basis for democracy in the West, and (2) the projected "unification of Western Europe" around the "Franco-German couple."

By its original aspirations, the working-class movement was best suited both to strengthen the social foundations of democracy in each country and to develop a consciousness that could serve as the basis for an international citizenship. The decline of the labor movement is weakening this first fundamental role, while the Socialist parties have drawn from recent history two conflicting versions, French and German, of "common sense," exemplified by the opposing interpretations of such a historic symbol as "Munich."

LOSERS ON THE WINNING SIDE

The Franco-German war is over, but its interpretation tends to be quite different, even opposite, in the French and German Left, based on contrasting historical experience. With Hitler, Germany took imperial conquest to its ultimate extreme and experienced as a result a total defeat. This experience fully discredited warlike nationalism. The German Left dissociated itself doubly from nationalism and war, not only because it led to defeat and national destruction, but also because of the crimes along the way. The French experience was more ambiguous and harder to distill into such a simple, clear historical lesson. In 1940 France lost the war, in a traumatizing defeat even worse than 1871. However, inasmuch as Nazi Germany was eventually defeated by the Soviet Union, Britain, and the United States, France ended up on the winning side, against a regime revealed as horrifyingly evil. The war that taught Germans to renounce nationalism actually revived French nationalism and blocked any critical rejection of the French chauvinism that had contributed to the debacle of Europe.

Traditional French chauvinism resurfaced in the 1980s attacks on the German peace movement, with occasional echoes in the United States. Although the West German peace movement had many direct contacts in the United States, notably through Protestant churches, and because of participation in common German-American NATO strategic debates from which France withdrew two decades ago, the review *Telos*, oddly enough, chose in the early eighties to present the German peace movement to American readers through the distorting prism of the French intellectual critique.

This was odd because *Telos* was ostensibly on the Left, whereas

16

the French view of the German peace movement coincided with that of the Reagan administration. However, the network of academic contacts was probably the decisive factor. The so-called "second Left" of French intellectual theorists on "unreal nonexisting socialism" appealed to American academics attracted to the largely virgin fields of American Marxism by the tumult of the sixties, yet anxious to mark their difference from the "real existing socialism" of the Soviet bloc. Nobody had more prestige in this field than André Gorz.

The spring 1982 issue of *Telos*, number 51, had a long special section on European peace movements which took the French side. In his introduction editor Paul Piccone made sweeping attacks on the German movement which echoed the French: "Most of the German Left's responses betray a failure to transcend the old myths concerning, for example, the most outrageous fraud in the 20th century (the October Revolution), or to understand adequately the social and political character of either the United States or the Soviet Union." The attacks conveyed the impression that the German Left and the German peace movement were made up of orthodox pro-Soviet Communists, or else resurgent German nationalists, or perhaps both.

Telos reproduced Gorz's January 1982 interview with *Der Spiegel*, in which he claimed that "there are nations whose destiny is connected with the idea of freedom, such as Poland, France, Great Britain, and, in spite of everything, the United States. And there are nations whose destiny is not linked to the idea of freedom." This of course meant Germany. "Such nations stand for no universal values. Their identity is simply based on the love of the fatherland and self-glorification and thus, as in Switzerland, on national egoism and provinciality. People of other countries pay little attention to these nations."

Gorz acknowledged that German social democracy could be liberating and internationalist, but that did not count because then it was "antinationalist." In short, Germans could be either nationalist or internationalist, but only France had a unique and almost mystical capacity to be both at the same time. Gorz put Poland in that same wonderful category. And (grudgingly) the United States.

In the same interview Gorz broached the subject of "Munich." "We charge that the Germans are now making the mistakes we made 50 years ago, and are treating the Russians as we did Hitler in 1938," he said.

Praise for Poland's "universal" significance in the same breath with "Munich" detaches these "universal values" from mere historical fact. For it is a fact that in September 1938, just before Munich, the Polish government took its cue from Hitler, voicing threats and getting set to invade Czechoslovakia to detach a piece of territory for Poland.

THE MEANING OF MUNICH

Why such French hostility to "pacifism"? Lothar Baier asks. The usual answer is Munich. "Apparently convincing, the reasoning which attributes to the 1938 accords the present rejection of the peace movement does not, however, stand up to an examination of the facts."

"Munich" has been absorbed into post-World War II Cold War mythology primarily as a false analogy. The original event has been simplified in the West as giving in to a brutal aggressor in a misguided (because counterproductive) desire to preserve peace. As such, it is invoked as the clinching argument for being strong and not giving in to an adversary's demands. Munich means "appeasement," and appeasement leads to war. "Munich" is used to justify a high level of armament and suspicion of negotiated peace settlements.

The simplification has another, retrospective purpose: a more or less deliberate repression of the multiple national failures surrounding that event. Because France was most directly involved, this repression function of simplification is stronger in France, no doubt, than in the United States.

The "Munich" problem in Franco-German relations in the 1980s begins with the hasty and nearly unanimous French condemnation of the German peace movement as a dangerous reappearance of the same sort of "pacifism" that led to the 29 September 1938 accords in Munich by which Britain and France agreed to let Hitler dismember Czechoslovakia. The accusation was repeated in countless editorials and declarations in France, echoed with satisfaction by the German Right.

The accusation was rightly felt as slanderous in the German peace movement. It was based on false assumptions about the Munich accords, about the German peace movement, and about the parallel that might be drawn between two very different historical situations.

In the West, the Munich legend has made "appeasement" primarily responsible for war. The matter naturally looks a bit different from a German viewpoint: it would be irresponsible for Germans to put all the blame on British and French appeasement rather than on Hitler.

The real problem, however, has to do with the meaning of "appeasement" at Munich and whether or not it allows parallels with "pacifism" in other situations. A review of the record[5] suggests that "pacifism" was above all the public excuse used by British prime minister Neville Chamberlain and French premier Edouard Daladier for a policy whose motives were altogether more political and less moralistic.

Chamberlain's policy served to get France off the hook of its treaty obligations to defend Czechoslovakia. Twenty years after the Versailles treaty, Western leaders were ready to admit that the new boundaries they had drawn in Central Europe, ostensibly in the name of ethnic regrouping, had erred in including the Sudetenland, with three and a half million Germans, in a country supposedly made up of Czechs and Slovaks. Prague was obliged to agree to cede the Sudetenland. But Hitler was still not satisfied and demanded immediate German military occupation of the Sudetenland. Thus the crisis of September 1938. Hitler insisted on a method of recuperating the territory that would assert Germany's role as decisive power in Central Europe. What could make this ultimately acceptable to Chamberlain and Daladier was that the rival power in that unstable region was the Soviet Union.

In terms of the sacrosanct military balance, Germany was not at that time stronger than its adversaries. France, backed by Britain, was quite as well armed. Moreover, the Soviet Union was bound by treaty to help defend Czechoslovakia if France did so. And that is precisely why Chamberlain and Daladier sought a pretense of mediation from Mussolini at Munich, rather than the international mediation suggested by Moscow or offered by the United States. Chamberlain wanted to prevent a situation that had already been

5. For instance, Paul Nizan's *Chronique de septembre*, 1939, reissued by Gallimard in Paris in 1978; mentioned by Lothar Baier.

successfully avoided in Spain: the alliance of the Western democracies with the Soviet Union against fascism.

At the time Western commentators described the Munich accords as a defeat for the Soviet Union. Moreover, by openly stressing London's unwillingness to involve the British Empire in a war in Central Europe, Chamberlain tacitly assigned to Nazi Germany its own area of imperial expansion. Certainly many conservatives in the West were ready to sit back and watch Nazism attack, and perhaps eliminate, Bolshevism. What went wrong was that Hitler pushed his advantage in 1940 to invade France. It was a face-saving fiction to attribute this Western error in realpolitik calculation to "pacifism."

A year after Munich, while he sat out the "phony war" on the Maginot line writing letters and diaries,[6] Sartre saw why Britain and France could appease Hitler's demands on Czechoslovakia at Munich in 1938 and then declare war against Germany over Hitler's aggression against Poland the next year. "It's the bourgeoisie which prevented war in 1938 and decided the capitulation at Munich, from fear of victory even more than of defeat"—fear war might benefit communism. In September 1939 on the other hand, war was welcomed by the bourgeoisie—because the Molotov-Ribbentrop Pact (Stalin's response to Munich) had meanwhile discredited communism and because "everyone now realizes that this war, which is being waged directly or indirectly against the Soviets, will necessarily be accompanied by a police operation domestically." In fact, the French Communist party was banned only weeks after the September 1939 declaration of war. "Beneath its trappings of a national war, it's to a great extent a civil war," Sartre observed.

"War in '38 could have been the occasion for a revolution—in '40 it's the occasion for a counterrevolution. The war of '38 would have been a 'left' war—that of '39 is a 'right' war," Sartre concluded. The Hitler-Stalin pact enabled the French bourgeoisie to use the war to eliminate the internal enemy, communism, and turn it into an external (Soviet) threat.

Pacifism was also a retrospective excuse for an erroneous appraisal of the strategic situation. It was believed in France that France and England, connected by the Atlantic Ocean to the U.S.,

6. *The War Diaries of Jean-Paul Sartre* (New York: Pantheon, 1985).

were in the position to win a war of attrition. The strains of war effort would defeat the encircled German economy, causing it to collapse from within. The inaction on the western front known as the phony war, while Germany and the USSR polished off Poland and Finland to the east, was understood in France as part of the economic war.

The French had concluded from World War I's stagnant trench warfare that modern industrial nations' strong defenses had rendered offensive war useless. The specter of total war was thought to be an effective deterrent. The defensive posture behind the Maginot line was all the more comfortable for the French in that they had got all the territory they wanted from the previous war. "Thus the French armies on the German frontier have no purpose other than to force Germany to adopt a war economy destined to make their blockade effective," Sartre wrote.

Sartre himself hoped for an antimilitarist victory of sheer economic power. The visibly low morale of French soldiers, the "dissolution of the military spirit," was a sign that war was being "civilized" in industrial society. Wealth rather than heroism would finally win. He was "reckoning on a war without 'greatness'—principally economic. In that case, 'decadence' can . . . become a positive factor."

Germany was indeed finally defeated by American wealth, but also by Russian heroism. In any case, for the French the 1940 collapse confirmed: (1) the assumption that the human element, "morale," or the military spirit, has declined too far to be relied on for the defense of France, and thus (2) reliance on some other factor of superiority to secure a purely defensive strategy vis-à-vis more vigorous European nations. This factor is no longer economic strength but an assumed technological superiority or simply the nuclear threat.

Thus General Pierre-Marie Gallois, theoretician of Gaullist nuclear deterrence strategy, calls Europeans "fat bourgeois who won't defend themselves except by technology." France is not disciplined for war, and therefore, the only thing it can do is "to make a little deterrent that would leave us in peace."

Indeed, the French nuclear deterrent is probably a contemporary equivalent of the Maginot line, a purely defensive, if ultimately useless, contraption. Its danger most likely lies in the example it sets for nuclear proliferation rather than in any probability of French use of nuclear weapons. However, to be credible, it entails a psychological and political as well as purely technological component: the bluff of readiness to "press the button" and blow up the world.

This element of bluff got mixed up in the Franco-German debate of the early eighties. André Glucksmann led the charge of "new philosophers" against the craven "pacifists" who would "rather be red than dead." Nuclear deterrence depends on the opposite assumption. Glucksmann became a champion of nuclear weapons as the embodiment of a moral superiority, a willingness to die (indeed, to become extinct) for a political ideal.

This pretension soured the discussion irreparably. True, the French tone has softened considerably since, and efforts are being pursued, especially by German Social Democrats and French Socialists, to find some common understanding. But so long as the French continue to give priority to their nuclear deterrent, they are unlikely to give up the bluff that carries with it the quite unmodern, untechnocratic claim to be ready to plunge the world into primeval chaos.

This bluff was expressed by French writers like Glucksmann who extolled the French "spirit of resistance"—the comforting illusion that France as a whole is standing up successfully to the "Soviet threat" because it has nuclear weapons. Very few French intellectuals[7] have bothered to notice and point out how inappropriate it must be to require that the Germans strike a similar pose.

Some Germans[8] have suggested that France has never really come to grips with the trauma of 1940 and that the "Soviet threat" has served as a "projection" of the Hitler Germany that was not successfully resisted in 1940. The illusion of nuclear resistance to the Soviet Union may be a compensation for the failure of 1940.

Lothar Baier suggests that "serious debate on the political lessons to draw from those accords and their disastrous consequences for all Europe would make it possible to drop the charges against 'pacifist quibbling' in favor of an analysis of the blindness caused yesterday by a visceral anti-Sovietism that is found again today in other forms among the heralds of antipacifism."[9] Munich, he told a

7. French intellectuals able to appraise the German movements fairly—notably Claude Bourdet, as well as Jean Chesneaux and Jean-Marie Vincent—were largely ignored.
8. For instance, Dan Diener at a March 1986 symposium of French and German intellectuals in Paris.
9. See n.1 on p. 7.

symposium in Paris in 1986, is a cadaver that has never undergone a proper autopsy.

PACIFISM OR ANTICOMMUNISM

In France, religious and intellectual traditions leave little place, and no influence, to genuine pacifism. Opposition to war has generally been selective, based on appreciation of national or class interests.

The Franco-German war was opposed from the start by the international working-class movement. In September 1870 the German Social Democratic Workers' Party issued a protest against German annexation of Alsace and Lorraine. And the first workers' International in London issued a statement drafted by Karl Marx calling it an absurd anachronism to fix national boundaries according to military considerations. Bismarck wanted to defend Germany starting from the Vosges mountain range, whereas France would feel safer if its boundaries began at the Rhine. Any boundary fixed by the victor would be contested by the other side and bear seeds of a new war, Marx warned.

This pacifism failed notoriously to prevent war in 1914. But after the 1914–18 slaughter, "pacifism," in the limited sense of desire to keep peace, prevailed on the Left (Socialist as well as Communist) in France all the more easily in that France had got all it wanted at Versailles and was henceforth a status-quo power. Only the extreme nationalist Right around *Action Française* pursued the vendetta against defeated Germany. In his *Histoire de deux peuples: La France et l'empire allemand*, the foreign editor of *Action Française*, Jacques Bainville, had presented his thesis that the French and the Germans are eternal enemies because France naturally seeks to extend its boundaries to the Rhine. Bainville had excoriated the Bonapartists for neglecting, in their pursuit of imperial grandeur, France's traditional foreign policy of keeping Germany broken up in small states ("German chaos") and allowing the "catastrophe of all catastrophes" (unification of the German Empire under Bismarck) to occur. After Bainville died in 1936, Henri Massis carried on the crusade against the "German mentality" with its leaning toward the "unsoundable depths of free thought," while admiring Italian fascism and Portugal's dictator Salazar. In 1939 a translation of Bainville's book, subtitled *Frankreichs Kampf gegen die deutsche Einheit* (France's fight against German unity), was served

23

up to the German public as proof that France was an implacable enemy of the Germans.

This was far from the whole truth. But the thirties were a period of nearly inextricable confusion as the rise of Nazism in Germany followed by the Popular Front in France and the civil war in Spain dramatically reversed the positions of political camps toward Germany. The Left, especially the Communists, who had defended the "German working class" and peace, began to demand resistance to fascist and Nazi war preparations. In France the Left government of the Popular Front, led by Socialist Léon Blum, lasted a mere year, from June 1936 to June 1937, but granted benefits to the working class (pay raises and annual vacations) that, as ambassador Stefan Osusky reported to Prague, were "a terrible blow to the French middle classes and bourgeoisie."

In his report to his government on the French political situation in March 1938, Czechoslovak ambassador Stefan Osusky pointed out that up until two years before (that is, the fascist attack on the Spanish republic), it was the Left in France that had been "pacifist" and the Right that was "patriotic," but that now the roles had been switched. The Communists were resolutely antifascist. But the Socialists were split: some of the most conservative, such as Jules Moch (who as postwar interior minister went down in history for tough suppression of Communist-led strikes) advocated appeasement.

The Czechoslovakian ambassador's March 1938 analysis indicates that it was middle class and bourgeois resentment against the Popular Front that set the stage for France's failure to hold to its commitments to Czechoslovakia. "The French middle classes, those guardians of French patriotism, stopped playing that role. Just as the French nobility rallied, after the great French Revolution, to foreign states to fight their own country against the defenders of the French Revolution, so the French contemporary middle classes and bourgeoisie are seeking to align with foreign forces to combat those who have governed France since the 1936 elections." The bourgeoisie and middle classes combated the French working class by a fierce rejection of any French involvement on the other side of the Rhine.

The Right dropped its tirades against the Germans and returned to an old fin de siècle theme: French decadence, which made France unable to stand up to Germany. The disorders of the Popular

Front—spoiling the workers with pay raises and holidays on the beach—were proof of that decadence. *Anti-Semitism was the bridge that enabled the nationalists to drop their anti-German theme and eventually rally to collaboration with Nazism.* Everything—French decadence, the Popular Front (Léon Blum was a Jew), Bolshevism, the economic crisis, even the old hostility between French and Germans—could be blamed on the Jews.

As so often in France, political alignments were to be explained by the struggle between class interests. This is a feature of French social history which must not be overlooked, even if Karl Marx can be proved wrong to have extended the French model of class struggle to the world in general.

This does not exclude a great deal of confusion. The shift of the Right toward accommodation with Germany and of the Left toward resistance to Nazism was a general trend, with many exceptions. The most notorious were those who started out on the Left and ended up as ardent Nazi collaborators: the former Communist Jacques Doriot and the former Socialist Marcel Déat. Déat shared with the extreme Right a fascination with the dynamism of fascism, as opposed to the limp passivity of comfortable France. He shared with Doriot a powerful hostility toward the Soviet Union. The "pacifism" of Déat and Doriot stopped when the enemy was no longer Germany but the USSR. After Hitler sent his armies to invade the Soviet Union, they helped organize the Legion of French Volunteers against Bolshevism to fight on the eastern front.

The most important discrediting link between socialist pacifism and collaboration with the Nazis was former Socialist premier and Vichy government leader Pierre Laval. Like Déat and Doriot, Laval's pacifism was selective, as shown by the radio message that, after the war, brought him the death sentence for treason: "In these combats I hope for a German victory, because without it, tomorrow bolshevism will be installed everywhere."

In short, what led to "Munich" was not "pacifism" (something that scarcely existed in France) but *anticommunism*. And after the war, precisely to promote militant anticommunism, the buck for "Munich" was passed to "pacifism."

In the Cold War, the West has studiously avoided the sort of analysis applied by ambassador Osusky to the French situation prior to Munich. The very mention of "class struggle" stigmatizes an analysis as "doctrinaire Marxism" or some such. Certainly there

25

are limits to what can be explained by Marxist class analysis. But the systematic avoidance of that dimension is a self-imposed handicap in a diagnosis of Nazism that flails about looking for traits and parallels and ends up in the sticky domain of guilt by association. Example in the form of reduction to the absurd: Nazis professed love for nature, therefore love for nature smacks of Nazism.

That is the hysterical new philosopher version. A politer version is expressed by French Socialist Jean-Pierre Chevènement,[10] who confided his misgivings to German Social Democrats:[11] "I fear that the hostility to technique, even among [German] Socialists, conceals irrational, even anti-Enlightenment tendencies. The mythologizing of 'Nature' seems to me more an expression of civilization fatigue than a clear idea."

Implicit in this statement (and many, many other similar contemporary French comments on Germany) is the assumption that German concern about weapons or environmental destruction is based on pure philosophy, on "ideas," rather than on perception of facts. This assumption is all the easier when the French observer makes sure to overlook the facts in question. This is not a place to fill the gap, but it must be stressed that the German peace and environmental movements churn out mountains of extremely carefully documented factual descriptions of the problems that concern them and that this content is never noticed, much less taken into account, by the French critics of "the German mind" or "German Angst."

This production of documentation makes it clear that the Germans, far from being systematically hostile to modern technology on the basis of some atavistic German nature worship, are quite at home in modern technology—sufficiently at home in it to be able to analyze what is going wrong and to develop discrimination about what sort of technical development is desirable and what is not.

In contrast, the French elites of the past couple of decades have notably lacked enough confidence in France's place in modern technology to dare afford the luxury of discriminatory criticism. Instead everything that belongs to modern technology is accepted uncritically as marvelous—starting of course with nuclear power and nuclear weapons—and defended as the very embodiment of

10. Named defense minister in the first government of prime minister Michel Rocard on May 12, 1988.
11. In the June 1987 issue of *Die Neue Gesellschaft/Frankfurter Hefte.*

"rationality" from supposedly backward German ecologists.

The very mechanism of guilt by association works differently in France and Germany because of different notions of what Nazism was all about. In France the Nazi ideological praise of "nature" is taken very seriously as part of the Nazi essence. This may seem more plausible in that Vichy France, inspired by deep hostility toward industrial society, especially since the short-lived working class triumph in the Popular Front, did indeed promote a return to rural society and its values.

Lothar Baier[12] points out that "contrary to the long-prevailing view of National Socialism in France as 'a relapse into barbarism,' in Germany it was a matter of a *forced progress* movement. In its short existence, National Socialism accomplished an extraordinary leap, often covered by the folkloristic aspects used to show itself off." France had a contrary experience. This difference in historical experience explains the greater challenge today in Germany to the concept of technological progress, Baier suggested. Thus the German Left is particularly alert to misuse of genetic engineering because of the notorious Nazi biological experiments on human beings, all in the name of scientific progress.

The French guilt by association of ideas is selective: traces of the Nazi taint are readily found on "pacifism" and "nature," but not on the creation of "Europe" as a great power independent of both the Soviet Union and the United States. It is in the name of this "Europe" that many a French intellectual goes into the battle of ideas against "neutralo-pacifism" in order to "anchor Germany to Europe," that is, to the great new power to be built out of the Western European community.

But if "pacifism" can be stigmatized as a form of precollaboration with totalitarianism, then "Europe" recalls collaboration itself. The fundamental motivation of the ardent collaborationists in Paris, such as Marcel Déat, Jacques Benoist-Méchin, Robert Brasillach, or Pierre Drieux La Rochelle, was the creation of a dynamic united Europe—under German domination, of course, because only the Germans were determined to defy both the Bolsheviks and the Anglo-Saxons, especially the British who had always schemed to keep the Continent weak and divided.

12. At a March 13, 1986 public debate between French and German intellectuals at the Pompidou Center in Paris.

Not only Nazis dreamed of "Europe"—so did anti-Nazis who fought against them. But this observation again raises the question of the political content of the unification process.

The very difficulty of communication between political cultures favors increased reliance on images and symbols. But, like "Munich," such images and symbols may impoverish the political culture by blocking analysis of Europe's formative history.

2 TWENTY YEARS ON
May '68 Revisited

Daniel Singer

The ghost of communism is not haunting Western Europe. Paris is no longer the capital of revolutionary hope. A visitor returning there after a long interval could hardly believe that this was the same town where twenty years earlier the established order was trembling, and imagination was supposed to seize power. Ironically, to celebrate the twentieth anniversary, the French staged one of these general elections which, for all the apparent pomp and passion, in no way question the nature of the regime—no more, that is, than do similar polls held in Britain, Germany, or the United States. Mutatis mutandis, Prague is not the only European city to have gone back to "normal." Does it mean that the hopes aroused by the uprising of May 1968 were mere illusions, that the issues raised by rebellious students and striking workers, in dramatic if utopian fashion, have become irrelevant? Before trying to argue the opposite, I should reveal my vested interests.

When the sudden French crisis showed the depth of discontent hidden beneath the glittering surface of capitalist society, and the general strike, by paralyzing the country, confirmed the social power of the working class, I raised the question of whether Marxism might not be returning to its original terrain, in a book eloquently entitled *Prelude to Revolution*.[1] Naturally, I could plead that publishers don't like question marks and that the optimistic message, as every reader of the book will admit, was hedged with all sorts of qualifications. Such pleading, however, would be

---

1. Daniel Singer, *Prelude to Revolution: France in May 1968* (New York: Hill & Wang, 1970).

superfluous. Once again "the golden tree of life" proved much greener than all the theoretical predictions. Even we who denied that capitalism had discovered the secret of permanent growth—and we were not many at the time—did not know that a major economic crisis was just round the corner and would entirely alter the political horizon (paradoxically, in the short run, strengthening the establishment and weakening its radical opponents). Even we, who had accused the French Communist party of selling its revolutionary birthright for a mess of electoral pottage, did not guess that it would pay the penalty so rapidly, helping the Socialist party to recover and François Mitterrand to perform the part of "normalizer." Even we, who had learnt in our Marxist textbooks that the ruling ideology is the ideology of the ruling class, did not imagine how quickly capitalism would carry out this task, how easily intellectuals could be bribed into betrayal. These disappointing years were at the same time quite instructive. Yet before we look at the facts and draw lessons from them, we must, at least for the sake of a new generation, recall if only in shorthand what did actually happen in that jolly month of May.

THE FRENCH MAY AND ITS SPECIFICITY

It all started on May 3d when the rector of the Paris Academy, presumably on orders, called in the police to the Sorbonne to evict a few hundred student activists. This highly exceptional move had an extraordinary sequel. The "ringleaders" arrested, the students did not make verbal protests. They counterattacked, with the Parisian cobblestone (le pavé) soon matching the hand grenades. There followed a week of bloody skirmishes and joyous demonstrations. The tougher the repression, the larger the number of students beaten up or arrested, the stronger the movement grew. The student strike spread throughout the country. Professors, researchers, young workers from the suburbs joined the demonstrators in Paris. By May 10th the leaders of the growing movement could no longer play for time. When the government refused to respond to the main slogan of the protesters—"free our comrades"—and surrounded the Sorbonne with an armada of policemen, they just could not tell the demonstrators to disperse and go home. Staying put in the Latin Quarter and facing a police armed to the teeth, the students began spontaneously to put up barricades.

The whole nation was watching or rather listening to the dramatic confrontation, as much of the dialogue was held live on the radio. Would the government opt for compromise or would it dare to strike? At two in the morning the order was given to clear the streets. At dawn the Latin Quarter was a sorry sight. Battered and beaten, the students were militarily defeated and politically victors. The government now yielded on all issues, proclaimed not even negotiable the day before. The left-wing parties, and particularly the Communists, who on the eve had been giving the students sermons on law and order, had to rally behind them. On May 13th Paris witnessed one of its biggest demonstrations ever, a million or so people marching behind the banner "Students, Teachers, Workers—Solidarity." The slogan was an omen.

In the official conception, the solemn march was to have been the beginning of the end. It proved to be the end of the beginning. The students had shown that courage paid and the mighty state was not unyielding. On the morrow of the great *demo* the first strike started near Nantes. The day after it was the turn of the Renault car works in Normandy. That evening, the Communist-dominated CGT, the biggest labor confederation in the country, decided to join the movement and spread it in the hope of keeping control. It was high time as the tide was now sweeping the country, invading province after province and branch after branch. After ten days the number of strikers was put at ten million, or roughly half the working population (an American equivalent would be something like sixty million). The country was paralyzed.

When everything was at a standstill, the minds started to move in a different fashion and the crisis changed nature. Students began to dream aloud about changing the world; technicians, researchers, and teachers started debates about their function in society; while workers in some occupied plants talked about their role in production and the meaning of the hierarchical order. With red flags flying over many factories, the employers and their government concluded it was high time to get down to business. The CGT was eager to oblige. During the night of May 28th, the revolutionary students and their allies, having chanted "we are all German Jews," set rather symbolic fires inside the Bourse. The day after, a Saturday, the representatives of the government, the employers, and the labor unions sat together in search of a deal. The concessions made to the workers, mainly the promise of bigger pay packets, were quite impressive by normal standards. Only the times were not normal, and the CGT leaders who went straight from there on Monday morning to face their supporters at the Renault works in Boulogne-Billancourt probably expected no more than a conditional approval. What they had not bargained for was total rejection. This resounding *no*, echoed in factories throughout France, precipitated an unexpected third act, three days of political interregnum when everything looked apparently possible.

The dynamic wing of the movement gathered its forces at the Charléty sports stadium not knowing where it was heading. Left-wing politicians thought their hour had struck. François Mitterrand, assuming an impotent de Gaulle would resign, offered his services for the presidency; in the interval, matters could be run by a government headed by Pierre Mendés-France and including the Communists. The latter, not to be treated as junior partners, staged an impressive mass demonstration as proof of their strength. The government was in a state of panic: the general had vanished. Actually, as everybody was burying him, de Gaulle was in the process of resurrection. Up until then, as the social movement was rising, he seemed at a loss. But by now he had grasped the crucial lesson: the Communists had no wish to push the movement forward and, if challenged openly, they themselves would help to demobilize it. To dramatize the situation, de Gaulle traveled to Baden-Baden to get the blessing of the armed forces from General Massu of Algerian fame. Back in Paris on May 30th, he announced a general election and threatened all those who would try to prevent it by paralyzing the country. As soon as his broadcast was over, it was the turn of his supporters to demonstrate.

Were the Gaullist marchers in the Champs-Elysées as numerous as the left-wingers who had crossed Paris on May 13th? Probably not quite, yet it does not matter. The two huge demonstrations symbolized a country split in two, and for a spell it looked like a collision course. Only for a spell. The day after, Georges Séguy, the Communist leader of the CGT, proclaimed that his confederation would impede nothing, that it was eager to negotiate not only at the top but at all levels. The army of labor was thus being disbanded. Knowing that an unfinished upheaval is no preparation for a poll, the Communists had opted for electoral defeat. It proved rather difficult to bring the strikes to an end, but by June 30th the Right was duly returned to office. The *événements* were virtually over.

What lessons can be drawn from the events, summarized here as briefly as possible? If the French crisis had ended with the march on May 13th, it would have differed only marginally, in drama and color, from other student revolts that year spreading from Berkeley to Tokyo. What made France, and later Italy, qualitatively different was the response of the workers, however ambiguous and filtered through the Communist party (CP) it may have been. The student revolt in Paris had precipitated the biggest general strike in the country's history. In a centralized system, an elected monarchy, the problem of power was rapidly put on the agenda. What is more, the progressive paralysis of the economy led people to question all values and all institutions. Only this and nothing more. An immediate revolutionary solution was never at stake. Those who would—the students, the revolutionary "grouplets"—couldn't. Those who could, or had claimed that capacity as their birthright—the Communists—wouldn't. (Whether the situation was potentially revolutionary is, in this context, irrelevant. Viewing the situation, like all the other parties, in electoral terms, the CP refused to push the movement as far as it could go.)

The other feature was fairly classical. The young rebels wore yesterday's clothes to tackle the issues of tomorrow. The active minorities that inspired the movement and gave it a sense of direction may have felt that they were reenacting the seizure of the Winter Palace, and some of their leaders that they were playing the part of Lenin or Mao. Yet it was one of the first Western rebellions for a long time without a model: the Soviet one had been discredited, and this was part of the problem with the CP; the "cultural revolution" fashionable at the time had little to do with its Chinese original. Even if in often crude and clumsy terms, the young rebels were raising questions connected with problems facing advanced capitalism: not only the distribution of the product, but the very purpose of growth; the reasons for the hierarchical division of labor or for the artificial expansion of the unwithering state. However utopian their solutions, they were groping toward a radical alternative, revealing a glimpse of the future.

THE RESTORATION

Naturally, the general election of 1968 brought nothing to an end, bar the counting. General de Gaulle's departure in 1969, to take but

33

one example, was a direct consequence of the previous year's crisis. What mattered most for the French establishment, however, was to obliterate the glimpse of an alternative; and this, because it concerned mainly its supporters, was the task entrusted to the respectable Left. It was up to the Socialists and to the Communists to convince their electorate of two connected points: that the reborn belief in radical change, in a revolutionary break, was based on a hallucination; that a proper use of the ballot, on the other hand, could enable people to "change course" (*changer de cap*, the title of the Communist program) or even to "change life" (the title of the Socialist one). Because it was socially stronger and in greater need of a substitute for its shattered "revolutionary" reputation, the Communist party was ready to make much bigger concessions, which may seem ironic in retrospect. By 1972 the two partners produced their counterpoint to the May movement, the Common Program of government, arguing that important reforms could be carried out gradually, without a break, within existing institutions.

It took them so long because the protest movement was far from spent. It had undermined the ruling ideology in the schools, the university, and the cultural media. It had sapped the belief in the work ethic. And it was still spreading. The two crucial newcomers of this half-century—the ecological movement and feminism—were both late developments in France, following and not preceding 1968. If, despite the undermining of its pillars, the ideological edifice still stood, it was because the various currents never coalesced, since each sought its own direction.

Simultaneously, the "grouplets"—whether Trotskyist, Maoist, or libertarian—had become groups (though not parties). The Maoist *Gauche Prolétarienne*, or GP, with the help of its famous fellow traveler, Jean-Paul Sartre, did steal the limelight for a time. It managed to focus attention on such relevant issues as the plight of prisoners or the exploitation of immigrant labor. But its propaganda was as crude as it was spectacular. The GP seemed to live in a world of make-believe where every summer was to be hot, where foreign workers were the vanguard of the proletariat, where the Communists (that is, the "revisionists") were the "principal enemy" and the revolution was just round the corner. Reality refusing to conform to such a vision, an organization of this kind was bound to collapse sooner rather than later.[2]

Yet the GP was not alone. Finally, it was the movement as a

whole which proved short-lived. Imagination never seized power after 1968. Questioning the role of political parties, the May movement never invented an organizational substitute. It never elaborated a project capable of bringing its warring factions together for long-term action. It did not outline the contours of a hegemonic coalition. Thus, though it did raise all the problems that marked the period, the May movement never looked like a realistic alternative, and without one the Common Program, however uninspiring, gradually emerged as the only possible "solution."

If one defines the May movement as the force groping toward a solution beyond the confines of established capitalist society, it was last seen acting, or rather reacting, collectively at the time of the takeover by the employees of the Lip watch factory at Besançon in 1973. The leaders of this "work-in" never claimed that theirs was a case of self-management, of *autogestion*; you don't build socialism in a single factory. But the workers running their plant by democratic means and selling the watches through a militant network all over France in complete breach of the law did capture the imagination of the *contestataires*. Actually, when the death of Georges Pompidou precipitated a presidential election in 1974, there was question of picking Charles Piaget, the leader of Lip, as the symbolic candidate of the New Left.

Though it did not come off, the very idea showed to what extent the preoccupations were by then electoral. Indeed, it may be argued that the presidential poll of 1974 marked the highest point in the potential rise of social democracy in France. François Mitterrand, the recently chosen first secretary of a renewed Socialist party, was then the candidate of a United Left. The Communists, on that occasion, dutifully and even eagerly performed their part as juniors in the coalition, and the two partners ran their campaign on the hopeful assumption of a Japanese rate of growth. And Mitterrand missed victory by a cat's whisker.

THE ECONOMIC CRISIS RESHAPES THE LANDSCAPE

The irony is that this moment in 1974 of near fulfillment for French

2. Why it did not cross the line leading to terrorism, as in Italy or Germany, is another matter requiring longer explanation.

social democracy was also the time when the premises on which its success rested really collapsed. It is by now generally admitted that the crisis which hit that year was not caused by the jump in the cost of crude oil; it had been duly heralded by a fall in the rate of profit. On the other hand, the dramatic rise in petroleum prices did accelerate the process and reveal the crisis to the general public. Indeed, so deep was the conviction that capitalism had found the secret of eternal growth that the economic crisis took everybody—Left, Right, and center—by surprise. This is not the place to analyze the nature of this crisis, or to ponder how the system will emerge from the resulting predicament, but since it has completely altered the political equation, we must look at its consequences for the European Left in general and the French movement in particular.

The shock of 1974–75 was so stunning because it came after thirty years of unprecedented prosperity and deep changes in the social structure of the population. The May uprising, it must be remembered, came during this long cycle, while the going was apparently good. It revealed the seamy side of the "miracle," the depth of pent-up discontent. There is no doubt, however, that the doubling of living standards within a generation helped the opponents of the May movement to plead that life could be altered within the existing system.

In France probably the most striking social change during this postwar period was the mass migration from country to town. The virtual vanishing of the peasant was coupled with a slow growth of the industrial proletariat and a much more rapid expansion of white-collar workers. The boom years required a substantial import of foreign labor, while the shift to tertiary employment involved the mass entry of women into the labor market. The crisis preserved this last trend, while affecting all the others. Despite the closing of frontiers to foreign labor, the industrial slump led to a return of mass unemployment, with the traditional strongholds of the working class, such as mining, iron and steel, the car industry, and shipbuilding being particularly affected. Labor unions would have had difficulty coping with all of these trends even if they had a strategy, but they clearly had none.

Politically, the respectful Left was even more bewildered. The relative success of the capitalist economy had been such that even the Communists, with the Soviet model shattered, were resigned to seeking solutions within the system. In France the Left, guided by conditioned reflexes, refused to face the new situation. In 1981 it reached office in a country entirely open to foreign competition with a nice Keynesian program, as if nothing had happened—one reason for its rapid ideological and practical bankruptcy.

Failure of the old Left does not mean success of the new. In a sense, the temporary blunting of radicalism by the economic crisis is not unusual; in the short or even medium run, unemployment tends to moderate the temper of the working class. This time, however, the change was more profound. The 1960s had seen the makings of a new trend. Some sections of the labor movement had begun to make qualitative demands, to question the logic of the system, to refuse monetary compensation for, say, unhealthy working conditions, to ask for a reduction in the hours of work and even for some form of workers' control over the organization of labor. But the social climate created by the economic crisis was very unpropitious for this budding plant. Who cares about "enrichment of tasks" or meaningful work when one's immediate preoccupation is to get (or keep) a job, of any kind whatsoever.

Worse was still to come. Qualitative demands had been linked with a strategy known in Italy as one of "structural reforms" and in France as "revolutionary reformism." Its objectives were always somehow ambiguous. Were the reforms, as the protagonists of this strategy claimed, links in a chain leading beyond the confines of capitalist society, or were they designed to improve it and ensure its survival? In France, the economic crisis and the subsequent accession of the left to office gave a clear answer. The spokespeople of the so-called *Second Left*—Michel Rocard or Jacques Delors, the Socialist ministers, or Edmond Maire, the leader of the CFDT—dispelled any possible doubt. Capital was for them the ultimate horizon and flexibility was thus designed to make the system work better. It was not compromise but surrender, and their conduct must have discredited, at least for a time, what had looked like a search for a radical alternative.

But let us not anticipate. The drastic changes in the economic climate, according to pure logic, should have affected the Right even more than the Left. After all, it was restoring the image of capitalism to its true colors and, by the same token, destroying the fashionable new myth of "capitalism without crises." The gospel of growth had become the religion of the Western world, the establishment's perfect counter to the egalitarian aspirations of the

37

people. Now, this smokescreen dispelled, the nature of capitalist society would seem plain to see, with its injustice, inequality, and absurdity illustrated once again by mass unemployment.

Here, then, there seemed to be a serious risk that revulsion against this society in crisis might unify the various protest movements, provide them with a common purpose, turning sporadic confrontations into a frontal attack and skirmishes into a decisive battle. The paradox is that the Western Right, pretty shaken by 1968 and apparently threatened by the economic crisis, found in it the means for a spectacular ideological recovery. France is a good example to show how Western capitalism, without the *gulag*, can produce at the right time and in the right place the "universal ideas" required for its survival.

THE IDEOLOGICAL DEFEAT OF THE LEFT

Thus, what the capitalist establishment feared most was that the economic crisis could bring with it a threat of united action. What was, therefore, required was an ideology damning the very search for a global project. To proclaim that our system, however bad, was better than "all those that have been tried from time to time" was fine, though no longer enough, since the young rebels themselves had abandoned the Soviet model. It was indispensable to convince them that, if individual rebellion might be right, any form of collective action was bound to turn society into a vast concentration camp. This was the message needed in the midseventies and, with the help of Solzhenitsyn's *Gulag Archipelago*, it was the message duly delivered by the so-called *nouveaux philosophes*. There is no necessity to bother here with the intellectual content of this cheap remake of *The God That Failed*, patched up entirely with borrowed ideas. What is of interest for our purpose is the tremendous success of this exercise in propaganda and, particularly, the indispensable part played in it by "children of May" turned preachers against the evil of revolutionary solutions. Yet in order not to exaggerate the importance of a few turncoats, one must put the relationship between the movement and the so-called new strata in its proper context.

The students rebelling against society in 1968 were also questioning their futures and as such were finding an echo among teachers and researchers, social workers, and all sorts of cadres unhappy with their own role. Nineteen sixty-eight can be described as a portent of things to come, insofar as it outlined an alliance between the fast-changing working class (including the newly alienated white collars and the highly skilled technicians quite close to the social frontier) and the fast-growing sections of the professional intelligentsia. It foreshadowed not a marriage with the middle classes but a cleavage within the latter. But it only foreshadowed. With the movement defeated and the New Left having failed to appear as a credible alternative, these cadres who had been tempted for a time had to seek other solutions to defend their immediate rather than long-term interests. Incidentally, it can be argued that the electoral advantage of the Socialists over the Communists is largely due to their greater success in wooing these "new strata."

Another point to keep in mind is that the turncoats are not typical. Many youngsters active in 1968, once the movement collapsed, went back to cultivate their own gardens, devoted their energy to their profession, or even when they resigned themselves to rallying to the Socialist party, did so without any illusions, faute de mieux. Those who have been most in the limelight are precisely the people who now preach the perpetuity of capitalism or the necessity for the Left to love private enterprise with the same passion with which yesterday they had forecast the doom of capitalism and advocated civil war. Indeed, in the case of some Maoists turned new philosophers, they altered their ideas without changing their manner of thinking. They used to chant Marx, Engels, Lenin, Stalin, Mao, and Lin Piao. Then, ten years later, in the same primitive fashion, only reversing the line, they described Karl Marx as the grandfather of the *gulag*. What made French converts peculiar and some of their pronouncements so distasteful was their smugness and self-satisfaction. They seem to be as proud of their past as they are pleased with their present: the French breed of convert is righteous rather than repentant.

Even weathercocks need an element of stability, a rod around which to turn with the wind. For the French recanters this stability is provided by "anticommunism." To be more precise, while the word is the same, the content is not. The born-again champions of capitalism used to attack the French CP as insufficiently anticolonialist because it had not backed the Algerian insurgents enough and was advocating merely peace in Vietnam instead of victory for the FLN. Now, though the white man's burden rather than the wretched of the earth marks their vocabulary, they are still true to themselves, because they remain anti-CP. Yesterday, they branded Communist apparatchiks as traitors to the cause and described CGT bosses as the main obstacle between the working masses and power. Today revolution is for them the supreme sin, but they remain faithful to their "anticommunism." They have to cling to this concept as the only element of artificial continuity in their life. Indeed they are rather proud of their achievement. They have rendered their country a great service. They were the prime movers in getting rid of a powerful Communist party.[3] But was it such a great service, and are they not claiming too much?

THE COMMUNIST VOID

The second question can be answered quite easily. They do exaggerate their importance. François Mitterrand did much more to bring the CP down to size, and Georges Marchais, taken here symbolically for the CP leadership as a whole, incomparably more. Seen in perspective, the conduct of the French Communist party in the last twenty years looks as if it were guided by a death wish, by some obsessive passion for suicide.

May 1968 undoubtedly played a significant part in this dramatic decline of the CP. Its essentially electoralist line had been initiated earlier. The crisis of 1968, however, revealed that, whatever the rhetoric, the party had no revolutionary option and therefore a popular front alliance with the Socialists was imperative. Could not the French Communists take advantage of the situation and, like their Italian counterparts, gain a hegemonic position on the French Left? To do so, the French CP would have had to break its close links with Moscow earlier and proceed with its own transformation much faster. It managed to take half-measures halfheartedly, to move in two directions and, finally, to lose both ways.

Under the leadership of Marchais, the CP dropped some of its major concepts, such as the dictatorship of the proletariat. It did it without any genuine debate and without any attempt to fill the resulting ideological void. Previously, the French CP had con-

---

3. Herve Hamon and Patrick Rotman, *Génération*, vol. 2, *Les Années de poudre* (Paris: Seuil, 1988), pp. 640–42.

demned the Soviet invasion of Czechoslovakia in 1968 only to resign itself to its "normalization." Subsequently, it distanced itself from Moscow during its "Eurocommunist" phase in the mid-seventies, only to approve the invasion of Afghanistan and General Jaruzelski's coup against Solidarity in Poland afterwards.

The relationship with the Socialists was no less contradictory. To begin with, the Communists, needing a partner, helped the Socialists to recover. Then, having found out that the alliance favored the more moderate partner, they suddenly discovered that the Socialists were no "revolutionaries." Breaking the pact, in 1977, they brought about the unthinkable—the defeat of the Left in the parliamentary elections of the following year. Three years later they paid the price: Marchais was badly beaten by Mitterrand in the first ballot of the 1981 presidential poll. The Communists then entered his government without any preconditions. They stayed in, without real influence, for three years, including two years of austerity, proclaiming that this government was better than any previous left-wing administration. The day after their departure, they called it an example of bourgeois betrayal.

Indeed, it was their own behavior that was probably the main reason for the Communist downfall. The CP was ready to admit past mistakes, including its behavior in 1968, though never to cast doubt on its current infallibility.[4] It even got converted to self-management, to the famous *autogestion*, for years dismissed as the sin of the *gauchistes*. Yet who could believe in this conversion when every year the stifling of debate and the elimination of successive oppositions confirmed that the CP could not conceive of power as something that was not flowing from above? It deserved to lose and did so spectacularly. For a party committed to an electoral road, the milestones of its decline are plain to read. Before 1968 the CP used to get well over one-fifth of the votes cast in France. In the presidential poll of 1981 Georges Marchais captured 15.5 percent. In the parliamentary election of 1986 the CP was down to 9.7 percent, on a par with Le Pen. In the presidential poll of 1988 André Lajoinie got no more than 6.8 percent.[5]

4. See, for example, the speech of Georges Marchais at the 25th congress of the French CP in *L'Humanite*, 7 February 1985.
5. It is true that there are precedents for such an electoral fall. The Gaullists, who had approached 40 percent in local elections and still gathered 20.4 percent of the poll in the parliamentary election of 1951, had only 4.4 percent in the parliamentary

DANIEL SINGER

There remains the question of the effect, the consequences of this spectacular fall. Drawing the lesson from the events of 1968, Sartre's *Les Temps Modernes* made the bitter comment: "We knew we could not make a revolution without the Communists. We now know we cannot make it with them." It was common knowledge, these lines suggested, that no revolutionary break could take place in France without the mass of the workers who supported the CP; it was now obvious that the leadership of that party had no intention of participating in such an upheaval. From these premises the conclusion was drawn by the movement that whatever form the break should actually take, no radical transformation of French society was possible unless the Communist party changed its very nature, or, since this seemed unlikely, until it was swept aside. There was disagreement as to what would fill the resulting void. In the post-1968 mood, many took it for granted that the forces so unleashed would be harnessed by a really radical movement. Others, less vocal at the time, assumed that the disappearance of the CP would simply help them to play politics without risks, in the style of France's northern and western neighbors.

The coexistence of such expectations illustrates the dual role performed by the French CP in the postwar period. On the one hand, by its reputation, its revolutionary rhetoric, its Marxist vocabulary, it was helping to preserve the belief in the radical break, in the possibility of genuinely altering life through political action (and this distinguished France and Italy from, say, Britain or Germany). On the other hand, its system of command from above, its absence of inner life, its ideological sclerosis ensured that this favorable opinion would never be exploited. In 1968 it partly contributed to create a situation in which its revolutionary impotence was revealed. Thereafter, its fate may well have been sealed. The snag is that, as its decline coincided with the turn of the tide, instead of helping the rise of a new radical movement, it prepared the ground, at least temporarily, for the normalization of France.

For this, however, the French Left still had to learn that there was no scope for reforms either. To teach this, the Socialists had to get

poll five years later. But the Gaullists were not a normal party. They were a Rally (the *Rassemblement du Peuple Francais* or RPF) around General de Gaulle and by 1956, his first assault repelled, the general had retired to his tent or rather to Colombey-les-deux-Eglises.

into office with the Communists as very junior and very useful partners.

NORMALIZATION AND THE GHOST OF MAY

François Mitterrand always wanted to "redress the balance" of the French Left, that is to say, reduce the weight of the Communist party, and he made no bones about it. At the same time I do not think, for reasons explained elsewhere, that he intentionally planned the surrender of the Socialists in office.[6] The defeat of the Left was written into its electoral victory in 1981, which coincided with ideological subservience, the absence of a social movement, and the lack of any analysis of the economic crisis. Once the Socialists, so disarmed, discovered that their Keynesian program was leading them nowhere, Mitterrand altered his line altogether. Since he could not gain laurels as a socialist reformer, he would go down in history books as the man who brought France into the established Western pattern by depriving it of dreams of a different future.

Within less than two decades the supporters of the French Left had been submitted to a tough ordeal. In 1968 they had recovered hope together with a vague belief in a real alternative. It took quite a time to convince them that, if May was an illusion, something similar could be achieved by parliamentary means. By the time they seemed converted, the sudden collapse of the Socialist-Communist alliance deprived the Left of certain victory in 1978. Then, in 1981, the disenchanted leftists had electoral victory thrust upon them in the presidential poll; it was not so much their victory as the defeat of the other side. Still, one does not look a gift horse in the mouth. But after a year of illusion, the Left was to find out that its side was following in the footsteps of its predecessors, that Socialist austerity did not differ greatly from that practiced by the conservatives. The road led from hope to hopelessness and resignation.

If May 1968 was essentially the rebirth of hope, the end of marginalism, the rediscovered belief in change beyond the confines of the system, then Mitterrand can be fairly described as the

6. Daniel Singer, *Is Socialism Doomed? The Meaning of Mitterrand* (New York: Oxford University Press, 1988).

gravedigger of May. He was not alone, nor did he set out to earn that title. The Socialists had actually begun by borrowing the vocabulary of the May movement. Yet once in office, presiding over a perfectly orthodox policy of austerity, they had to convince their supporters that there was no alternative and could be none; they had to persuade them to expect no "miracles," electoral or otherwise. The drop in the support for the Socialists and their president was a measure of the disappointment among the electorate of the Left. The recovery of that support was a sign of the resignation of that electorate. The French, like their neighbors, had to accept that there was nothing beyond the capitalist horizon.

How a birthday is celebrated is often symbolic. For the twentieth anniversary of May, the French staged a presidential election, the main significance of which was its relative insignificance. As in other Western countries, it did not even pretend to cast doubts on established institutions, to threaten the regime, to raise problems clashing with the existing order. If May 1968 was a passionate reassertion that history never comes to a full stop and that there is a future beyond capitalism, the election of 1988 was its counterpoint. It was not an anniversary celebration for May, rather its belated funeral oration.

Yet dead and duly buried, the ghost of May refuses to lie down. The spirit of May is clearly not more alive but undoubtedly more relevant than it was at the time. The questions raised in 1968—over the meaning of growth, the purposes of the social division of labor, the menacing size of the ruling Leviathan and its real function— could be and were dismissed as rather utopian or not very urgent at a time when the economy was apparently forging ahead, incomes were rising, and the welfare state was ensuring unprecedented security. Today in a Europe with millions of jobless, where our inventive ability leads to longer lines of unemployed, where the welfare functions of the state and social security in general are being threatened, these are no longer abstract or distant questions. The capitalist establishment continues to rule not because it provides valid answers, but because it has managed to foster the spirit of inequality, to divide the working people between the skilled and the unskilled, the better paid and the worse off, the employed and the unemployed. The Left will not stand a chance again until it tackles the questions raised in 1968, builds its answers into a coherent project, opposing its own logic to that of capital.

What are its chances? In France there is no denying that its original advantage, the belief in an alternative, has been shattered. Its future is partly dependent on the answer to two connected questions: is the resignation, a natural result not only of the economic crisis but of a series of letdowns, a lasting phenomenon? Can the revolutionary tradition, two centuries old, be dissolved as easily and as permanently as the vote for the Communist party? Of the latter collapse, incidentally, we have only seen so far the negative effects, the service this has rendered to the ruling ideology. It remains to be seen how the void is being filled. If the Soviet model as such is obviously destroyed, the Soviet bogey, since *perestroika*, no longer scares. There are vague signs of a changing mood—notably the student demonstrations and spontaneous strikes in France toward the end of 1986—suggesting that the young generation is not quite as Americanized and submissive as it had been painted. Mitterrand's normalization may prove ephemeral after all.

But what is now required is more than a mere revolt limited to national frontiers. It is, to begin with, a vast project appealing to the working people of Western Europe. There can be no question of looking back, hoping to repeat the seizure of the Winter Palace in entirely different surroundings. To get a response, the project will have to deal with such matters as labor and leisure, culture and communications in the age of the robot and the computer. It will have to face various issues of which the sixty-eighters were only dimly aware; our place in the universe and survival in the still-nuclear world; the new role of women both today and in the projected society. It will have to succeed where May failed, in inventing new forms of organization and democracy both on the shop floor and in the country at large. The task is undoubtedly tremendous, yet the movement will not even begin to fulfill it unless it is willing to reassert its own logic, ready to clash with the allegedly beneficial rule of the market, the wisdom of profit, the presently undisputed reign of capital.

"Be realistic, ask for the impossible" remains the message of 1968 most relevant for our day, provided it is not interpreted poetically as just a flight into fancy. The limits of the possible are being defined for us all the time by our environment, our media, our pundits and preachers—it is what our society is ready to tolerate. The allegedly "impossible" leads us straight to the classical dilemma of socialism, namely, that the questions it raises and the

45

struggle it must carry through are rooted in existing society, while the answers it should provide lie ultimately beyond the frontiers of that society. The Right is now dominant in the world not because of what it offers, but because of the absence of another vision, of a radical alternative.

With so many great expectations shattered, I will not end with any forecast, only with two remarks. The first is rather gloomy. Even if the existing order is "built on sand," it does not mean that another, our own, is ripe and ready to take over. The second is one of cautious optimism. History, the French say, offers no second helpings, *l'histoire ne repasse pas les plats*, which is quite clearly inaccurate. The snag is that its conception of time differs from our impatient calculations. The lean years in between, as we have bitterly learned, are measured in scores rather than sevens. All the more reason to prepare the alternative assiduously during the lengthy intervals of seeming immobility so as not to miss the appointment during the privileged moments when history, as in 1968, beckons us to action.

3 JENSEITS DES HISTORIKERSTREITS
The Significance of the Controversy

Charles S. Maier

What is the *Historikerstreit* about? By now the major texts are familiar. On one side four main elements have appeared: (1) the various appeals of Chancellor Kohl and other political leaders for a historiography that did not dwell exclusively on the crimes of the Nazi era; (2) Andreas Hillgruber's *Zweierlei Untergang*,[1] whose full title bracketed the end of the German national state with the destruction of the European Jews and claimed that the historian must "identify" with the Wehrmacht defending the eastern borders of Germany in the winter of 1944–45; (3) Michael Stürmer's essays[2] which argued that West Germans were searching for a meaningful historical identity and that their history should provide national orientation as a reliable member of the Western alliance; and, most egregious, (4) Ernst Nolte's claim, supported by the editor of the *Frankfurter Allgemeine Zeitung* (*FAZ*), Joachim Fest, and now redefended in Nolte's book-length response to his critics[3] and in a further Nolte volume[4] that the Gulag Archipelago was "more original" than Auschwitz and that in some ways Soviet terror served as the predecessor for Hitler's genocide.

On the other side two major streams can be identified: (1) essays of protest by leading historians—Eberhard Jäckel, Hans Mommsen, Jürgen Kocka, and Martin Broszat, among others; and most

1. Andreas Hillgruber, *Zweierlei Untergang* (Berlin: Siedler, 1986).
2. Collected in Michael Stürmer, *Dissonanzen des Fortschritts* (Munich: Piper, 1987).
3. Ernst Nolte, *Das Vergehen der Vergangenheit* (Frankfurt/Main: Ullstein, 1987).
4. Ernst Nolte, *Der europäische Bürgerkrieg, 1917–1945* (Frankfurt/Main: Ullstein, 1987).

significant, (2) Jürgen Habermas's polemical response to the conservatives with its evocation of "constitutional patriotism," a commitment to a national *Rechtsstaat* of the West as a counterideal to a "conventional" national identity. These pieces,[5] plus dozens of additional essays, polemical responses,[6] related volumes,[7] and the argument over the plans for a "German historical museum" in Berlin have been the key documents of the historians' controversy.

But what is the significance of this massive set-to among the German academic intelligentsia? Is it just the artifact of a feuilleton war between *FAZ* and *Die Zeit*? Exemplification of the penchant for self-laceration that a close academic community encourages? A battle over which way to "historicize" the Nazi past such that, in the judgment of Saul Friedländer, misguided "functionalist" interpretations favored by the Left, which sought to make the Third Reich normal and explicable as ordinary politics, ended up sanctioning the Right's claim that indeed the Third Reich was normal politics?

It is revealing that the controversy has not gripped all educated readers equally. One historian in his late thirties proposed to me this past summer that the argument was the affair of those in their late forties or over, a preoccupation perhaps like cholesterol levels and college tuitions that one faces on the backtrack of life. He had a point: has the *Historikerstreit* been generation-specific? If so, why? And in any case, why this dispute now when the Federal Republic is not outwardly passing through any political or social crisis; when it has not yielded to the ugliness of a movement like the Front National across the Rhine; when the economy (at least through the summer) continues its usual exemplary performance; when no great national issue such as *Ostpolitik* causes tremors of angst; when Fassbinder is dead, Lafontaine is all sweetness and light, the last prisoner of Spandau has been gathered to his fathers, and when the world's most illustrious Germans, Steffi Graff and Boris Becker, could hardly be expected to remember the chancellorship of Willy Brandt?

The *Historikerstreit* is about memory, politics, and the writing of

5. Now collected in *Historikerstreit* (Munich: Piper, 1987).
6. Viz. Andreas Hillgruber, "Jürgen Habermas, Karl Janssen, und die Aufklärung Anno 1986," *Geschichte in Wissenschaft und Unterricht* (December, 1986).
7. To wit, Christian Meier, *Vierzig Jahre nach Auschwitz* (Munich: Deutscher Kunstverlag, 1987); Hans-Ulrich Wehler's disputatious *Entsorgung der deutschen Vergangenheit?* (Munich: Beck, 1988).

history. It is about memory because only a particular crisis of memory satisfactorily explains why it erupted in 1986. It is about current politics and what Gramsci would have called hegemony—control of political discourse based upon who determines the relevant political and historical comparisons. Finally, it is the specifically West German form of a wider transnational phenomenon: the rise of what might be called postmodern historiography.

MEMORY: WHY NOW?

Explanations can be tentative at best, but I will suggest three possibilities.

1. At one level the answer is contingency, a series of contested commemorations unleashed by the fortieth anniversary first of D Day (the Germans could not be included), then of V-E Day (the Germans did not know how to be included). But why did these fourth-decade commemorations matter more than those of a decade earlier? Perhaps because two generations were caught at once. Some of those who fought the war or experienced the events as young adults felt the need to justify German sacrifices (including brothers slain in service); they did not wish to repress the ambivalences of German defeat. And those moving into midlife positions of influence still had sharp memories, if only from early childhood. Fathers and sons, who were now (to speak metaphorically) grandfathers and fathers, were engaged simultaneously at a moment of importance in their respective life trajectories. If 1968 was a revolt of sons against fathers, the *Historikerstreit* of 1986 was a more complicated generational interplay: on one side fathers, now grandfathers, striking back; on the other side sons, now grown fathers, no longer abjuring their elders' past, but insisting on their own implication, *Befangenheit*, within it. For all the annoyance foreign observers can feel about the so-called revisionist campaign to reduce the implications of National Socialist crimes, it should be recognized that the controversy has also generated more convincing and widespread arguments for continuing German co-responsibility than at any point since Karl Jaspers and Theodor Adorno's essays of the postwar period.

2. There is a more general circumstance. One might call it, after Günter Grass, "the Onion Cellar revisited." Readers of *The Tin Drum* will recall Oskar's postwar Düsseldorf *Lokal*, where clients

49

received with their drinks an onion and a paring knife so that they might finally be able to weep. Those tears, which forty years ago only lachrymogens could unleash, now flow on their own: the trials of Klaus Barbie and Ivan Demjanjuk, the construction of Holocaust museums and deportation memorials throughout the diaspora, the demand of Poles, Armenians, Ukranians, and others for the certification of *their* "holocausts"—all this suggests that there is a universal need to let sadness and memory claim the public space that may have earlier been withheld. The Mitscherlichs' "inability to mourn" has been overcome; even now, or perhaps only now, *sunt lachrimae rerum at mentem mortalia tangunt.*

Memory becomes not just a gateway to the past, but a subject of contemplation and wonder in its own right. Saul Friedländer's *Speak, Memory*, with its conflation of private and public spheres, is an affecting example of the genre. The preoccupation with memory claims academic enterprise as well: the revival of the hermeneutic or *verstehende* approach in the social sciences, a new wrestling with subjectivity, sympathy for cultural and anthropological approaches in history, for *Alltagsgeschichte*. There is a broad cross-cultural thirst to redeem the past, with tears if need be, with memorials, to retrieve the names of *all* the dead (whether at the Vietnam Memorial on the Washington Mall or in the 1986 *Gedenkbuch* that lists all traceable German-Jewish victims of Nazism).

3. Is this turn toward memory, the revival of history—but not *Annaliste* history or *Strukturgeschichte* so much as the history of events, the narrative—just an accident? It follows upon the collapse of faith in the great reformist projects of the 1960s—the erosion of the Keynesian premises and expectations of robust growth that shaped a generation after the war. The preoccupation with history, evident in Germany and elsewhere, may testify to a certain general loss of future orientation, not to a simpleminded failure of faith (although is it just an accident that birthrates are dropping below replacement ratios, most strikingly in West Germany?) but to a need at least to recognize the past as constraining, problematic, and formative.

A POLITICAL CONFLICT

Even as it reveals the grip of an ambivalent memory, the *Historikerstreit* has been a political battle. It is a dispute over the controlling public discourse of the Federal Republic. The most spectacular issue of the dispute has concerned the question of whether the Holocaust is comparable to other twentieth-century genocides or mass killings, above all to the Soviet purges and terror. Indeed Ernst Nolte did not claim just comparability, but historical priority for the *gulag*—a charge that he has elaborated in his newest volume, *Der europäische Bürgerkrieg*. This study fills out an argument already suggested in *Marxismus und Industrielle Revolution*[8] that fascism was a reaction to the strivings for "transcendence" on the part of the European Left. The civil war referred to was the National Socialist response to Bolshevism; the Nazi murder of the Jewish race was an answer to the Bolshevik liquidation of the bourgeois class. Nolte does recognize that the murder of the Jews was "biological," that is, literal, whereas class liquidation was often structural—but that does not inhibit his flights of analogy. In effect, Hitler becomes a rather anxiety-ridden champion of the bourgeoisie. This thesis is far less original than Nolte's own self-advertisement as the last real practitioner of "philosophical history" would suggest.[9] After all, Marxist wags of the 1940s described Stalingrad as the great confrontation between Hegelians of the Left and Right. But no matter what the originality (or the validity) of Nolte's assessment that he is writing the first real history to ground totalitarian theory, the thrust of the analogy is to suggest that Nazi crimes can be assimilated into the broader currents of human experience. To suggest otherwise Nolte argues—erroneously I believe[10]—would be to imply there is absolute evil and thus to forsake history for utopianism.

The point to be underlined is that the dispute is one over relevant comparisons. Nolte and Joachim Fest, who has seconded Nolte's argumentation, do not claim Auschwitz is like the *gulag*. They pose the pseudohistorical question, namely, whether it is impermissible to ask if Auschwitz is like the *gulag*. Agreed: the historian cannot place any comparison off-limits in advance. But if comparison is honest, it must be over the substantive issue and not the pseudo-question, "Is it not permitted to ask?" Moreover, any honest comparison will lay as much stress upon the distinctions between

8. Ernst Nolte, *Marxismus und Industrielle Revolution* (Stuttgart: Klett-Cotta, 1983).
9. Ernst Nolte, "Philosophische Geschichtsschreibung Heute," *Historische Zeit-schrift*, 242 (1986): 265–89.
10. Ernst Nolte, "Die Ausschau nach dem Ganzen," *Frankfurter Allgemeine Zeitung*, July 18, 1987.

the cases compared as upon the similarity and will stress equally what is specific as well as generic. What the *Historikerstreit* has confirmed is that to "control" the universe of relevant historical comparisons is, in effect, to set the parameters of political discourse and legitimacy. Rudolf Augstein expressed disbelief that in the year 1986 Germans could seriously debate whether Auschwitz was more or less modeled on Soviet terror. He had a point. As several commentators have suggested, the questions raised legitimate a type of exculpatory agenda that hitherto marked only the fetid growth of rightist publications. The *Soldatenzeitung* has been *rehabilitiert*, and that means that the quasi-constitutional restraints on historiography are being lifted. No "stab-in-the-back" thesis has been advanced, but the implications raised about the 20th of July resisters by the thrust of Hillgruber and Nolte's historiography may yet play a similar role. The *Historikerstreit* has revealed that a nationalist and apologetic interpretation of the past serves (as Michael Stürmer reminds us) as a mainstream ideological orientation. Just as 1968, in effect, temporarily opened the narrow West German political spectrum to Marxist options, so 1986 has opened the spectrum to a conservative nationalism. Bonn is not Weimar, but intellectually it is a bit closer than it was.

A CHAPTER IN HISTORIOGRAPHY

The historians' controversy is also part of an international debate over the limits of history. It is the German form under which postmodern historiography has challenged the claims of history as a would-be social science and has contested any implicit theory of progress or development. Jürgen Habermas can be taken as the Federal Republic's preeminent spokesman for what might be called the liberal-democratic or social-democratic "metanarrative"—the conviction that knowledge substantially reflects the real world, is progressive, and can change politics and society. Postmodern historiography, in effect, is attempting to fill a void left by the erosion of the earlier social-democratic premises of post-1960 history and politics. The major thrust of postmodern historiography is the unanchoring of politics from social structure. Discourse tends to be granted the causal preeminence that Marxists earlier reserved for economy and class structure. Language becomes an active agent for the postmodern historians, just as it serves as a force of opaqueness for Derrida or of oppression for Foucault. Similarly, memory itself becomes not a simple act of recall, but a subject in its own right. The German version of these trends is the invocation of "history," less as a record of events than as a socially constitutive act, a problematic construction of identity.

The political agenda of postmodernism is indeterminate. The point is not that it need be reactionary; it can be radical. So too in the *Historikerstreit*, its thrust is unclear. The demand for "historicization" expresses the ambiguities. It licenses the Right as well as the Left. There is considerable potential for conservative interpretations. What fills the gap between social structure and cultural or political outcome can be a neo-*Historismus* that justifies the past by appealing to the good conscience of those who committed it. What can also fill the gap is a revived distaste for mass democracy. Not inappropriately, Michael Stürmer remains fascinated by handicrafts and ideas of luxury, as well as by authority. Not surprisingly does his critique of the *Kaiserreich* focus on the incapacity of its elites to channel constructively mass impulses such as democratic nationalism. In the hands of a cruder historian such an interpretation could lead to the reactionary aestheticism of an Ernst Jünger. Not that the stance is not legitimate: conservatives and neoconservatives are all entitled to their own history. The point is merely to show the possible political implications of different approaches and to understand the contending approaches that have collided in the *Historikerstreit*.

Perhaps Habermas, along with many others (including myself), tended initially to interpret the *Wende* too narrowly. The "shift" since the mid-1970s was not just a simple turn to neoconservatism. It followed upon a more general exhaustion of an earlier historical faith, revived with the forces of democracy in 1945, but seemingly worn out after 1968. The institutional form of this earlier ideological buoyancy was the easy triumph of the welfare state in an era of prolonged economic growth. But this trend has been arrested. It may be that the educated public turns to history for consolation or as a respite from future-oriented thinking. German history offers less consolation than others, so the task is more problematic.

What sort of social and historiographical reconstruction will in turn follow the contemporary postmodern vogue is unclear. Social scientists and historians will not simply be able to restore the earlier transparent sociology that envisaged the economy, the political system, and the cultural systems mutually influencing each other in an easy and unproblematic relationship. The accumulated critiques of such diverse postmodern thinkers as Foucault, Derrida, Lyotard, and Rorty have rightly shaken earlier assumptions. How a postmodern Left might define a nonsimplistic program is unclear. How it will attempt historical "understanding" is also uncertain. To be sure, German social thought has not produced postmodern critics with the stature of the French theorists. The absence of postmodern originals (Habermas still transcends his critics at home) is not only because the Germans had a different 1968 (which they did)—one that was less anarchic and more intimidating, less targeted on a social order and more focused on individuals—but also because the Germans had 1933, with its devastation of an intellectual community that is still felt; 1933, to borrow a line from Ernst Nolte, was "more original" than 1940 in France.

Without postmodern theorists of the stature of the French, West German postmodern critiques have tended to take the form of revivals: neo-*Historismus* (Hillgruber and Stürmer), neoconservatism, and neo-structural functionalism (represented preeminently by Niklas Luhmann). For this reason the *Historikerstreit* has not produced compelling theoretical documents that will remain as significant philosophical statements, with the exception perhaps of Habermas's efforts to work out concepts of national identity. But if the Bonn Republic has rarely produced thinkers of the verve that Paris has encouraged since the 1960s, its intellectuals can still draw upon predecessors that lend their debates sophistication and style, such as Benjamin and Adorno.

Consequently, the *Historikerstreit*, focused on an intensely German issue of responsibility, is part of a larger conflict. On one side are those for whom history, if hardly a story of progress, is still a summons to enlightenment and to the advance of reason through the analysis of violence and repression; on the other are those for whom history bears witness to obscure drives, unavoidable suffering, and universal reversions. This opposition would all be terribly familiar were it not for the fact that the slogan of historicization serves both sides in the conflict. It is the ambiguity of this methodology—its reformist call to see through the structures of a society and its reactionary potential to justify the most destructive anxieties—that heralds a postmodern historiography and not just a rerun of earlier clashes.

4 THE MODERN VERSUS THE POSTMODERN
The Franco-German Debate in Social Theory

Mark Poster

In a recent overview of the current state of social theory Perry Anderson laments, "Paris today is the capital of European intellectual reaction."[1] This judgment of 1984 refers not to the notoriously anticommunist *nouveaux philosophes* but to the poststructuralists —Foucault, Derrida, Barthes, Lacan, Baudrillard, Lyotard, Deleuze —all of whom, Anderson notwithstanding, have participated in leftist politics and most of whom align themselves with the project of emancipation.[2] For Anderson the political climate in the mid-1980s is so conservative that he is able to name only one Continental theorist of stature, Jürgen Habermas of Frankfurt-am-Main, who escapes the negative epithet. Indeed the current battle over high theory, over the foundations of critical theory, may be studied as a duel between Habermas and the poststructuralists.

In some ways the debate, however acrimonious, represents an improvement in Franco-German intellectual relations. Since the Enlightenment French and German intellectuals have largely ignored one another despite geographical and at times even spiritual proximity. The exceptions to this situation, while important, are surprisingly few: Goethe's interest in Diderot, Marx's interest in Fourier and Saint Simon, Victor Cousin's interest in Hegel, the symbolist poets' fascination with Wagner, Sartre's interest in Heidegger, the recent interest of many French intellectuals in Nietzsche, and several others. Even if the list is doubled or tripled,

1. Perry Anderson, *In the Tracks of Historical Materialism* (Chicago: University of Chicago Press, 1984), p. 32.
2. Barthes, Lacan, and Foucault are of course no longer with us.

55

the generalization would seem to hold that these two proximate cultures have been well insulated from one another for two centuries. Americans are routinely astonished at the ignorance induced by the vapors of the Rhine. I recall asking Habermas in the mid-1970s if he had read Baudrillard since both worked on the problem of language in critical social theory. No, he had not, was the reply. Within the year I had the occasion to ask Baudrillard, who was trained as a Germanist, if he had read Habermas: no, he said, but he had heard of him. In this historical context the interest of the French poststructuralists in the Frankfurt school and the critical attention Habermas has given of late to the French must be taken as a step forward in international understanding.

The current rift between Habermas and the French may be traced back to the politically intense days of 1968. While most French intellectuals supported the New Left, Habermas had serious difficulties with the German student movement. His essay on the SDS reproached them for their radical antiauthoritarianism and for their regressive tendencies and advised the students to confine their reforming zeal to the halls of the university.[3] Lack of working-class support for SDS limited its revolutionary potential, he warned. Discounting the fact that eight or nine million French workers went on strike in solidarity with the students in that nation, Habermas surmised that these workers also "resisted" the May 1968 events.[4] In the course of the late 1960s and early 1970s, Habermas at times softened his critique of the New Left.[5] French intellectuals were less grudging in their attitudes. The future poststructuralists hailed the Paris spring as a new age in revolutionary struggles. Baudrillard, Foucault, Deleuze, Barthes, Derrida, Lyotard, Lacan all discerned hopeful signs of democratization in the massive protest movement.[6]

The disparity in the enthusiasms of Habermas and the French intellectuals for the politics of 1968 may be attributed in part to the

3. Jürgen Habermas, "The Movement in Germany," in *Toward a Rational Society*, trans. Jeremy Shapiro (Boston: Beacon, 1970), p. 46.
4. Ibid., p. 37.
5. See his comments in an interview published as "Political Experience and the Renewal of Marxist Theory," in Jürgen Habermas, *Autonomy and Solidarity: Interviews*, ed. Peter Dews (New York: Verso, 1987).
6. For a critical view of the role of intellectuals in May 1968 from a conservative perspective see Luc Ferry and Alain Renaut, *La Pensée 68: Essai sur l'anti-humanisme contemporain* (Paris: Gallimard, 1985).

difference in the nature of the movements in their respective nations. The radical students in Germany were isolated from wider political and social groups; the French were backed by popular opinion at large, by non-Communist unions, by Mitterrand and the Socialist party, by many skilled technical workers and virtually the entire artistic and intellectual community with the notable exceptions of Louis Althusser and Raymond Aron, at one in an unusual moment of agreement. In response to this new political situation and to the general socioeconomic changes of "postindustrial society," Habermas and the French were moving in different directions. I will now broadly summarize the two directions of thought to provide a background to the confrontation of their positions.

Recognizing general weaknesses in existing social theory, Habermas set out to "reconstruct" historical materialism.[7] In broad outline, he introduced the following revisions:

1. Define the conditions for a "public sphere" separate from the private interests that could serve as an arena for consensual reform.[8]
2. In advanced capitalism the state enters the economy, shattering the superstructure/base distinction. The legitimacy of the state is in crisis because economic issues are now politicized.[9]
3. In advanced capitalism science is integrated into the economy and takes its place as part of ideology.[10]
4. In the new social context blind adherence to working-class politics must yield to a more general demand for the conditions of free public discussion. Marxist theory must be revised to account for what Habermas variously terms symbolic interaction, communicative action, or language.
5. The problem of theory is to outline a universal pragmatics of language that may serve as the condition for public debate or, in

7. Jürgen Habermas, *Zur Rekonstruktion des historischen Materialismus* (Frankfurt/Main: Suhrkamp, 1976). For a good sense of the way Habermas's recent positions have been received in the English-speaking world see John B. Thompson and David Held, eds., *Habermas: Critical Debates* (Cambridge, Mass.: MIT Press, 1982) and for a reliable overview of Habermas's work see Thomas McCarthy, *The Critical Theory of Jürgen Habermas* (Cambridge, Mass.: MIT Press, 1978).
8. Jürgen Habermas, *Strukturwandel der Öffentlichkeit* (Neuwied: Luchterhand, 1971).
9. See Jürgen Habermas, *Legitimation Crisis*, trans. Thomas McCarthy (Boston: Beacon, 1975) for a full analysis of this issue.
10. See "Technology and Science as 'Ideology,'" in *Toward a Rational Society*, pp. 81–122.

his more controversial formulation, "the ideal speech situation."[11]

6. Since the problem is sociolinguistic, critical theory must ground reason not in a concept of consciousness but in a concept of communicative action.[12]

7. The revised Habermasian dialectic now interprets history as a set of moral, cognitive, and aesthetic advances. In the current stage of history, autonomous rational individualism is possible if the conditions of communicative rationality are achieved. Such a moral change would align practical reason with the more developed instrumental reason, *Wertrationalität* with *Zweckrationalität*. This evolutionary schema is intended not as a classic philosophy of history but as a heuristic model that can orient concrete studies.[13]

The French poststructuralists look at things very differently.[14] At the outset it is well to remember that the term poststructuralism has most currency in the United States. It certainly defines no unified movement. At best it designates a vague theoretical tendency, one often identified with postmodernism, and it includes as much disagreement as agreement among those who are listed under its rubric. Nonetheless the term has been used effectively and intelligibly by both proponents and detractors.

The French poststructuralists are particularly concerned with the foundation and limits of theory. They are animated by a rereading of Nietzsche, especially by his far-reaching and virulent critique of truth.[15] The lesson they learn from Nietzsche is that truth is not a transcendent unity. The persistent attempt in European philosophy to unify truth, be it by means of a scientific method or a dialectical totalization, has unfortunate epistemological and political implications. The tendency in poststructuralism is therefore to regard truth as a multiplicity, to exult in the play of diverse meanings, in the process of continual reinterpretation, in the contention of opposing claims. Accordingly text replaces mind as the locus of enunciation,

11. Jürgen Habermas, *Communication and the Evolution of Society*, trans. Thomas McCarthy (Boston: Beacon, 1979).

12. Jürgen Habermas, *The Theory of Communicative Action*, Vol. 1, *Reason and the Rationalization of Society*, trans. Thomas McCarthy (Boston: Beacon, 1984).

13. Jürgen Habermas, "History and Evolution," *Telos* no. 39 (1979): 5–44.

14. For an opposing view of the relative merits of Habermas and the French poststructuralists see Peter Dews, *Logics of Disintegration: Post-structuralist Thought and the Claims of Critical Theory* (New York: Verso, 1987).

15. The important but by no means the only essay in the rereading of Nietzsche was Gilles Deleuze, *Nietzsche and Philosophy*, trans. Hugh Tomlinson (New York: Columbia University Press, 1983; original ed. 1962).

and difference replaces identity as the strategy of reading. Those not sensitive to what the poststructuralists regard as the epistemological dangers of consensual truth are highly irritated by this celebration of "the undecidable," to cite one of Derrida's terms.

Having abandoned the assumption of the transcendent unity of truth, of truth as a totalizing closure, poststructuralists redefine the position of the theoretical subject and its relation to politics. The place of theory cannot be a center, a privileged locus, a solid point of origin for the progressive movement of society, either in a liberal or a Marxist sense. When theory is the ground of politics the results are invariably authoritarian, as the Jacobin and Leninist examples indicate. Favoring a strategy of the dispersal of truth, poststructuralists also take a cue from Nietzsche's association of truth with power. Truth is enunciated in discourses. These in turn are coordinated with power, or better, are forms of power since they shape practices. Far from the Olympian position of the cogito, truth for them is a mundane, "always already" political affair, a multiplicity of claims without a final arbiter.

The theorist's situation, for poststructuralists, contains certain dangers. Theorizing with no guarantee of certain truth, poststructuralists are to many observers in a cynical, or as Habermas argues, conservative, position. These critics see little difference between the poststructuralist retreat from theory and similar moves by figures as diverse as Edmund Burke and Karl Popper. The response of Foucault, Derrida, and Lyotard is, however, that the quest for certain truth and the claim of having attained it is the greater danger. The logocentric philosophic tradition, with its strong assertions about truth, is for them complicit in the disasters and abominations of twentieth-century Western history. On this difficult, even tragic issue of the relation of politics to truth, poststructuralists in general strive for a cosmopolitan position that makes every effort to recognize differences, even uncomfortable or disagreeable ones, and for a theory of truth that is wary of patriarchal and ethnocentric tendencies that hide behind a defense of reason as certain, closed, totalized. Above all poststructuralists want to avoid forms of political oppression that are legitimized by resorts to reason, as this has been, in their view, one of the paradoxical and lamentable developments of recent history. In the end it seems to me that the poststructuralists have by no means attained their goal of developing a nonauthoritarian form of discourse, and they are even further from achieving an adequate politics, one consonant with that discourse.[16]

With these necessarily simplified characterizations of the positions before us, we may now turn to the confrontation of Habermas and the poststructuralists.

The poststructuralists hold no uniform view of the Frankfurt school. Lacan and Barthes rarely if ever refer directly to the Frankfurt school, though Barthes' *Mythologies* has affinities with the analysis of the media that is found in Adorno. Deleuze's *Anti-Oedipus* explicitly opposes the Freudo-Marxist synthesis that is associated with the Frankfurt school in the works of the early Fromm,[17] Horkheimer's *Studien über die Familie*, and Marcuse's *Eros and Civilization*. Nonetheless his call to liberate the schizoid impulses of the libido might be viewed as a variation on the Freudo-Marxist theme. As for Derrida, I do not recall seeing a single mention of the Frankfurt school or its members in any of his works.[18] Baudrillard's case is more complex. His early works are directly parallel with the themes of the Frankfurt school,[19] though after 1972 his position drifts more and more away from that problematic.[20] Lyotard's writings have been the most explicitly antagonistic to the Germans. The collection of essays, *Des dispositifs pulsionnels*, mounts a strong attack against the Frankfurt school, especially Adorno's negative dialectic.[21] *The Postmodern Condition* is

16. The current state of poststructuralist thought on politics may be evaluated by looking at the recent spate of books on Heidegger, the Nazis, and the Jews. This discussion is highly complex but one of its motifs is the relation of philosophy to politics. See Philippe Lacoue-Labarthe, *La Fiction du politique* (Paris: Christian Bourgois, 1987); Victor Farias, *Heidegger et le nazisme*, trans. Myrian Benarroch and Jean-Baptiste Grasset (Paris: Verdier, 1987); Jacques Derrida, *De l'esprit: Heidegger et la question* (Paris: Galilée, 1987); Jean-François Lyotard, *Heidegger et "les juifs"* (Paris: Galilée, 1988); Avital Ronel, *The Emergency Call: A Politics of Technology* (Lincoln: University of Nebraska, 1988).
17. These are collected in Erich Fromm, *The Crisis of Psychoanalysis: Essays on Freud, Marx, and Social Psychology* (New York: Fawcett, 1970).
18. The only exception is Walter Benjamin in Derrida's *The Truth in Painting*, trans. Geoff Bennington and Ian McLeod (Chicago: University of Chicago Press, 1987) but he was on the periphery of the Frankfurt school.
19. This would include *Le Système des objets* (1968), *La Société de consommation* (1970) and *Pour une critique de l'économie politique du signe* (1972).
20. See Mark Poster, ed., *Baudrillard: A Reader*, trans. Jacques Mourrain (Stanford: Stanford University Press, 1988) for a selected overview of his writings.
21. Jean-François Lyotard, "Adorno come diavolo," in *Des dispositifs pulsionnels* (Paris: 10/18, 1973), pp. 115–33; translated by Robert Hurley as "Adorno as the Devil," in *Telos*, no. 19 (Spring 1974): 127–37.

equally vehement against Habermas.[22]

Foucault is the only poststructuralist who actively sought to associate his work with that of the Frankfurt school. In *Discipline and Punish* Foucault criticizes an obscure neo-Marxist analysis of prisons by two associates of the Frankfurt school, Rusche and Kirchheimer. At the time, in 1975, even this attention to work by the Frankfurt school was exceptional in France. Foucault here refers to Rusche and Kirchheimer's "great work" as providing "a number of essential reference points" for his own analysis.[23] Though Foucault's analysis differs considerably from the Frankfurt schoolers', he respected it enough to pay these compliments. On a number of occasions Foucault complained that his own education in France offered no introduction to the work of the Germans: "When I was a student I can assure you that I never heard the name of the Frankfurt School mentioned by any of my professors."[24] The project that increasingly engaged Foucault's interest toward the end of his life was a critique of scientific reason that the Frankfurt school, following Weber, had pioneered and explored at length. While Foucault was not completely happy with the direction of the Germans' work, he was eager to cooperate with Habermas and others in what he saw as a common enterprise.

If the poststructuralists' attitude toward the Frankfurt school was mixed, the same cannot be said of Habermas's disposition to the French. From the Adorno Prize address of 1980, to the Boston speech of 1982, to the Paris lectures of 1984, Habermas took the occasions of public speaking engagements to denounce the dangerous errors of the French poststructuralists.[25] Before that time

22. Jean-François Lyotard, *The Postmodern Condition: A Report on Knowledge*, trans. Geoff Bennington and Brian Massumi (Minneapolis: University of Minnesota Press, 1984).

23. Michel Foucault, *Discipline and Punish: The Birth of the Prison*, trans. Alan Sheridan (New York: Pantheon, 1977), pp. 24ff. It is of course difficult to know how seriously to take Foucault's praise in this sentence.

24. Gérard Raulet, "On Post-Structuralism: An Interview with Michel Foucault," trans. Jeremy Harding, *Telos*, no. 55 (Spring 1983): 200 and also in conversations I had with him.

25. These are respectively "Modernity versus Postmodernity," *New German Critique*, no. 22, (Winter, 1981): 3–18; "The Entwinement of Myth and Enlightenment," *New German Critique*, no. 26 (Spring/Summer 1982): 13–30; and *Der philosophische Diskurs der Moderne: Zwolf Vorlesungen* (Frankfurt/Main: Suhrkamp, 1985); translated by Frederick Lawrence as *The Philosophical Discourse of Modernity* (Cambridge, Mass.: MIT Press, 1987). Habermas first mentions Foucault in a 1977

Habermas paid scant notice to philosophy across the Rhine. Martin Jay, the noted historian of the Frankfurt school, rightly observes that Habermas is no sectarian who restricts his interests to a narrow circle of thinkers. Habermas, Jay points out, bolsters his position with "arguments of a wide range of thinkers, most notably Weber, Luhmann, Parsons, Piaget and Kohlberg."[26] Indeed Habermas is truly a cosmopolitan intellectual taking cues where he finds them, except, that is, from France. Jay's list of influences on Habermas includes after all two Germans, two Americans, and a Swiss.[27] In the 1980s then Habermas's relation to French poststructuralism shifted from a simple avoidance to an outburst of hostility. In estimating the reasons for the change one would want to take into account the fact that during the early 1980s Habermas had just completed his major work of reconstructing Marxism as a defense of Enlightenment rationality. *The Theory of Communicative Action* appeared in 1981 in two large volumes. Perhaps the time was ripe to turn one's attention to opposing points of view and what better place to search for those than across the Rhine.

Habermas casts his differences with the poststructuralists as a debate over the nature of modernity. He defines modernity in the sociological terms of Max Weber: the differentiation of science, morality, and art into autonomous spheres. The process of modernity is the fulfillment of each of these spheres and their incorporation into the life world, the full development of each sphere, and the subsequent transformation of daily life on the basis of that perfection. What was missing from Weber's definition, in Habermas's eyes, was a specification of the conditions in everyday life that enabled the transfer of science, morality, and art back on to

essay entitled "Ideologies and Society in the Post-War World," referring to him as an anarchist. This is noted in Habermas, *Autonomy and Solidarity: Interviews*, p. 46. In a 1978 essay, "Conservatism and Capitalist Crisis," which appeared in Italian, Foucault fell into "irrationalism."

26. Martin Jay, "Habermas and Modernism," *Praxis International* 4, no. 1 (April 1984), 5; reprinted in Richard Bernstein, ed., *Habermas and Modernity* (Oxford: Blackwell, 1985), pp. 125–39. In an interview with Perry Anderson, Habermas made up his own list of influences, some fifteen names most of which were German and only one, Emile Durkheim, was French. See "Jürgen Habermas: A Philosophico-Political Profile," *New Left Review*, no. 151 (May–June 1985), 76.

27. It might also be noted that the French were absent from the well-known collection of debates with Habermas, *Habermas: Critical Debates*, which included a reply by Habermas. The critics were Britishers, Americans, and West Germans in approximately equal number.

society. In *The Theory of Communicative Action* Habermas provided those conditions with the concept of the universal pragmatics of language. If public speech were structured properly the autonomous cultural domains of science, morality, and art would be integrated into society, thereby achieving human emancipation, the synthesis of reason and society, and the fulfillment of the project of modernity as outlined by the Enlightenment.

According to Habermas the French move to postmodernity was a retreat from the challenge of the Enlightenment, not an advance beyond it. What bothered Habermas most about the French rejection of the Enlightenment project was their critique of reason and their resort to counterrationalist positions like those of Bataille and Heidegger. In 1980 then the French, in a "line" that led "from Bataille via Foucault to Derrida," are "Young Conservatives"[28] who turn their backs on the unfinished project of modernity. In 1982 the poststructuralists, disciples of Nietzsche's antirationalism, betray a "regressive turn [that] enlists the powers of emancipation in the service of counter-enlightenment."[29] By 1984 Habermas had undertaken an intensive investigation of the French writers. His lectures of that year demonstrate a sustained, serious reading of poststructuralist authors. Habermas's masterful ability to digest vast corpora of theory and rigorously analyze them in relation to his own position is brilliantly on display once more in the Paris lectures.[30] But the intensive reading of the French texts did not alter Habermas convictions. In 1985 he complained that poststructuralism "bales out" on the Enlightenment, falsely thinking it can find a "cure for the wounds of Enlightenment other than the radicalized Enlightenment itself."[31] Finally in 1986 the French "mystify peculiarly modern experiences."[32]

28. "Modernity versus Postmodernity," p. 13.
29. Habermas, "The Entwinement of Myth and Enlightenment," p. 29.
30. Jürgen Habermas, *Der philosophische Diskurs der Moderne: Zwölf Vorlesungen* (Frankfurt/Main: Suhrkamp, 1985); translated by Frederick Lawrence as *The Philosophical Discourse of Modernity* (Cambridge, Mass.: MIT Press, 1987).
31. "Jürgen Habermas: A Philosophico-Political Profile," p. 82.
32. Habermas, *Autonomy and Solidarity: Interviews*, p. 203. The full quotation reads: the French thinkers project the experience of unreason "backwards into archaic origins, onto the Dionysian, the pre-Socratic, the exotic and primitive. This kind of *nachgeahmte Substantialität* was completely alien to Adorno and Benjamin. It never occurred to them to mystify peculiarly modern experiences in this fashion. For that is what this radical criticism of reason in effect amounts to, with its fabulation of pre-civilizational states. We have had all that, in Germany, so

A full treatment of Habermas's position on poststructuralism would require a detailed evaluation of *The Philosophical Discourse of Modernity*, a work largely based on lectures given in Paris and Ithaca, New York. While there is no space for such a discussion in the context of this essay, one peculiarity of the book is worth pointing out: Habermas appropriates the poststructuralist critique of reason for his own ends. Instead of condemning the French attack on Enlightenment humanism, Habermas surprisingly argues that he does it better than they do. In the passage cited below he attributes to his own theory of communicative action, not to deconstruction and not to discourse analysis, the true critique of logocentric reason.

> The furious labor of deconstruction has identifiable consequences only when the paradigm of self-consciousness, of the relation-to-self of a subject knowing and acting in isolation, is replaced by a different one—by the paradigm of mutual understanding, that is, of the intersubjective relationship between individuals who are social-ized through communication and reciprocally recognize one another. Only then does the critique of the domineering thought of subject-centered reason emerge in a *determinate* form—namely, as a critique of Western "logocentrism," which is diagnosed not as an excess but as a deficit of rationality.[33]

The important shift in Habermas's argument in this passage, and therefore in the impact of the book as a whole, is that Habermas ascribes to his own position the critique of Enlightenment reason that is at the heart of the poststructuralist position. Poststructur-alism serves Habermas well by filling a gap in his own argument. His *Theory of Communicative Action* introduced a shift from a problematic of consciousness to one of language, but the justifica-tion for this move was not adequately explained. A major weakness in Habermas's position, one that dates back to his essays from the late 1960s, is the flatfootedness in his move from the concept of labor to concepts of "symbolic interaction," "language," or "mutual understanding." This move (away from classical Marxism) is pre-sented as a simple supplement or addition to an existing position. Until *The Philosophical Discourse of Modernity* Habermas never

immediately at hand that you can smell it ever afterwards: the artificial mystifica-tion of something so close into something supposedly so primordial." Poststruc-turalism is thus associated with the Third Reich.
33. *The Philosophical Discourse of Modernity*, p. 310.

persuasively argued this shift or cogently justified it. Poststructuralism provided Habermas with a sharp critique of the inadequacy of Marx's position on reason, the legacy of this flaw in his concept of labor, and the resulting need to rethink critical theory from a perspective rooted in language theory. In a sense therefore Habermas's conquest of Rome from the north has made him something of a Roman. But his self-presentation as the one who has done properly what the French do badly undermines his critique of poststructuralism as "irrationalism" and calls his own project into question. For himself Habermas claims that he has merely given up a false concept of reason in favor of a more suitable one.

Habermas's attack on poststructuralism is most revealing when he is compelled to distinguish the positions of Horkheimer and Adorno in *Dialectic of Enlightenment* from those of the French. The Frankfurt school itself, it could be argued, preceded poststructuralists in the critique of the Enlightenment. In the dark days of the 1940s the forces of science and reason appeared to promote, not to dissipate, domination. There are no more fitting testimonies to the Nietzschean critique of reason than the technical rationality in the organization of Auschwitz and the scientific creativity of the Manhattan Project that made feasible Hiroshima. Adorno and Horkheimer did not shrink from the fact that enlightenment produced economical mass extermination in gas chambers and instant incineration with the atom bomb. No wonder the late Foucault admired the work of the Frankfurt school: the Germans, like the Frenchman, were impressed with the interconnection of reason and power, reason as technical mastery becoming the domination and destruction of human beings. The Baconian maxim of knowledge as power received new meaning in the 1940s.

Faced with the disturbing pessimism of *Dialectic of Enlightenment*, Habermas pleads for a judicious, balanced judgment: "bourgeois ideals" contain "elements of reason." Habermas writes:

> I mean the internal theoretical dynamic which constantly propels the sciences—and the self-reflection of the sciences as well—*beyond* the creation of merely technologically exploitable knowledge; furthermore, I mean the universalist foundations of law and morality which have *also* been embodied (in no matter how distorted and imperfect a form) in the institutions of constitutional states, in the forms of democratic decision-making, and in individualistic patterns of identity formation; finally, I mean the productivity and the liberating force of an aesthetic experience with a subjectivity set free from

the imperatives of purposive activity and from the conventions of everyday perception.[34]

But Horkheimer/Adorno and the poststructuralists do not dispute that there are "elements of reason" in liberal culture. What they dispute is the lens that discerns "reason" in law and democracy but not in gas chambers and atom bombs, the Habermasian lens of distorted perception that espies in bourgeois reason a mirage of "universalist foundations" when there is nothing more in sight than yet another human discourse. When Habermas defends with the label of reason what he admires in Western culture he universalizes the particular, grounds the conditional, absolutizes the finite.[35] He provides a center and an origin for a set of discursive practices. He undermines critique in the name of critique by privileging a locus of theory (reason) that far too closely resembles society's official discourse.

Of course two different things are being spoken about and confounded, as is the case in many disputes. Like Weber, Habermas distinguishes between instrumental rationality and communicative rationality. Instrumental rationality characterizes practices in what he calls "the system," that is, in institutions like the bureaucratic state and the economy that achieve social solidarity through "steering mechanisms." Communicative rationality characterizes actions in what he calls "the life world," that is in areas of social action where socialization and cultural reproduction are at issue. Communicative rationality designates the ability of speakers to raise "validity claims" to those they address and to problematize those claims in a general effort to achieve mutual understanding. When "the system" intrudes upon "the life world," as it increasingly does in technically advanced societies, "pathologies" are produced. Communicative action is aborted because efforts at mutual understanding are replaced by hierarchically distorted verbal exchanges in which each party instrumentally manipulates the

---

34. Habermas, "The Entwinement of Myth and Enlightenment," p. 18.
35. There may well be a political motive for Habermas's defense of bourgeois liberties since the Federal Republic of Germany recently has suffered a wave of repression similar to the McCarthy era in the United States. Fred Jameson discusses this situation in "The Politics of Theory: Ideological Positions in the Postmodernism Debate," *New German Critique*, no. 33 (Fall 1984): 59. Such a valid political intervention still does not justify, at the level of theory, an absolutist defense of reason.

other, with the state, for example, having a considerable advantage in the manipulation game over a welfare mother.[36]

Communicative rationality in Habermas's view is not subject to the poststructuralist critique of reason. Only instrumental reason supports domination and is therefore open to the poststructuralist objection. Communicative rationality requires a democratic context in which anyone may question the argumentative claims of anyone else, so long as each party aims at consensus and agrees to concur with positions that he or she cannot refute. The issue in the Franco-German debate is whether such a notion of consensus contains elements of domination. Lyotard for one thinks that it does: the "sort of unity Habermas has in mind" is restrictive in the postmodern context which is characterized precisely by a multiplicity of cultural expressions (*le différand*).[37] Habermas's notion of reason as consensus, in Lyotard's view, introduces constraints upon the most desirable manifestations of cultural development in postmodernity: the play of unrecuperable differences. No sharper opposition can be posed than this: Habermas defending reason in the form of consensus and Lyotard denouncing reason as a danger to dissensus.

From a certain vantage point Habermas and Lyotard veer toward one another, despite their acrimonious hostility. Habermas wants to allow for critique and dissent as determinants of public policy; Lyotard implies but does not assert a consensus over differences, that his reader ought to assent to the justice of his claim for the play of multiple discourses. Yet beneath this point of convergence a fundamental opposition divides the two positions: Habermas defends modernity as the *rationality* of communicative action; Lyotard defends the postmodernity of an *aesthetic* model of a multiplicity of cultures. Sharply posed, the issue then is which of these positions better accounts for critique in the context of postindustrial society, or what I call the mode of information. To the extent that Habermas's position can be said to presuppose or support a notion of the subject that invokes the autonomous individual of bourgeois

36. Jürgen Habermas, *The Theory of Communicative Action*, Vol. 2, *Lifeworld and System: A Critique of Functionalist Reason*, trans. Thomas McCarthy (Boston: Beacon, 1987), p. 183.

37. Jean-François Lyotard, "Answering the Question: What Is Postmodernism?," trans. Régis Durand, in *The Postmodern Condition* (Minneapolis: University of Minnesota, 1984), p. 72.

society and the class consciousness of the proletariat, his position recuperates the elements of domination in the "dialectic of enlightenment." To the extent that Lyotard opens the scene for the entry of hitherto excluded configurations of subjectivity (women, gays, minorities), his position must be said to throw up a critical posture against established forms of authority. However, if no form of freedom is possible beyond that envisaged in the metanarratives of liberalism and Marxism, Habermas secures more firmly than Lyotard existing levels of democracy and Lyotard, by challenging that democracy, opens the path to directions that may regress beneath whatever freedom is currently enjoyed.

Habermas seriously underestimates the difficulties of the current conjuncture in democratic societies. His defense of reason appropriates discursive practices that are highly dangerous. He uncritically legitimizes science, for example, as an achievement of consensus: "Modern science . . . [is] governed by ideals of an objectivity and impartiality secured through unrestricted discussion."[38] Yet modern science largely operates with an exclusion of women and minorities from its discourse, an exclusion that is legitimated precisely by the apparent procedural neutrality of "unrestricted discussion," of communicative rationality. Modern science instantiates the figure of the rational individual; it constitutes the subject of its discourse in a thoroughly Cartesian manner that excludes rhetoric, fiction, art and invalidates culturally determined subjects, such as women, who somehow do not have the "communicative competence" to engage in "unrestricted discussion."

Habermas claims simultaneously that this notion of reason is (1) counterfactual, that it has never existed and will never exist, and (2) that all of human history is moving toward a condition in which this communicative reason may become actual. He eats from the cake of communicative reason as a universal necessity of logic and yet keeps it for another day as an historical tendency, one being actualized in the successive release of communicative competence in the modern world. He argues that this double strategy, simultaneously transcendental and empirical, avoids the element of domination characteristic of the same posture in earlier formulations of Enlightenment reason. In different ways Adorno, Horkheimer, Foucault, and Derrida agree that the dilemma of reason is

38. Ibid., p. 91.

that it postulates itself as transcendent, thereby constituting the world as one of objects, while also empirically positioning reason as another thing in the world. This subject/object identity or "birth of man" introduces domination into those discourses, such as science, which ground themselves in transcendental reason while figuring empirical subjects as also rational. When Habermas reinscribes reason in the new register of communicative action he reproduces this doubling effect as the rhetorical figure of his own discourse. He writes, for example, "Society's knowledge of itself is concentrated neither in philosophy nor in social theory."[39] "Society's knowledge of itself" is contained in Habermas's discourse as the imperative to act so as to bring about consensus, to release potentials of communicative competence, to utter speech with the aim of mutual understanding. His own discourse contains the same, hidden "performative contradiction" he attributes to his French opponents: to read *The Theory of Communicative Action* as an instance of communicative reason, fictionally to establish communicative rationality as the already existing empirical context of its very enunciation and emergence as a position, to accord the privilege to Habermas of an authorial voice with no elocutionary or rhetorical aims so that his position, his defense of communicative reason may emerge without the violence or force of repressing oppositions to it.

According to Habermas, Horkheimer and Adorno manage to preserve the critical function, whereas Nietzsche and the poststructuralists undermine it. An inverse hypothesis works much better: *Dialectic of Enlightenment* is a product of disenchantment and despair with the universalizing values of reason, be they liberal or Marxist. Poststructuralists move a step beyond this negative reversal: the problem for the poststructuralists is not that reason has "turned into" domination, but that all discourses are always already implicated in power. The problem is not that an absolute ground has been swept out from under us by certain historical events but that such grounds are the source of the theoretical problem in the first place. Adorno and Horkheimer historicize their critique of Enlightenment reason; the poststructuralists treat it also at the levels of epistemology and language.[40]

39. *The Philosophical Discourse of Modernity*, p. 377.
40. Again *The Philosophical Discourse of Modernity* introduces subtle confusions. Hab-

Confronting this dilemma, the American philosopher Richard Rorty provides an interesting alternative point of view. He rejects the solutions of both Habermas and the poststructuralists, opting instead for the pragmatism of John Dewey by dispensing with the baby of critique along with the bathwater of universal reason. Rorty writes, "What links Habermas to the French thinkers he criticizes is the conviction that the story of modern philosophy . . . is an important part of the story of the democratic societies' attempts at self-reassurance."[41] With a humility not atypical of an Anglo-American philosopher, he suggests that social emancipation has nothing to do with theoretical critique. If Habermas wants emancipation, Rorty argues, he should work on concrete reforms; if the French want elegant theory they should practice it for its own sake. The disarming simplicity of Rorty's position is a tribute to the American discipline of philosophy. In short, why all the fuss, why bother with critique? As Stanley Fish once said in a similar spirit, responding to a talk by Edward Said which pleaded for politically engaged criticism, in effect: "We don't need it. We are comfortable enough."[42]

The pragmatist position paradoxically assumes the same Cartesian position that it rejects. Descartes, Rorty complains, gave us "the false lead . . . that made us think truth and power *were* separable."[43] The defense of the cogito is thus, for him, the exemplar of all the difficulties. But if truth and power are not separable, as he argues in agreement with the poststructuralists, then how can one struggle for democratic reform without reference to discursive truth? The answer is not that theoretical discourse is

ermas slides from the effort to keep separate the Frankfurt school tradition and the French poststructuralists to a lumping of the two into the same camp. In the conclusion of the book Habermas *fully includes* Adorno in the camp of the poststructuralists: "The radical critique[s] of reason . . . give no account of their own position. Negative dialectics, genealogy, and deconstruction alike avoid those categories in accord with which modern knowledge has been differentiated" (p. 336). Thus Adorno's negative dialectics is *no different from* Foucault's genealogy or Derrida's deconstruction.

41. Richard Rorty, "Habermas and Lyotard on Postmodernity," *Praxis International* 4, no. 1 (April 1984): 38.

42. Oral intervention at a conference at SUNY, Binghamton in 1978. Edward Said's paper is available as "Reflections on Recent American 'Left' Literary Criticism," in William Spanos et al, eds., *The Question of Textuality: Strategies of Reading in Contemporary American Criticism* (Bloomington: Indiana University Press, 1982), pp. 11–30.

43. Richard Rorty, "Habermas and Lyotard on Postmodernity," p. 42.

extra baggage on the voyage to a free society but that it cannot be avoided. And if it cannot be avoided the issue becomes, as both Habermas and the poststructuralists recognize, how may the discourse of theory intervene in practice without bolstering domination? The sorry truth for the American philosopher is that the difficult labor of sublimation is not a language game played only in the fields of academe but one inextricably entangled in the fate of society.

Habermas insists that theory must find a universal ground in reason. He claims to have done so in the historically totalized concept of the ideal speech situation, the universal pragmatics of language that provide validity claims for public discourse in nations that have attained moral maturity. The poststructuralists disagree with this conclusion, but differ seriously among themselves about the best discursive strategy to choose. Baudrillard offers to decode the new age of "hyperreality" in which self-referential media languages constitute simulacra of communications.[44] Derrida proposes an interminable deconstruction of the Western philosophical tradition, interminable because the internal structure of writing is trapped in an abyss of binary oppositions.[45] Lyotard advocates a celebration of multiple, competing discourses, an acceptance of the justice of the *différand*, of the impossibility of consensus.[46] Foucault proposes the self-constitution of the critical theorist through a practice of opposition to the dominant discourses of the present conjuncture.[47] While none of these provisional solutions is entirely adequate (nor are they claimed to be so), none of them are fairly labeled "conservative" or "counterrevolutionary." In my view, each has the advantage over Habermas in facing squarely the limits of totalizing, universalist discourse and in recognizing the limitations or historical failures of the great "metanarratives" of liberalism and Marxism. If critique is to be "reconstructed," as Habermas wishes, it must be accomplished on the difficult terrain of a

44. Baudrillard's most recent statement of this position may be found in *Les Stratégies fatales* (Paris: Grasset, 1983).
45. To my thinking the best statement of this position remains Jacques Derrida, *Writing and Difference*, trans. Alan Bass (Chicago: University of Chicago Press, 1978).
46. Jean-François Lyotard, *Le Différand* (Paris: Minuit, 1983).
47. This position was being elaborated in the multivolume project *The History of Sexuality* when Foucault's life abruptly ended. See for example Michel Foucault, *The Use of Pleasure*, trans. Robert Hurley (New York: Pantheon, 1985).

Nietzschean view of the truth.

To my mind, the most interesting effort to conserve traditional forms of (Marxist) critique is the work of Fredric Jameson, particularly in his attacks on poststructuralism. Jameson's treatment of poststructuralism is complex and ambivalent. From one side Jameson's Marxism has led him, like Anderson and Habermas, to condemn poststructuralism as counterrevolutionary. He characterizes Lyotard's *The Postmodern Condition*, for example, as "indistinguishable from anti-Marxism."[48] Marxist analysis leads Jameson to regard poststructuralism as the ideology of a new, multinational stage of capitalism.[49] This political condemnation of poststructuralism comes from the mid-1980s and represents a change in his thinking. Earlier, in *The Political Unconscious*, Jameson was eager to incorporate the best features of poststructuralist thought within the wider framework of a totalizing Marxist position. He generously suggested that "Marxism subsumes other interpretive modes or systems . . . [but] the limits of the latter can always be overcome, and their more positive findings retained, by a radical historicizing of their mental operations."[50] But by 1984, when he completed the "radical historicizing of [poststructuralist] mental operations," Jameson's posture was one of defensive exclusion of a dangerous ideological opponent.

From another side, as a reader of culture, Jameson presents the most coherent depictions available of poststructuralism. His immanent critiques of the phenomenon are brilliant examples of the genre. So cogently does he present poststructuralism that his texts make a compelling case for its importance and richness.[51] He treats poststructuralism as one side of postmodernism, stressing the relations between French theorists and primarily American cultural expressions in architecture, film, television, and so forth. He is careful to distance his position from that of leftists like Christopher Lasch, who virulently attack recent culture.[52] With an almost

48. Fredric Jameson, "The Politics of Theory," p. 61.
49. Fredric Jameson, "Postmodernism and Consumer Society," in Hal Foster, ed., *The Anti-Aesthetic: Essays on Postmodern Culture* (Port Townsend, Wash.: Bay Press, 1983), p. 125.
50. Fredric Jameson, *The Political Unconscious: Narrative as a Socially Symbolic Act* (Ithaca: Cornell, 1981), p. 47.
51. This is especially so in "Postmodernism and Consumer Society," and in "Postmodernism, or The Cultural Logic of Late Capitalism," *New Left Review*, no. 146 (July–August 1984): 53–92.
52. Ibid., p. 71.

loving brush he portrays the lines of an emergent cultural form as no one before him. His essays on postmodernism can be readily recommended to anyone who is curious about it.

From yet another side, Jameson presents the contemporary world as being intelligible only from the point of view of post-structuralism. In this mode he openly admits the inadequacy of Marxism to comprehend the present conjuncture. The Marxist concept of ideology, he writes in Althusserian terms, explains the "gap" or "rift" between "existential experience and scientific knowledge." In our situation the concept of ideology no longer works. The radically new "space" of postmodernism, which undermines all efforts of self-location, of referential self-coordination, requires entirely new categories of thought, an "aesthetic of cognitive mapping" in order to achieve

> a breakthrough to some as yet unimaginable new mode of representing . . . in which we may again begin to grasp our positioning as individual and collective subjects and regain a capacity to act and struggle which is at present neutralized by our spatial as well as our social confusion. The political form of postmodernism . . . will have as its vocation the invention and projection of a global cognitive mapping.[53]

In rigorous honesty Jameson admits "confusion," acknowledges the inadequacy of Marxism, and calls upon poststructuralism, no longer viewed as an anti-Marxism "ideology," as the only hope for a reconstituted critical theory.

Holding all three positions in tense, ambivalent balance, Jameson opens a path, however narrow, to an accommodation with poststructuralism. Surely he and Habermas are correct to point out tendencies in that intellectual stance that are not conducive to critical social theory. But I would contend, in agreement with Jameson's third position, that poststructuralism contains some of the elements for the beginning of an adequate analysis of the present. More particularly, certain of Foucault's positions clear away obstacles to an intellectual movement in that direction. These advances need to be outlined. After doing so, I will add my reservations about poststructuralism along with suggestions for new strategies to supplement the strengths of the position.

First, Foucault, like many poststructuralists, cogently addresses

53. Ibid., p. 92.

the problem of the theoretical subject.[54] Since Descartes, theorists have assumed that a rational voice was also a universal one; that the theorist strove for rationality as the main trait of his or her theoreticity; that attaining such a position was equivalent to being able to speak for humanity, for every man, woman, and child on earth. The problem with this theoretical voice is not simply that it is ethnocentric but also that rational subjects in possession of knowledge are now, in the advanced societies, in positions of power. Biologists, chemists, and physicists do not only generate knowledge which is regarded as the highest form of truth; they are inserted into key positions in high-tech corporations, the military, and the government. Claims of the universality of reason may have always been epistemologically unfounded: today they are something worse than that since reason is also the handmaid of institutions of unimaginably enormous force. Reason now legitimates and promotes institutions, both in the East and West, whose only universality is their threat of total destruction.

The issue for theory then is to elaborate a position for the theoretical subject that acknowledges the contingency of its validity claims, the embeddedness of theory in the present, in the political conjuncture, without however relinquishing the critique of domination or the project of emancipation. In other words the problem is to generate discourses whose power effects are limited to the subversion of power. How such power effects will avoid legitimizing new powers is not at all clear. Habermas is right to see serious dangers in such an enterprise, dangers of antirationalist conservatism and fascism. The greater danger today may come not from those who shout "blood and soil" but from those who scientifically plan for war in the name of freedom. These are the people whose trigger fingers represent the culmination of Western reason.

Second, earlier theory posited a rational social subject, be it the bourgeois individual or the proletariat, as the reference point of freedom. Today theory must proceed without such stable signposts: if there are social positions that are aligned with emancipation (women, gays, minorities) they are positions of oppression associated with marks of exclusion. Reason lies not with the oppressed but with the scientifically administered bureaucracies

54. See especially "Truth and Power," trans. Colin Gordon et al., ed. Colin Gordon, in *Power/Knowledge: Selected Interviews and Other Writings: 1972–1977* (New York: Pantheon, 1980), pp. 109–33.

that are the agents of oppression. None of the oppressed groups can promise a free society as the outcome of their emancipation, as the long line of thinkers from Locke to Marx thought. In this conjuncture, Foucault generates his discourses about excluded terms (sex, insanity) and oppressed groups (prisoners) not as the solution to the riddle of history but as part of the problem. The texts of the critical theorist are discursive interventions in a field of contending forces that might be of assistance in clarifying the position of the oppressed. They attempt to avoid to the greatest extent possible possession of a hegemonic position within the movement, a fate that befell the discourse of Locke in 1776, Rousseau in 1789, and Marx in 1917 and 1949.

The intellectual's will to power is stashed in his or her text in the form of universal reason. The art of appropriating the universal was the main business of the Enlightenment. The philosophes were master impressionists whose textual voice mimicked that of humanity. Diderot elevated the philosophes' polemic into a morality. The captain of the Party of Humanity, Diderot's deepest wish was immortality in the memory of an emancipated mankind, although he had another far more skeptical voice as evidenced in *Rameau's Nephew*.[55] Still, the future of modern politics was mapped by the editor of the *Encyclopedia*: in generations to come, those who spoke for humanity automatically resurrected the saints of Enlightenment. By specifying the universal truth of the ideal speech situation, Habermas's text, echoing the Enlightenment, becomes the blueprint of freedom, his mind the noumenon of liberation. Foucault and the poststructuralists offer far less.

Third, the theorist constitutes him- or herself as textual agent through a critique of discursive practices that celebrate contemporary hegemonic institutions. For Baudrillard the target of criticism is the media, for Foucault it is the human sciences associated with the welfare state, for Derrida it is the Western philosophical tradition. The poststructuralist intervention endeavors to locate the place of power in the discursive formation, to analyze how this power operates on the subject, and to elaborate strategies to reveal the play of that power. Habermas instead aims to locate the point where he can speak the truth, define its conditions and accordingly plot the

55. Denis Diderot, "Encyclopedia," trans. Jacques Barzun, in *Rameau's Nephew and Other Works* (New York: Bobbs-Merrill, 1964), p. 288 passim.

next stage of human emancipation. His goal is to outline a position against which one can only be defined as a counterrevolutionary. His strategy is that of Marx, Freud, and the Enlightenment: to oppose him is to be an enemy of mankind, *l'infame* whose only fate is to be crushed. Habermas's strategy is one of totalization: to encompass the position of rational enlightenment to such an extent that all opponents are irrational.[56] The poststructuralist project is far more modest. It aims at a detotalized position which finally is uncertain of itself, a strategic intervention in an indeterminate field of forces whose outcome is contingent.

In one respect Habermas is right to be wary of the poststructuralists or at least of Foucault. So reluctant is Foucault to totalize his position that to a fault he avoids conceptual clarification and systematic argument. The consequence of his timidity is a failure of generality, of indicating the lines of force of his themes in the present, however much he orients his work to that end. To help rectify this weakness, I have proposed that the poststructuralist position may be developed into a critical theory of the mode of information, a regional theory of new language situations characterized by electronic mediation.[57] I suggest that what Jameson terms our current spatial "confusion" may be due in part to the structurally new ways in which we are constituted as subjects in electronically mediated language formations. TV ads, data bases, and computers, to select some cogent examples, position the individual outside the binary oppositions of freedom/determinism, subject/object, identity/difference, thereby undermining the reference points of theory. If that is the case, domination is no longer only a question of (political and economic) action but relates to discursive forms through which the subject is positioned in cultural space.

This presentation of the controversy between Habermas and the French poststructuralists is necessarily a fictional invention since the actual relations between the two positions have not been extensively argued. The "debate" between German and French theory clarifies the issues for the further development of criticism in

56. There is a similar totalizing element in some of the positions of the poststructuralists. To the extent, for example, that one cannot criticize Derrida's position without being open to the charge of logocentrism, at least from the vantage point of deconstruction, a totalizing enclosure is put into place.
57. See Mark Poster, *The Mode of Information* (New York: Blackwell, forthcoming).

the age of the mode of information. Without abandoning the emancipatory aims of critical theory, as currently presented by Habermas, this further work will benefit from the criticisms of logocentrism enunciated by poststructuralists.

5 DEFENSE POLICY UNDER MITTERRAND MARK 2
Toward the Collapse of "Consensus"?

Jolyon Howorth

In his March 1988 electoral epistle, *Lettre à tous les Français,* candidate François Mitterrand took obvious pleasure in stressing the major differences of opinion and policy that had separated him from his prime minister, Jacques Chirac, over the preceding two years. Nowhere did this pleasure manifest itself more acutely than in the area of defense and foreign policy where, if Mitterrand was to be believed, Chirac had "demonstrated considerable abnegation in repeatedly giving in to decisions with which he disagreed." Twisting the knife, Mitterrand added: "The fact that he did this out of concern for the unity of our foreign policy and respect for the constitution rather than out of any desire to please me is something on which I can only congratulate him."[1] The areas of fundamental disagreement that Mitterrand chose to reveal (thereby exploding the carefully nurtured myth of "consensus"[2]) covered everything from SDI to Chad, from tactical nuclear weapons to Lebanon, from Latin America to France's plans for a new strategic weapon. But the area which was potentially the most revealing (and on which, in fact, Mitterrand was at his most laconic) was the question of French responses to Gorbachev's INF[3] proposals.

Lifting a diaphanous veil which had already been somewhat shredded by early press coverage of the ragbag of responses which

1. François Mitterrand, *Lettre à tout les Français* (Paris, March 1988), pp. 8–14.
2. See Jolyon Howorth, "Consensus of Silence: The French Socialist Party and Defence Policy under François Mitterrand," *International Affairs* 60, no. 4 (1984): 579–600.
3. Intermediate Nuclear Forces.

JOLYON HOWORTH

Gorbachev's February 1987 proposal had elicited from within the governing circles,[4] Mitterrand noted that the agreement signed in Washington in December 1987 was one "which I approved of, but which the main leaders of the government, either publicly or secretly, rejected." Behind this significant understatement can be detected a growing rift within the French political class over the entire configuration of defense policy for the year 2000. At issue are most of the major problem areas still awaiting a clear policy direction from Paris: the future shape of strategic nuclear defense; the role and function of France's tactical (from 1983, renamed "prestrategic") nuclear weapons; deployment (or not) of the neutron weapon; equipment for the conventional armed forces; France's relationship with NATO; France's role in the defense of Europe (which is not necessarily the same thing); France's relationship with the Federal Republic (which may be the same thing). Underlying all these questions is the basic issue of how France interprets the Gorbachev phenomenon. On all these matters a deep divide now exists between Mitterrand, backed by the majority of the Socialist party on the one hand, and, on the other hand, most leading right-wing defense specialists, from Jacques Chirac to Raymond Barre and from Valéry Giscard d'Estaing to André Giraud. In a nutshell, the socialists trust Gorbachev and seem to believe in the doctrine of defensive sufficiency or minimal deterrence, while the conservatives insist that the very notion of "trusting" the Soviet Union is naive and hope that the nuclear gaps left by American ratification of the INF treaty can be plugged by France.

The re-election of François Mitterrand on 8 May 1988 and the subsequent partial socialist victory in the parliamentary elections of 5 and 12 June 1988 suggest that, in this clash of wills over the future of French defense policy, "reasonable sufficiency" is likely to prevail over escalation. That is probably true, but matters are not as simple as that. For the French, the recent imperative to present to the world an apparently unshakable united front on defense policy constitutes a political-cultural context giving some leverage to the defeated Right, especially to the crucially important center parties. Mitterrand's stated intention (and Rocard's sincere desire) to create a workable extended majority embracing acceptable elements of the political center is likely to break down, first and foremost, over

4. *Le Monde*, 6 March 1987.

80

defense policy. It is possible that concessions will be made in this area in order not to prejudice the grand design of marginalizing the "hard" Right. Moreover, interservice rivalry within the military is stepping up, and the apparent desire to shift the balance of French defense procurement away from the massive nuclear escalation of recent programs will meet with stiff resistance from the armed forces.[5] Pressures from the arms manufacturers are bound to intensify as the imbrication of arms sales, the national economy, prestige, research and development, and nationalized industries grows stronger by the day.[6] Moreover, both Mitterrand himself and his defense minister Jean-Pierre Chevènement attach overriding importance to the pursuit of the most advanced scientific and technological research, in particular in those areas where the military interest (if not in fact the military impetus) is paramount: space, nuclear programs, aviation and marine exploration.[7] It will be extremely difficult for mere politicians (even if their office is situated in the Elysée Palace) to exercise the necessary control over the consequences and implications of much of that research.

The role in defense planning of the new prime minister, Michel Rocard, might also seem to be a guarantee that "reasonable sufficiency" will win the day. Those close to the prime minister confirm that he is personally sceptical about the long-term prospects for French nuclear weapons, whether strategic or pre-strategic. For obvious reasons he cannot afford to be too assertive about this as long as public attachment to the fading verities of "Gaullism" remains so strong. But a close analysis of his recent defense pronouncements suggests that he sees the future far more clearly in conventional rather than in nuclear terms.[8] However, it is here that his attempts to coexist with the center-right may prove a complicating factor. In order to obtain a clearer grasp of the evolving clash over defense policy, it is instructive to look back to the events of 1987 and to analyze the conflicting responses in France

5. See *Défense Nationale* (June 1987 and July 1987), in which the commanders in chief of the army and the air force make their respective cases for more resources.
6. See Edward A. Kolodziej, *Making and Marketing Arms* (Princeton: Princeton University Press, 1987), esp. pt. 3, "Arms and the State."
7. *Lettre à tous les Français*, p. 30. In this section Mitterrand notes that Michel Rocard also shares these objectives.
8. "Un entretien avec Michel Rocard," *Le Monde*, 11 July 1987 and 3 June 1988; see also Rocard's book *Le Coeur et la raison* (Paris 1987) and an interview with Rocard about the book in *Politique Internationale*, no. 37 (Autumn 1987): pp. 7–24.

to the "Gorbachev revolution." Those responses must be situated within the context of a much-heralded "consensus" on defense issues which filled the headlines after Mitterrand came to power in 1981, but which was already beginning to fall apart during the two years of "cohabitation" after the Right regained parliamentary control in 1986.

FROM CONFRONTATION TO CONSENSUS AND BACK AGAIN

De Gaulle's original reservations about NATO, formulated in the context of an ever-increasing world role for Washington, were essentially motivated by his fears about the *automaticity* involved in NATO membership. His quest for national independence was first and foremost a refusal to be automatically embroiled in every quarrel the superpowers chose to pick with one another. This was especially so given widespread scepticism, following the development of a Soviet intercontinental ballistic missile capacity, about the *automaticity* of American response to any Soviet attack in Europe. The bitter wrangling over flexible response only confirmed him in his view. Although de Gaulle himself believed that, one day, Europe would have to get its defense act together with relative autonomy from the United States,[9] neither the historical period nor the general's personality were then appropriate to the task. France was left to stew in her own independent juice, which, for de Gaulle, could only be nuclear. Thus "Gaullism," which began as an attempt to extricate Europe from the dangerous clutches of the superpowers, came essentially to be identified with nationalism and nuclear escalation.

Opposition to Gaullism, as formulated both from the center and from the old Socialist party (SFIO), was based far less on any principled objection to nuclear weapons as such than on a political fear that the general's independent stance would destroy the necessary solidarity of NATO.[10] At the time, one of the features of

9. Both the Fouchet Plan and the Franco-German Pact of the early 1960s were attempts to move in this direction. See Edmond Jouve, *Le Général de Gaulle et la construction de l'Europe 1940–1966* (Paris: LGDJ, 1967), vol. 2, pp. 441–65.
10. See my chapter in Jolyon Howorth and Patricia Chilton, eds., *Defence and Dissent in Contemporary France* (London: Croom Helm, 1984), pp. 95ff; also Jolyon Howorth, *France: The politics of peace* (London: Merlin, 1984), chap. 4; Pascal Krop, *Les Socialistes et l'armée* (Paris, PUF, 1983).

NATO particularly valued by its supporters was precisely the automaticity of the solidarity that membership appeared to confer. These objections to the general's disruptive attitude were coupled in most quarters with considerable scepticism about the credibility of what the socialists disparagingly referred to as the French *bombinette*.

By the early 1970s both of these major objections to Gaullism had begun to evaporate. The development of a strategic triad of authentically French nuclear weapons was a phenomenal gamble, but one which seemed to have paid off. By 1974 France was fast emerging as a superpower in miniature, a potential threat that could no longer be ignored by the Kremlin. At the same time, as the memory of the general's disruptive influence began to fade and as French defensive "dissidence" within the Atlantic Alliance was seen to have had no fundamentally negative impact on NATO, France's independent stance, especially with the advent of a profoundly Atlanticist president, Valéry Giscard d'Estaing, was officially declared, at the Ottawa meeting of the NATO council in 1974, to be an enhancement of deterrence. The multiplication of "nuclear decision centers," it was decided, increased the level of uncertainty and therefore compounded the Kremlin's planning problems. Overnight, Gaullist "dissidence" as such ceased to be a liability in the minds of those who had previously berated it. Thereafter the alignment of the left-wing parties was only a matter of time. The seeds of "consensus" were sown.

However, such consensus as did emerge was only paper-thin. Although all four major parties agreed that France should preserve her independent stance and should rely on her strategic nuclear systems for her own national "sanctuarization," there was precious little agreement once attention shifted from the banner headlines to the small print. In the context of fundamental shifts taking place in the global and European strategic picture, new and difficult problems were appearing. Globally the United States, having "lost" Southeast Asia, began to look, under President Carter, less and less like a superpower. At the same time there were frequent warnings from prominent Americans such as Mike Mansfield and Henry Kissinger that Europe should not expect Washington's "protection" to last forever.[11] That "protection" was, in any case, being

---

11. For a recent survey see Phil Williams, "The Limits of American Power: From Nixon to Reagan," *International Affairs* 63, no. 4 (Autumn 1987): 575–87.

made infinitely more complicated by developments on the old continent. The reinforcement of the European Economic Community (EEC), which seemed to imply, sooner or later, a (West) "European pillar" of NATO, was paralleled by the Federal Republic's *Ostpolitik*, which suggested that that pillar might one day have nothing to support (If East-West tension could be reduced by political or diplomatic means, the threat of military confrontation became less and less real). These developments complicated life for French defense planners, but in somewhat contradictory ways. European integration, because it was still anathema to large sections of traditional Gaullism and to the Communist party, served to perpetuate anti-Atlanticist discourse within the defense establishment, even though large sections of the liberal center and socialist Left were anxious to bury the past. *Ostpolitik*, because it aroused French fears of "neutralist drift" suggested, on the contrary, a reinforcement of Atlanticism. In general these complexities served to delay the much-needed renewal of French strategic discourse. That delay was the more significant in that Soviet progress toward "counterforce" capability in nuclear systems, particularly the deployment of the SS-20, hung an increasingly large question mark over the credibility of France's exclusively "countervalue" nuclear deterrent.[12]

The new, detailed questions that began to crowd onto the French defense agenda in the second half of the 1970s and early 1980s were only in part a reflection of these sea changes in the global order. Also crucial to the debate was the increasingly urgent need to consider options for the modernization or replacement of the defense systems planned in the 1950s and 1960s, deployed in the 1970s, and due to come to the end of their active life in the 1990s. Which new strategic systems, and how many? What type of "tactical" nuclear systems and where to deploy them? How to modernize the rather neglected conventional forces and for what purpose? Above all, in what way to modify the familiar incantations of classical Gaullism concerning national independence and relations with the allies? President Giscard d'Estaing made a brief attempt to

---

12. With Soviet "counterforce" weapons (i.e., of sufficient precision to be targeted not on population centers—"countervalue"—but on missile silos) came the thesis of the "window of vulnerability." See on this Robert H. Johnson, "Periods of Peril: The Window of Vulnerability and Other Myths," *Foreign Affairs* 61, no. 4 (Spring 1983).

draft a new score, notably by speaking of a "single strategic space" in Europe and by attempting to shift the balance of the defense budget away from nuclear systems and in favor of conventional ones.[13] But Giscard had overestimated the strength of his own position. Dependent on the Gaullists for a parliamentary majority, he had recently lost the services of Jacques Chirac as prime minister. Chirac was busy building up his new power base in the Rassemblement pour la République (RPR) and, as mayor of Paris at the Hôtel de Ville, was not terribly interested in defense policy in any case; he was therefore only too happy to allow the traditional Gaullist "barons" such as Michel Debré and Pierre Messmer the freedom to maul Giscard to their heart's content.[14] The socialist leaders, intent on showing off to the electorate their recently acquired Gaullist accoutrements, were only too pleased to make what political mileage they could out of Giscard's "Atlanticist sins." When they finally came to power in 1981, détente was in a state of collapse; Germany was in turmoil and, to many a paranoid French mind, drifting rapidly into "neutralism"; Eastern Europe was challenging the Kremlin gerontocrats in alarmingly destabilizing ways; and the French electorate was clamoring for "Gaullist" reassurance. The time was not ripe for any major socialist redrafting of the national security agenda.

A new approach is only just now (in 1988) beginning to emerge with any clarity. The process leading to its emergence has, since 1983, shown up the extent of the cracks in the old Gaullist edifice. After two years of mediatized obeisance to the notion of "consensus," during which President Mitterrand strove hard to secure his place in the pantheon of strategic conformity, two major signs of a new direction began to emerge. The first was the intensification of Franco-German defense cooperation, whose consequences are still being worked out but which, from the very beginning in the autumn of 1982, implied a major redefinition of France's relations with her NATO and European allies. From the establishment, in 1982, of a joint defense commission to the creation, in 1988, of a

13. See the article by Giscard's chief of staff, General Méry, "Une armée pour quoi faire et comment?" *Défense Nationale* (June 1976) and Giscard's speech to the Institut des Hautes Etudes de Défense Nationale in ibid., July 1976.
14. Admiral Paul Delahousse, a senior member of the UDF defense commission, told me in an interview in Paris in December 1984 that Giscard was frequently given ultimatums by the Gaullist barons who threatened to withdraw their parliamentary support unless he toed the defense line.

joint defense council,[15] it has been clear that the Paris-Bonn axis is intended to lay the foundations of that elusive "European pillar" of the Atlantic Alliance which, whatever de Gaulle's "real intentions" in the early 1960s, effectively takes France beyond Gaullism. We shall explore in the second half of this essay the different interpretations of that cooperation which can be found in France today. The second development in 1983 was that the resource issue finally came home to roost. Giscard d'Estaing had simply ignored the financial implications of the strategic differences between the Gaullists and himself by writing *both* nuclear *and* conventional expansion into his 1976–81 defense white paper. According to the Cour des Comptes, that white paper was almost fifty billion francs short of its real cost.[16] This allowed Charles Hernu, the new socialist minister, the luxury of avoiding the preparation of a new white paper until 1983, arguing that the former program needed to be completed first. When the socialist defense program for 1984–88 was formulated in 1983, it became obvious to everybody that France simply could not afford the type of expansion in every domain which had hitherto been taken more or less for granted. From 1983 onwards the defense debate in France has been informed by an intractable resource problem that has forced *choices* onto the security agenda. Again, the consensus has broken apart as the political parties face up to the painful fact that France cannot afford to maintain the bluff of superpower status.[17] Most of the right-wing criticism which, between 1983 and 1986, was leveled at the socialist defense budgets concentrated its fire not so much on the programs as such as on the general inadequacy of their budgetary base, a fact attributed to the inherent incapacity of socialists to manage money. Hernu's decision to concentrate the lion's share of resources on nuclear weapons in general and strategic weapons in particular meant serious cuts in the conventional wings of all three forces, as well as the abandonment of some of the more ambitious projects launched under Giscard, such as the mobile (SX) missile

15. The commission involved high-level bilateral talks at levels lower than ministerial. The council involves regular ministerial discussions.
16. See Charles Hernu, "Une défense moderne et crédible," *Le Monde*, 12 July 1985.
17. Jolyon Howorth, "Of Budgets and Strategic Choices," in George Ross et al., *The Mitterrand Experiment* (Oxford: Polity Press, 1987), pp. 306–23; and François Heisbourg, "Défense française: L'impossible statu quo," *Politique Internationale* 36 (Summer 1987): 137–54.

destined to replace the fixed-silo missiles on the Plateau d'Albion.[18] But the fact that the UDF and the RPR did not agree on the precise aspects of the budget cuts to deplore ensured that their most visible, joint public statements avoided the specifics nevertheless discernible in their respective detailed critiques of socialist defense planning.[19]

The defeat of the socialists in 1986 did little to resolve this resource issue. UDF and RPR stuck to their determination to present a common front and to demonstrate that they were able to put resources back into the defense budget by ordering up all sorts of items the socialists had either omitted to order or omitted to cost. Thus the conservative *loi de programmation militaire* for 1987–91 was all things to all men, calling for state-of-the-art equipment in every domain from battle tanks to satellites and introducing some new elements that had hitherto been shunned (such as chemical weapons). However, there was a curious division of labor on the Right. The defense ministry wrote the program, but omitted to offer any costing; the latter was left to the parliamentary defense commission, dominated by its energetic young Gaullist president, François Fillon. The former document comprised three pages of the *Journal Officiel*. The latter ran to three hundred and seventeen.[20] In the uncertain circumstances surrounding *cohabitation*, it was clear that nobody was prepared to make the necessary choices until they were forced to. Controversy over some of those choices began to escape into the public domain. The first to appear was a short-lived exchange over President Reagan's Strategic Defense Initiative (SDI). François Mitterrand and his last socialist defense minister Paul Quilès refused categorically to associate France with the American scheme, arguing that they preferred to ensure the future of *European* high-technology research and industry by launching the Eureka program. As the elections approached in 1986, five conservative "heavyweights," in the shape of Valéry Giscard d'Estaing, Jacques Chirac, Michel Aurillac, André Giraud, and, rather

18. Jolyon Howorth, "Defense and the Mitterrand Government," in Howorth and Chilton, eds., *Defence and Dissent in Contemporary France*.

19. UDF, *Redresser la défense de la France* (Paris: UDF, 1985); RPR, *La Défense de la France, quatre ans de gestion socialiste: Propositions pour le renouveau* (Paris, 1985).

20. *Journal Officiel: Lois et Décrets*, Saturday, 23 May 1987, pp. 5648–50; Assemblée Nationale, "Rapport fait au nom de la Commission de la Défense Nationale et des Forces Armées sur le projet de loi de programme (No. 432) relatif à l'équipement militaire pour les années 1987–1991," No. 622.

later, François Fillon fired off articles attacking this attitude and calling either for French participation in the American project, or for a European SDI, or both.[21] This was, in fact, something of a phony war, since nobody on the Right had any real idea what was involved in either an American or a French/European SDI program. Even as early as the summer of 1986 it was becoming clear that Reagan's "dream" was in fact a fantasy. As Mitterrand noted, once the new government was in place: "The discussion didn't last long. I reiterated my refusal. They never mentioned it [SDI] again." But the skirmish over SDI was symptomatic of the battles to come and those which are now raging in France. For the conservatives what matters are prestige projects and military might, whatever the cost. The socialists, mindful of the cost, if of nothing else, prefer to cut their coat according to their cloth. A second skirmish of a similar nature took place at the same time over the projected replacement of the missiles on the Plateau d'Albion. An initial decision had been taken under Giscard d'Estaing to develop a mobile missile similar to the American MX, and this had been corroborated by early statements from the ever expansive Charles Hernu. But the mobile missile had been the first clear victim of Hernu's shrinking budget and disappeared from sight around 1983. The conservatives resurrected the idea in the run-up to the 1986 elections, and a parliamentary report was commissioned.[22] Jacques Chirac, who was being very heavily lobbied by the potential manufacturers of the new ballistic missile, Aérospatiale, turned this into a trial of strength with the president.[23] Once again it was sufficient for Mitterrand to lay down the law, which he did in October 1986 at a speech at the military

21. Michel Aurillac, "Assez de gémissements," Le Monde, 11 January 1986; André Giraud, "Oui sur les grandes orientations, non sur leur mise en oeuvre," ibid., 12 February 1986; "M. Giscard d'Estaing fonde la sécurité de l'Europe sur l'arme à neutrons et un bouclier anti-missiles," ibid., 18 February 1986; Jacques Chirac, "Construction de l'Europe et défense commune," ibid., 28 February 1986; François Fillon, "Rompre avec la gestion précédente," ibid., 1 August 1986.
22. Journal Officiel, Assemblée Nationale No. 368, 3 October 1986, Rapport d'information par la Commission de la Défense Nationale et des Forces Armées sur la nouvelle composante des forces nucléaires stratégiques.
23. In his official speech to the Institut des Hautes Etudes de Défense Nationale on 12 September 1986, see "La Politique de défense de la France," Défense Nationale (November 1986): 10. Interestingly enough Fillon, Chirac's main defense adviser at the time, was in favor of developing a supersonic French cruise missile. He was overruled. . . .

camp of Caylus in Tarn-et-Garonne, for all talk of the SX missile to vanish from the public arena.[24]

More serious than these fairly academic exchanges over weapons systems (which, in any case, France could probably not afford) was the matter of reinterpretation of strategic doctrine, particularly in regard to prestrategic weapons. The precise function of shorter-range nuclear weapons has always been part of a "grey area" that military strategists prefer to keep as grey as possible. NATO doctrine has held that such tactical weapons are part of the battle-field panoply which, it is felt, would be needed at an early stage in an East-West war in order to compensate for an alleged Western inferiority in conventional systems. The doctrine of "flexible response" is deliberately fuzzy at the edges, partly because nobody can say in advance with any certainty under what circumstances and at what stage in the battle such weapons would need to be used and partly to increase the level of uncertainty which is seen as synonymous with deterrence. Many leading western strategists have recently revised their opinion of flexible response and called for "no first use."[25]

France, on the other hand, has always insisted on regarding short-range weapons as "prestrategic." Although the word only entered French military vocabulary under President Mitterrand, the doctrine it encapsulates has, through successive regimes, implied a refusal to accept the nuclear war-fighting implications of flexible response. The only exceptions to this golden French rule are the centrist Giscardians, who have never made any secret of their desire to see France align herself with NATO and embrace flexible response as the bedrock of deterrence.[26] As the post-1981 socialists reiterated prestrategic orthodoxy, increasing numbers of opposition spokesmen as well as leading defense commentators[27] began to agitate in favor of deployment of French short-range weapons

24. "M. Mitterrand réaffirme son autorité en matière de défense," Le Monde, 15 October 1986. The "new component" to replace the Albion missiles appeared in the 1987–91 white paper as an unspecified fixed-silo missile, but toward the end of 1987 André Giraud tried to reintroduce the idea of a mobile missile through the back door by linking it to the development work being done on the mobile tactical missile Hades.

25. McGeorge Bundy, George Kennan, Robert S. McNamara, and Gerard Smith, "Nuclear Weapons and the Atlantic Alliance," Foreign Affairs (Spring 1982).

26. UDF, Redresser la défense de la France, pp. 75–76, 81–83, 120–23.

27. See in particular Pierre Lellouche, L'Avenir de la guerre (Paris: Mazarine, 1985).

inside the territory of the Federal Republic, as battlefield systems. On the other hand, some prominent Gaullists questioned the very need for such (nonstrategic) systems and criticized the socialists for channeling resources into the new Hades program, which they had inherited from Giscard.[28] However, as Chirac approached the prize of political power, he allowed himself to be influenced not by his own purist Gaullist advisers but by the new breed of centrist "Atlanticists" and gradually began to argue in favor of battlefield deployment of France's short-range systems.[29] In his first speech to the establishment Institut des Hautes Etudes de Defénse Nationale (IHEDN), he went so far as to suggest that France had now shifted her strategic doctrine to envisage using these weapons in a battle-field situation.[30] He was sharply called to order—yet again—by François Mitterrand.[31] Clearly, there is in France no consensus whatever on this vitally important class of nuclear weapons. The fact that opinions vary so dramatically on such major issues as SDI, the new generation of land-based missiles, and the precise function of short-range missiles is a reflection of the rapid changes that have taken place in the global order over the last decade. The prescriptions of the 1960s and 1970s, when it became imperative for all French politicians to stand firm behind the defensive systems planned decades earlier, no longer held good. In particular, in the world of Mikhail Gorbachev, it was becoming increasingly difficult to continue to argue that nothing had changed. Nowhere was this dilemma more acutely felt than in French responses to Gorbachev's INF initiatives.

1987: THE YEAR MIKHAIL CAME TO STAY

Gorbachev's initial proposal, officially presented to the Geneva conference on 3 March 1987, was for a separate agreement between the United States and the Soviet Union to eliminate all intermediate

---

28. Hades is a longer-range (350 km) missile scheduled to replace Pluton in 1992. François Fillon, "A quoi sert l'armement nucléaire tactique?" *Le Monde*, 10 November 1984.

29. Jacques Chirac, "Construction de l'Europe et défense commune," *Le Monde*, 28 February 1986.

30. Jacques Chirac, "La Politique de défense de la France," *Défense Nationale* (November 1986; speech at IHEDN, 12 September 1986).

31. "M. Mitterrand réaffirme son autorité en matière de défense," *Le Monde*, 15 October 1986.

range (1000–5000 kms) land-based missiles from the territory of Europe. This became known as the "single-zero option," as opposed to the later proposal (eventually accepted by Reagan and signed in December 1987 in Washington) to eliminate both intermediate and shorter-range (500–1000 kms) missiles, which became known as the "double-zero option."

Initial reactions, which were forthcoming at the regular Wednesday meeting of the French cabinet on 4 March, were mixed. Mitterrand, seemingly backed by his prime minister Jacques Chirac (who confined himself to nodding affirmatively throughout Mitterrand's presentation and interjecting from time to time the words "he's right") insisted that the Gorbachev proposals were an important step in the right direction (disarmament) and that they should be responded to as positively as possible. André Giraud, the defense minister, seemingly backed by Foreign Minister Jean-Bernard Raimond, denounced the INF agreement as a "nuclear Munich" for Europe, a notion which, in subsequent weeks, was reiterated by many prominent spokespersons on the Right.[32] Those opposed to the treaty expressed fears of "denuclearization" in Europe, concerns that it might compromise France's own modernization program, worries that it represented a waning of the American commitment to Europe and misgivings about the future of "flexible response" (which France, ironically enough, had always officially denounced). Those in favor of the treaty, in addition to the president, included almost all the socialists, the communists, and former president Giscard d'Estaing.[33] They approved of the treaty for the obvious reasons but, for the most part (with the exception of the communists, who were gradually pulling away from the consensus on a variety of issues), sought to distance themselves from the more scaremongery attacks on it being formulated by the

32. See the lengthy reports in *Le Monde*, 6 March 1987; "Il faut mettre les occidentaux en garde contre un Munich américain," *Le Figaro*, 8 March 1987; Jean-Marie Daillet, "L'Option zéro: Munich II?" *Le Monde*, 10 March 1987; see also the extracts from the comments of most major politicians in *Politique Etrangère* 2 (1987).

33. See the *communiqué* of the Bureau exécutif of the Socialist party, dated 4 March 1987, in *PS Info*, no. 316, 7 March 1987; statement by the Bureau politique of the Communist party, *L'Humanité*, 4 March 1987. Giscard d'Estaing was very slow in making known his position publicly. However, as the host of the Guadeloupe conference at which the original NATO "two-track" decision had been made in 1979, he could hardly oppose the zero option. See his article, "Un bon accord, une chance pour l'Europe," in *Le Monde*, 23 September 1987.

"hard" Right. They denied that it would lead to "denuclearization" or that it would affect France's own programs or that it represented a dilution of US-European "coupling." Moreover, they all pointed out that, since the West had been the original architect of the "zero option" back in 1979, it was logically impossible suddenly to be opposed to it. In other words, those in favor of the treaty immediately sought to make clear that it actually changed very little in the world. The main differences between the treaty's supporters and its adversaries lay on two separate levels. First, they were divided as to its symbolic impact in the present. Second, they failed to see eye to eye over its repercussions for the future. The attitude of the French media was one of suspicion; this was faithfully reflected in an opinion poll published in *Le Figaro* on 21 April 1987 that found that 45 percent of respondents felt INF to be a "trap" cunningly laid for the unsuspecting West by the crafty Gorbachev, whereas only 35 percent felt the treaty to be a "good thing." However, despite Jacques Chirac's frenzied attempts to whip up hostility to the agreement in London and Bonn, both Mrs. Thatcher and Mr. Kohl expressed their eventual support, thereby effectively rendering ratification inevitable.[34]

In reality of course, Gorbachev, as many commentators noted,[35] had done little more than focus attention on questions which had been on the agenda for many years but which generation after generation of defense "experts" had fudged in one way or another—questions such as U.S.-Euro "coupling" or the precise intentions of France in the event of hostilities in Central Europe. Just beneath the surface of all those questions was the burning issue of the *European* defense of Europe and the role in that defense of nuclear weapons. For France such questions were more dramatic in their implications than for the other European NATO nations. First because France, far more than Britain, had over the years put more and more of her eggs into the nuclear basket. Second because France, having opted out of NATO, had lost the habit of thinking concretely in terms of the constraints and responsibilities of al-

34. Chirac's timing for these trips was rather unfortunate. Their purpose was to stave off Anglo-German support for the zero option, but they were followed rapidly (in the case of London, within twenty-four hours) by statements of support for the treaty from Mrs. Thatcher and Helmut Kohl. I was informed by a close associate of Chirac that he was particularly furious with "the Iron Lady" and considered that she had "made him look like a jerk."
35. Bernard Guillerez, *Défense Nationale* (April 1987): 143.

liances. Third because France, as a result of her geostrategic position both as a continental and as a maritime power (not to mention her self-perception as a *world* power) was bound to be located at the hub of whatever common security structures emerged from the new post-Gorbachev situation. The question facing French defense planners in 1988 was therefore the following: if France is to contribute a "specialist" role to the integrated defense of Europe, what role should that be? The natural inclination of most French respondents would be to opt for a nuclear role, leaving conventional specialization and updating to West Germany. Unfortunately, this French preference flies in the face of almost all the other variables: the actual requirements of the Federal Republic and other nations in Europe; the reluctance of those nations to see France "consecrated" in a different defensive league from themselves; the widespread desire across the Continent to de-emphasize, if not actually to eliminate, nuclear weapons; the progress of arms control and the inevitability of Franco-British involvement at some stage; last but not least, the difficulties of lending credibility to the notion of "extended deterrence." In 1987, for the first time, serious discussions took place between France and Great Britain over "nuclear collaboration" in Europe (coordinated targeting, submarine patrols, weapons procurement—especially a new "stand-off," air-to-ground medium-range missile). André Giraud, who speaks excellent English, and George Younger, Mrs. Thatcher's defense secretary, formed a close personal bond, but the president and the prime minister were clearly wishing to move in opposite directions.[36] However, it was not Franco-British relations which blossomed in 1987, but Franco-German.

FRANCO-GERMAN RELATIONS: THE COURTSHIP BLOSSOMS . . .

The intensity of Franco-German dialogue at the highest level, already impressive since the establishment in 1983 of permanent joint defense discussions, was stepped up considerably in 1987. Meetings between the respective heads of state or of government succeeded each other at almost monthly intervals, culminating in

36. Two "summit" meetings took place between the ministers, see *Le Monde*, 12 March and 2 October 1987. However, when Mitterrand and Thatcher got together in January 1988, relations became very strained, see *The Guardian*, 30 January 1988.

January 1988 in the twenty-fifth anniversary of the Franco-German treaty.[37] In April 1987 an opinion poll showed that 74 percent of respondents were in favor of automatic French support for Germany in the event of aggression, 63 percent were in favor of stationing French forces permanently inside the Federal Republic, and 51 percent were even prepared to "extend" the French strategic nuclear umbrella as far as the Elbe.[38] Public opinion was years ahead of the political class, which had not yet ventured beyond Charles Hernu's 1985 statement that "France and Germany share common security interests" or Jacques Chirac's 1986 formula to the effect that while France's security began on the Elbe, her survival began on the Rhine.

Despite the rhetoric and the media hype, however, the serious business of devising and implementing a joint Franco-German security strategy is riddled with problems. France has an interest in maintaining the division of Germany; German hankering after "reunification" sends shivers down many a French spine. For forty years Germans have looked to Washington for a defensive alliance of which, for the last twenty-five years, Paris has steadfastly refused to be a part. Over the same period Germany has been regarded by NATO as the inevitable battleground for any future hostilities (flexible response); France has believed her territory to be "sanctuarized" by her independent deterrent and, largely because of the policy of war fighting implicit in flexible response, has refused to be involved in NATO's strategic plans. Germany, forbidden by international treaty from possessing nuclear weapons, has put all her own defense resources into conventional systems; France has relied increasingly on nuclear weapons (and the forward procurement plans of the two countries perpetuate this disparity well into the next century). Large sections of popular opinion in Germany believe that nuclear war (which NATO plans to fight on German soil) would result in the obliteration of the German nation and are therefore uncompromisingly opposed to all nuclear weapons; French people have been told so often and for so long that *their* nuclear weapons will prevent them from being involved in any

37. On the Franco-German defense situation see GECSE, *Sécurité et défense de l'Europe: Le dossier allemand* (Paris: FEDN, 1985) and Karl Kaiser and Pierre Lellouche, eds., *L'Europe et sa défense: Volume I, Le Couple franco-allemand et la défense de l'Europe* (Paris: IFRI, 1987).
38. *L'Express*, 24 April 1987.

war that they see nuclear disarmament as a positive evil. The Germans, for geographical, historical, diplomatic, commercial, and cultural reasons, feel that good relations with Moscow and the Eastern-bloc countries (*Ostpolitik*) are a desirable fact of life; the French, having flirted massively with Communism for over fifty years, decided in the mid-1970s that Moscow was indeed the hub of the "evil empire." These are just some of the problems facing French and German security negotiators.

At the same time, both France and the Federal Republic share the liberal, democratic ethos of "Western" civilizations. Both countries feel a genuine sense of identity with the cause of (Western) European integration. Both are keenly aware that the American commitment to Europe, which has allowed Germany to reemerge as an industrial and economic giant and France to develop into a minor superpower, cannot continue indefinitely and that sooner or later the "Europeans" will have to put their money where their mouth is in security matters. Finally, both are conscious that, as the international order confirms the demise of nation-states and the desirability of continental units, cooperation at every level between and among European states is a condition of "independence" from the existing superpowers. How, therefore, to define a common security? Three major areas are: strategic nuclear deterrence; conventional solidarity; tactical nuclear weapons. The first two seem relatively straightforward, the third is a hornets' nest.

As the American commitment to Europe is brought into question and calls for the "European pillar" grow louder, the question of France extending her nuclear umbrella over the Federal Republic crops up from time to time. The French government has never officially suggested such a policy (on the contrary, the official line that French strategic nuclear weapons are exclusively for the defense of the "hexagon" has remained unchanged). For their part German-government spokespersons have repeatedly insisted that the Federal Republic has never asked and will not ask for any such development. But various leading politicians, including former ministers (and prime ministers), have proposed French "extended deterrence."[39] Moreover some prominent Germans, including former chancellor Helmut Schmidt, have not been averse to playing

---

39. Included in this list are Michel Aurillac, Giscard d'Estaing, Laurent Fabius, and Jean-Pierre Chevènement.

devil's advocate on this issue.[40] Yet everybody knows that such a development makes no sense, either diplomatic/political or military/strategic, so long as West Germany remains committed to NATO, indeed so long as NATO itself continues to exist. Equally clearly, it would radically alter the very basis on which France's military strategy has rested for over twenty-five years. Vast sea changes in defensive thinking on both sides of the Iron Curtain and on both sides of the Atlantic, not to mention both sides of the Rhine, would be required before any movement can be expected in this particular area. At this stage one has to conclude that all suggestions of extending French strategic deterrence to the Federal Republic, whether made by French or German actors, are geared more to producing a certain political or diplomatic impact, either in Europe or in the United States, than as serious strategic proposals.[41]

On the conventional front, however (the second of our possible areas of cooperation), there have been a few tangible developments. It was in October 1982 that François Mitterrand and Helmut Kohl set up a permanent Franco-German defense commission whose remit was to examine all means whereby the two countries could cooperate at a conventional level.[42] What the Germans required of the French in the first instance was some tangible sign that France was prepared to fight in the "battle for Germany." Such a signal was given in the spring of 1983 with the creation of the Force d'Action Rapide (FAR), combining five separate elite French divisions under a unified command. This polyvalent unit which combines maximum mobility (helicopter gunships and light tanks) with massive firepower (antitank precision guided missiles) was widely interpreted as a political gesture to the Federal Republic, indicating France's conscious move away from "Gaullism."[43] Al-

---

40. Helmut Schmidt, "La France, l'Allemagne, et la défense européenne," *Commentaire* (1984): 411–17. Schmidt's proposals were further examined in his *A Grand Strategy for the West: The Anachronism of National Strategies in an Interdependent World* (New Haven: Yale University Press, 1985). See also *Survival* (July–August 1987): 376.

41. I was told by a senior member of the SPD leadership, in London in May 1985, that Schmidt's only purpose was to shock the French into abandoning the canon of Gaullism by shattering the complacency (and ambiguity) of the previous twenty-five years.

42. *Le Monde*, 22, 23, 24–25 October 1982.

43. Dominique David, *La Force d'Action Rapide en Europe: Le Dire des armes* (Paris: FEDN, 1984); "La Force d'Action Rapide" (Dossier), *Armées d'Aujourd'Hui*, no. 96 (December 1984).

though the French made a great deal of the FAR, the Germans remained unimpressed. While symbols and gestures were not to be sneezed at, what Bonn really wanted was a practical show of strength. This was eventually forthcoming in September 1987 when joint military exercises (code-named "Saucy Sparrow" or "Moineau Hardi") were conducted by the Second German Army Corps and 20,000 men from the FAR. The exercises were commanded by a German general and observed by Mitterrand and Kohl, themselves closely watched by the world's television cameras. At a purely military level the operation was unimpressive. The "rapidly deployed" French troops did indeed demonstrate a capability to move men and equipment 1,000 kms within forty-eight hours and still have enough energy left to help their German allies "defend" a bridge over the Danube which was being "attacked" by a conveniently lethargic force of "Russians." However, when they were then sent by the German commander onto the counterattack, their performance led the *Economist* to the conclusion that they would scarcely scratch the paint on real Soviet tanks. There were problems of language (on one occasion it took more than twenty minutes for German and French tank officers to agree on a simple map reading), of codes and procedures, and of protocol. Above all, the Germans were incensed that the French insisted on vetoing the presence of NATO observers.[44] But the fact that the exercise took place at all was an event in itself and one which would have been unthinkable only a few years previously.

It was marked by an announcement from the French president that he and Helmut Kohl had agreed to establish a Franco-German defense council which would allow bipartite defense planning to move into a higher gear than had been possible with the commission established in 1982.[45] Clearly the two governments were doing their utmost to set a symbolic seal on their newfound desire to cooperate on the conventional front wherever possible. No doubt something will eventually come of all this, but many observers in Germany as well as Britain and elsewhere felt that, despite all the razzmatazz, "the Emperor was wearing little more

44. Pierre Lellouche, "Moineau Hardi: Envol difficile," *Le Point*, 5 October 1987, p. 29; Luc Rosenzweig, "Seule une ferme volonté a permis de surmonter de sérieuses différences de points de vue," *Le Monde*, 25 September 1987.
45. *Le Monde*, 27–28 September 1987.

than his shirt and underpants."[46] The sour grapes (if that was what was involved) stemmed not only from resentment at the "prodigal son" treatment being reserved for France, but also from a wide-spread sense that, before genuine military cooperation could be taken any further, a number of fundamental *political* problems would have to be solved.

The first involved the ultimate command of any such operation. Although in this instance the French president consciously placed the FAR under the "operational control" of the German Second Army, nobody missed the fact that that army is itself directly under the command of the supreme commander of NATO, General Galvin (whose invitation to the event was vetoed by the French!). Did this (despite the veto) represent a de facto French reintegration of NATO? More important still is the relationship between this exercise and the permanent (First) French Army Corps in Germany. The FAR had been projected into the so-called "forward battle" (on the eastern front) without the logistical backup of the regular army, whose function is seen in Europe as that of an operational reserve to be called into action in the event of a Warsaw Pact breakthrough in the east. Yet the First Army is, in French military thinking, directly linked, as a kind of "trip wire," to the strategic nuclear deterrent. This introduces the third major area where Franco-German military cooperation might exist (and which I have already described as a hornets' nest): that of tactical nuclear weapons.

It is in the field of tactical nuclear weapons that the greatest difference has always existed between France's strategy and that of her NATO allies, including West Germany. NATO's tactical nuclear weapons are, as their alternative name indicates, "battle-field weapons." Usually categorized as having a range of under 500 kms, they are intended for use in a situation of "controlled escalation," part of the panoply allowing for "flexible response." France's first Pluton missiles were deployed only in 1974 and from the very beginning were declared to be intimately linked to her strategic arsenal. They were officially intended to be used as a "warning shot," a test of enemy intentions, a signal that advancing enemy divisions should stop immediately in their tracks. If they did

---

46. Patricia Clough, "Building Europe's defence triangle," *The Independent*, 19 October 1987, p. 21; Luc Rosenzweig, "Le Scepticisme ouest-allemand demeure," *Le Monde*, 27–28 September 1987.

not do so, a strategic nuclear attack on enemy cities would be launched within forty-eight hours. These French tactical weapons have always been particularly offensive to the Germans. Prior to the Franco-German defense rapprochement of recent years, not only did Paris steadfastly refuse to give Bonn a guarantee of military backing in the event of a war, but the notion of the "tactical warning shot" suggested that a French response to a Soviet advance through West Germany toward the Rhine would be the release of a French Pluton missile whose range (120 km) ensured that it would explode on the territory of the Federal Republic. From a German perspective the announcement that a new weapon—Hades—was being developed with a greater range (350 kms) made very little difference. That Hades should be able to cross the Elbe and explode inside *East* Germany is hardly seen in Bonn as an improvement on the previous situation. In short, French tactical nuclear weapons have little to commend themselves to the Germans, but since they are operationally controlled by the First Army, part of which is stationed on the east bank of the Rhine, they also pose significant problems for conventional coop- eration between the two nations.

At the level of strategic theory, therefore, the rapprochement of French and German security efforts, which has been rendered almost inevitable by the success of Gorbachev's diplomacy, calls for considerable imagination and innovation. What the French are most able (and in almost every case most willing) to offer is some form of nuclear support. For many reasons, while not wishing to reject out of hand the prospect of discussions on this issue, the Germans would prefer to talk about other forms of cooperation. What the Germans have always wanted from the French and what they still feel would be the most appropriate manifestation of genuine solidarity would be the occupation, by the French conven- tional armed forces, of a specific sector of the eastern front. Such a proposal has always been regarded by France as unthinkable. Imaginative efforts to emerge from this impasse have been de- ployed by most leading French politicians in the course of 1987.

THE POLITICIANS AND STRATEGIC IMAGINATION

There can be no doubt that, among France's leading politicians, strategic thinking is dominated by François Mitterrand. Mitterrand has emerged, over the last decade, as a master of global strategic nuance. His command of detail and knowledge of military affairs has grown constantly, and the coherence of his approach has remained remarkably steady throughout a period of major change in the global strategic picture. Two concepts dominate and in a sense encapsulate the security thinking of the president—*strategic balance* and *nuclear deterrence*. Mitterrand arrived in the Elysée just as the controversy over the "Euromissiles" was reaching its paroxysm. His immediate position, which he has repeated incessantly ever since, was one of concern for *balance* between the superpowers. His stated preference was for that balance to be stabilized at the lowest possible level, but he believed that it were better to have a balance at higher levels rather than imbalance.[47] Mitterrand's position was dictated less by military considerations than by diplomatic ones. The alliance had made a decision to challenge the Soviet Union's deployment of SS-20s. It was far more important, in the president's view, to win the diplomatic battle over *balance*, if necessary through deployment of the Pershings and Cruises, than to pander to a public opinion that saw balance as irrelevant. In every major speech that Mitterrand has made as president he has reiterated his concern about *balance*. And the final test of his sincerity came in 1987 when the U.S. and the USSR eventually agreed on a disarmament treaty that did, in effect, represent balanced and verifiable reductions. While, at the outset, supporters for the zero option were exceptionally thin on the ground (and virtually nonexistent among right-wing politicians), François Mitterrand rapidly emerged as the firmest supporter of the INF treaty and, at the time of the treaty itself, he did not disagree when Jean Daniel, in a major interview, suggested that he must be "the European statesman who is most in favor of this treaty."[48]

Mitterrand's predilection for balance is inextricably linked to his faith in *nuclear deterrence*. Ever since Mitterrand rallied to the reality of the French nuclear arsenal (around 1969) he has believed that *deterrence* is the basis of France's security. Consequently, he has always harbored strong reservations about the function of France's

47. François Mitterrand, *Réflexions sur la politique extérieure de la France* (Paris: Fayard, 1986), esp. sec. 2, "De l'équilibre des forces." Of course many commentators, including myself, argued at the time that "balance" is an abstract concept when each side has the capacity to destroy the world several times over.
48. *Nouvel Observateur*, 18–24 December 1987, p. 40.

"tactical" nuclear missiles and has been fundamentally opposed to the concept of flexible response. It was under Mitterrand's impulsion that the term "prestrategic" was introduced to designate the former "tactical" weapons, and it was Mitterrand who insisted that these weapons be relocated under the direct control of the president of the Republic. Similarly, it was François Mitterrand, in 1987, who began to shift France's "declaratory strategy" decisively in favor of "all-out deterrence." Some observers believe that Mitterrand has always considered the development of tactical nuclear weapons to have been an error.[49] In 1986 he made it clear that he agreed with "experts" like Henry Kissinger and Robert McNamara who pointed to the absurdity of the theory of flexible response.[50] In February of that year he agreed to consult with the Germans about any eventual firing of a French short-range weapon (thus effectively ruling out their use other than in a situation where nuclear war might already have broken out). In the context of the "double-zero option" this whole issue became still more critical, especially for the Germans, since the only category of nuclear missiles left in Europe is precisely short-range ones. In Germany the saying goes that "the shorter the range, the deader the Germans." The vast majority of Germans (including Helmut Kohl) are therefore not entirely opposed to the notion of a "third" zero option, removing all tactical weapons from the European theater. For the vast majority of the French, however, that amounts to the "denuclearization" of the Continent and is to be avoided at all cost. Mitterrand was extremely sensitive to this dilemma when he paid an official state visit to Germany in late October 1987. It was on this occasion that the *petites phrases* uttered by the president began to cause quite a stir.

Mitterrand began his state visit on 19 October with a speech in which he let drop these tantalizing sentences: "There is no reason to believe that France's final warning shot against an aggressor would be delivered on German territory. . . . France's nuclear strategy is addressed to the aggressor and to him alone." The next day he drove the message a little further home: "Who dreamed up the idea

49. Jacques Amalric, "Les Tentations stratégiques de M. Mitterrand," *Le Monde*, 22 October 1987.
50. Mitterrand, *Réflexions*, p. 21. On the American debate see Robert S. McNamara, "The Military Role of Nuclear Weapons: Perceptions and Misperceptions," *Foreign Affairs* 62, no. 1 (Fall 1983): 59–80.

that the destination of France's nuclear weapons would be German soil? . . . Since the aim of French deterrence is to prevent an aggression, it is toward that aggressor, if he exists, that the threat must be addressed."[51] As usual, the president would not be drawn any further in the direction of strategic clarity and his remarks in Germany were subject to diverse interpretation. The defense correspondent of Le Monde, Jacques Isnard, inferred that Mitterrand was shifting toward a decision to deploy "prestrategic" missiles inside West Germany, as near the eastern front as possible.[52] But in a major interview with Jean Daniel, Mitterrand seemed, on the contrary, to imply that he was not certain there was any role for these weapons.[53] Indeed, on every occasion toward the end of 1987 Mitterrand went out of his way to insist that he was not convinced there was a real enemy anymore. The bottom line seemed to be that, for François Mitterrand, deterrence was total, sufficient, and effective. Thereafter, as the world began to move forward in the disarmament stakes, discussions between France and Germany on conventional collaboration would respond to the "real" perceived threat rather than to a preconceived notion of a world torn in half.

This presidential vision is—with certain variations—clearly shared by the entire Socialist party. In a series of statements throughout the year, the party reiterated its support for the double-zero option and for the further pursuit of disarmament in all areas; its belief in global deterrence; its abhorrence of nuclear war fighting or flexible response; its commitment to the conventional defense of West Germany; its faith in a new, more balanced relationship between Europe and the United States in which the Europeans would shoulder an increasing share of their own defense burden.[54] These official statements were echoed by a succession of articles from potential socialist presidential candidates.[55] Nuances

51. The full text of Mitterrand's speeches in Politique étrangère de la France: Textes et documents, October 1987, pp. 131–46. Extracts in Le Monde, 21 October 1987.
52. J. Isnard, "Des armes nucléaires préstratégiques le plus à l'est possible," Le Monde, 24 October 1987.
53. Nouvel Observateur, 18–24 December 1987.
54. Communiqué du Bureau exécutif du PS, 4 March 1987 in PS Info, no. 316, 7 March 1987, p. 1; Motion nationale d'orientation for Congress of Lille in Le Poing et la Rose, March 1987, p. 13; Communiqué du Bureau exécutif, 23 September 1987; "La France dans le monde," document presented by the Comité directeur, Le Poing et la Rose, September 1987, pp. 69–75; "Réflexions sur la sécurité européenne," text adopted by the Bureau exécutif, 30 October 1987, PS Info, no. 340.
55. Michel Rocard, "Le Coeur et la raison," Politique Internationale, no. 37 (Autumn

crept in on several issues. As to whether France should extend a "strategic nuclear umbrella" over West Germany, a matter on which Mitterrand has kept his cards very close to his chest, the post-May 1988 defense minister Jean-Pierre Chevènement's un-bridled enthusiasm was tempered by Laurent Fabius's suggestion that such a decision should remain a presidential prerogative (but he served notice that he personally was in favor) and by Michel Rocard's forceful rejection of the proposal (on the grounds that the Germans clearly did not want it).

In conclusion, therefore, it seems clear that the socialists are happy with the INF treaty, happy with the Gorbachev revolution, confident that the security of Europe is assured and that relations with West Germany will go from strength to strength. The same cannot be said for the right-wing politicians.

Jacques Chirac undoubtedly had the most uncomfortable ride throughout 1987. Strategic thinking has never been his strong point, and yet he felt obliged to assert the dynamism of govern-ment defense policy in a confused situation in which the position of François Mitterrand was clearly the one that counted most. In July he gave a foreign-policy interview to *Le Monde* in which he insisted that there were no divergences either between himself and the president or within the government team, but the net effect of the interview was unconvincing since the prime minister refused to be drawn into detail on a single aspect of policy.[56]

Chirac's main problem was in trying to emerge with an original position on Franco-German relations. The rapprochement between Paris and Bonn was so clearly the work of the Elysée and the thinking of Mitterrand and Kohl so obviously on the same wavelength that the prime minister was hard put to appear as anything other than the president's understudy. Twice he hazarded an original approach. On 19 September, on the occasion of the twenty-fifth anniversary of de Gaulle's address to the youth of

1987): 7–24; "Un entretien avec Michel Rocard," *Le Monde*, 11 July 1987; Lionel Jospin, "L'Option dissuasion," *Le Monde*, 5 December 1987; Laurent Fabius, "Pour un couplage franco-allemand," *Le Monde*, 20 August 1987; Laurent Fabius, "La Défense de la France à l'aube du XXIe siècle," *Défense Nationale* (November 1987): 9–24; Paul Quilès, "Du bon usage du consensus," *Le Monde*, 8 April 1987; Jean-Pierre Chevènement, "La Double Clé franco-allemande," *Le Monde*, 18 June 1987.
56. *Le Monde*, 8 July 1987. See also "Jacques Chirac diplomate," *Politique Inter-nationale*, no. 33 (Autumn 1986).

Germany, Jacques Chirac, in his own speech to several thousand young Germans, chose to lecture his audience on the dangers of "pacifism" and the historical torments that, in his view, could so easily lead the German people astray. Exactly one month later Mitterrand set out, during his state visit, to destroy those very stereotypes and misunderstandings which, as the *Le Monde* correspondent noted, Chirac had merely served to reinforce.[57] At the end of September Chirac found himself upstaged once again when the president used the "Saucy Sparrow" Franco-German military maneuvers as the opportunity to announce the forthcoming Franco-German defense council. Chirac responded swiftly with an exclusive interview in *Le Point*, implicitly minimizing the significance of that decision by referring to it as a "symbolic measure"[58] and by suggesting that the idea had not yet been fully thought through. Only days later, Helmut Kohl publicly disavowed the prime minister by revealing that he and Chirac had discussed the defense council at great length in September and that the prime minister had assured the chancellor of his complete support for the idea.[59]

Despite these various attempts to put across an "original" position on defense policy, Jacques Chirac had still not succeeded in enunciating a policy which was clearly distinguishable from that of the president. One final occasion presented itself when he gave the traditional prime ministerial address to the Institut des Hautes Etudes de Défense Nationale in December 1987. Presented by *Le Figaro* as "a profound shift in our military philosophy,"[60] his speech implied not only that France was prepared to extend her nuclear umbrella to the Federal Republic, which was henceforth to benefit from "immediate and unreserved" French support in the event of hostilities, but also that his country's short-range nuclear weapons would participate in the forward battle in Europe, presumably replacing the American ones that would have been withdrawn under the INF treaty. While Bonn reacted positively to the offer of immediate support, the Germans were less than happy about the reference to a new role for French short-range nuclear

57. Claire Tréan, "Jacques Chirac a tenté de briser la routine de la coopération franco-allemande," *Le Monde*, 22 September 1987.
58. *Le Point*, 5 October 1987, pp. 26–28.
59. *Le Monde*, 8 October 1987.
60. Ibid., 15 December 1987, p. 15; *Le Figaro*, 16 December 1987.

systems.[61] Once again it was left to Mitterrand to dot the *i*'s and cross the *t*'s. Asked whether the prime minister had effectively extended France's strategic deterrent to the territory of the Federal Republic, Mitterrand insisted that only the Atlantic Alliance could assume that role and that the French president alone would decide when France's "vital interests" were at stake. Asked about Chirac's implied conversion to "flexible response," the president was forcefully laconic: "There is no flexible response for France. That is also the opinion of the prime minister".[62]

Chirac's problem stemmed not only from the fact that he personally had no clear vision of defense policy. The Gaullist party was also in disarray on this matter. The "historic" figures like Michel Debré and Pierre Messmer were increasingly marginalized. But the new breed of Europeanist/Atlanticist, like François Fillon, was not yet able to make his mark. Nor indeed did the RPR wish to appear to be rallying to the UDF position. In short, Gaullist defense policy remains in a state of flux.

The same cannot be said of Valéry Giscard d'Estaing and Raymond Barre. The former president and his former prime minister have clear, but quite different positions. Giscard supported the double-zero option, while Barre denounced it. Giscard and the UDF have gone much further than anybody else toward a clear French return if not to NATO structures, at least to NATO doctrine. Barre has gradually elaborated a strategic discourse almost indistinguishable from that of Mitterrand. There is no real surprise in the first development. A series of UDF security documents throughout the 1980s has called increasingly unequivocally for France openly to embrace the doctrine of flexible response.[63] A major document published by the UDF defense "think tank" in May 1987, while stressing the dangers of total denuclearization in Europe, called on the European powers to seize the opportunity offered by the double-zero option to coordinate their defense policies. In particular the UDF invited the French to "weigh up the limitations of proportional deterrence" and to realize that, without the Atlantic Alliance, France's deterrent was of little value. France should therefore, according to the UDF, reintegrate NATO's

61. For Bonn's reactions, *Le Monde*, 16 December 1987.
62. *Nouvel Observateur*, 18–24 December 1987, p. 42.
63. UDF, *Une doctrine de défense pour la France* (Paris: UDF, 1980); *Défendre l'Europe* (Paris: UDF, 1984); *Redresser la dèfense de la France* (Paris: UDF, 1985).

planning committees and state "loud and clear that her security begins on the Elbe and that consequently she is ready, in agreement with her allies, to shift her strategic concept of 'final warning shot' . . . toward that of 'forward' deterrence."[64] Giscard d'Estaing, who in the spring of 1987 was elected chairman of the parliamentary foreign affairs commission, confirmed these options in September in an article that saw the INF treaty as a "good agreement" and a "chance for Europe." The UDF discourse is still dressed up in a number of conciliatory overtures toward Gaullist (or even socialist) concern for "national independence" but the basic strategic doctrine involves planning to join the "forward battle" and to use French short-range nuclear weapons as battle-fighting elements of a flexible-response strategy, now renamed "double deterrence."[65] No other political formation has gone as far as the Giscardians in the direction of an overt rejection of the "prestrategic" interpretation of short-range weapons. The UDF seems convinced that, if only France would put these weapons into the common European pool and openly abandon the notion of the "warning shot," then the political problems with the Germans would be resolved. For the moment, since the declaratory strategy of the president and of the government has not shifted, the Germans have not seen the need to make a statement on this hypothesis. It seems highly unlikely that they would be as keen on it as the Giscardians appear to feel.

Raymond Barre, amazingly, has avoided any specific comment on the role or function of French short-range nuclear weapons. "Amazingly," because M. Barre has consciously tried to emerge as a major strategic thinker in the course of the last few years.[66] Barre's discourse can be disassembled into two main parts: his attempts to make political capital out of certain stated disagree-

64. Groupe Renouveau Défense, "L'Affaire de l'option zéro" (Paris, UDF, mimeograph, 10 May 1987), p. 21.
65. Giscard d'Estaing, "Un bon accord, une chance pour l'Europe."
66. In particular, Barre's *permanence* in Paris publishes a regular bulletin, *Faits et Arguments*, which has issued several special numbers on defense: "L'Indépendance nationale et les exigences du présent" (November 1986); "Après le sommet de Reyjkavik," no. 41 (December 1986); "L'Affaire des Euromissiles," no. 47 (June 1987). Above all, see Barre's delivery of the Alastair Buchan lecture to the International Institute for Strategic Studies on 26 March 1987, which has been reproduced in *Faits et Arguments* (April 1987), *Défense Nationale* (June 1987), *Survival* (July-August 1987), and conferred upon him the stature of a major international strategist.

ments with Mitterrand and his own proposals—which resemble those of the president in almost every way. The former prime minister has, on every possible occasion, criticized Mitterrand for devising the slogan "neither Pershing nor SS-20" and has chosen, for obvious reasons of public popularity, to stress the potential *dangers* of the INF treaty. But in speech after speech and article after article he has insisted on three of the basic planks of Mitterrand's own defense platform: the indivisibility and absolute nature of French strategic deterrence (the president alone having the prerogative to decide whether France's vital interests begin at the Elbe or on the Rhine); the need to develop ever-closer conventional solidarity with the Germans and to enhance the conventional component of Europe's defenses; and the usefulness of the neutron bomb. Clearly Raymond Barre is seeking to occupy a doctrinal "slot" that is as close to traditional Gaullism as is compatible with the parallel attempt to be perceived as an original thinker. The difficulty with that objective is that such a "slot" is already occupied by the president of the Republic. Barre is therefore forced, not only for this reason but also because of his electoral need not to offend the "Atlanticist" lobby too deeply, to inject a few nuances into his discourse. One of these is that any future security arrangement in Europe must ensure the survival of a "flexible-response" capability on the part of NATO (even if France chooses not to be a part of it).[67] Another, which in effect amounts to the same, is that, if the zero option does strip Europe of these intermediary stages in her flexible response, then perhaps the role of France would have to be that of "piloting" the Continent toward replacement systems that would fill the gap left by the Americans.[68] But Barre is very firm in denouncing any interpretation of "flexible response" as implying war fighting and considers that there is "too much talk" about "forward-battle" and war-fighting strategies.[69] In other words, the main difference between Barre and Mitterrand is in their conception of which systems are necessary in order to ensure deterrence, the "grey area" being precisely that of short-range,

67. *Faits et Arguments*, special number (April 1987): 8.
68. *Le Monde*, 10 November 1987.
69. Assemblée Nationale, "Rapport fait au nom de la Commission de la Défense Nationale et des Forces Armées sur le project de loi de programme (no. 432) relatif à l'équipement militaire pour les années 1987–1991," *Annexe au procès-verbal de la séance du 2 avril 1987*, no. 622.

tactical, or pre-strategic weapons. It is precisely in this area that both men are at their least specific.

Some of the ambiguities can be cleared up by reference to the former defense minister André Giraud, who is considered to be very close to Raymond Barre. Giraud's overt hostility to the INF treaty was based on an exceptionally inflexible vision of the Soviet Union, which he continues to regard as overarmed and permanently threatening (an interpretation on which he actually diverges from Raymond Barre). But above all he fears the process of "denuclearization" in Europe and has emerged as the apostle of a new vision of deterrence that he is not afraid to call "flexible response." Nowhere was this approach spelled out more clearly than during Giraud's visit to London in March 1988. At a speech at the Royal Institute of International Affairs, he called for the installation in Europe of a complete new range of (French) nuclear weapons to replace the American ones removed under INF. He referred to this policy as one of "flexible response." In response to my question about his use of this expression, he said: "If flexible response means battle fighting, we are opposed; if it means war prevention, we are in favor."

Thus the major battle lines in France are drawn. On the one hand, the president of the Republic and the socialists, who will perpetuate one Gaullist vision of minimal nuclear deterrence, restricted increasingly to strategic systems. This they see as the most convincing form of "deterrence." At the same time they will enter more comprehensively into discussions with the Federal Republic on the requirements for a European defense of Europe in the context of the growing rapprochement between the two halves of the Continent. On the other hand, the totality of the right-wing, committed to a major increase in weapons systems of all types, nuclear and conventional. This right-wing is itself internally divided into a Giscardian wing which would like to align France with NATO's operational strategy (flexible response) and endow her with the weapons systems necessary to participate actively in the "forward battle." Some defense experts sympathetic to this position wish to go even further and formally abandon France's traditional declaratory ambiguity. These strategists argue that France should now state openly under precisely which circumstances she would engage in the conventional battle for Germany.[70] There is increasing evidence that this "pro-NATO" view is shared by Jacques Chirac. The opposite view on the Right is that encapsulated in the positions adopted by Raymond Barre, André Giraud, and, one suspects, François Fillon: a more traditional "Gaullist" view of national independence, with a continuing refusal to state openly where and when France's vital interests might be at stake. This camp is intent on re-arming Europe against the continuing Soviet threat and also talks of "flexible response," but with the emphasis firmly on war prevention, the traditional *refus de la bataille*. In the context of the long-awaited and very necessary decisions about the specifics of France's own defense modernization, these deep divisions within the political class are bound to help explode the myth of "consensus." François Mitterrand has remained the supreme arbiter of France's destiny throughout the 1980s. All the signs suggest that it will be his vision which will preside over the recalibration of Europe's defenses in the remainder of the twentieth century.

---

70. Thierry de Montbrial, "Sur la politique de sécurité de la France," *Commentaire* 10, no. 40 (Winter 1987–88).

6 THE GDR
UNDER THE SHADOW
OF *PERESTROIKA*

Günter Minnerup

For the last four decades the division of Germany has been at the heart of the European order. Their geographical frontiers determined by the identity of the occupation forces governing them after the collapse of Hitler's Reich, their political and social constitutions modeled on those of their postwar masters, their foreign policy and security stances tailored to the needs of their respective power blocs and military alliances, the two German states have been creations of the Cold War between East and West. Neither the Federal Republic of Germany (FRG) nor the German Democratic Republic (GDR) are, of course, entirely artificial constructs: both can lay claim to the inheritance of powerful German intellectual and political traditions. But the point is that each of them has had to be selective in the adoption of its—liberal-conservative or socialist-communist—historico-ideological lineage in order to conceal the fact that neither really owes its statehood to the victorious self-assertion of these traditions in Germany.[1] Without occupation and Cold War, neither the GDR nor the FRG would be in existence today.

The order built around the division of Germany has proved remarkably stable—so stable indeed that the question of whether two states so closely tied up with this order could survive any radical change in the external conditions of their existence hardly appeared worth asking. The terms of political discourse in Europe

1. Cf. the regular resurfacing of the West German uncertainties over *Vergangenheitsbewältigung*, as in the recent *Historikerstreit* or the East German ambiguities concerning the GDR's Prussian heritage.

were increasingly marked by an unquestioning acceptance of the immutability of the status quo—never more so than during the détente period of the 1960s and 1970s when progress and peace were largely synonymous with domestic reform within a framework of international stability.

The Second Cold War began to change all that. It was not only the Reaganite Right that resumed threatening talk of a revision of Yalta, but on the Left, too, the peace movement prompted some rethinking of previously unchallenged assumptions. If the détente between the superpower-led alliances had been so fragile, then perhaps these alliances themselves had to be reexamined? The hitherto largely economic strains between the U.S. and Western Europe gained a growing political dimension in a new "Europeanism" of the socialist and social-democratic parties in particular. In addition, through such channels as the European Nuclear Disarmament (END) movement the first tentative steps were taken toward a dialogue between the Western Left and the democratic opposition in Eastern Europe about visions of an alternative order in Europe.

And now there is Gorbachev, speaking of a "common European house," the prospect of a military withdrawal of both the U.S. and the USSR from Central Europe, and the democratization of "actually existing socialism." Few Europeans on either side of what used to be referred to as the Iron Curtain, whatever their political persuasion, fail to be fascinated by the spectacle of *glasnost* and *perestroika* because they all instinctively understand that they are more than mere spectators: a Soviet Union transformed would be a Europe transformed.

But if the entire old Continent has a stake in the restructuring of the USSR, it is the Germans more than anybody else who have cause to hope, or to fear, that their history may approach another turning point. For underneath all the carefully cultivated appearance of normality the status quo in Germany remains the most immediately sensitive to any change in the East-West equilibrium. Of the two Germanies, however, it is the GDR whose fate is more intimately tied up with the Soviet Union than that of any other state in Europe—not least because, to the present day, the strength of Red Army divisions deployed on its territory is more than twice that of its own armed forces.

Yet the leadership of the GDR's ruling party, the SED (Sozialistische Einheitspartei Deutschlands), is among the most determined opponents in the communist world of the "new thinking" emerging in Moscow. In an ironic reversal of the more familiar pattern of Soviet intervention against reformist deviations among the USSR's East European allies (Hungary 1956, Czechoslovakia 1968), it is the GDR's dissidents and democratic opposition who are today invoking Gorbachev's name against Honecker's Politburo and hoping for the Communist Party of the Soviet Union (CPSU)'s "fraternal assistance" in introducing reform and democratization. This essay is an attempt to explain this state of affairs and to venture some tentative, and unavoidably rather speculative, conclusions concerning the future of the GDR.

HISTORY AND NATIONALITY

The historical evolution, as well as the present and future dynamic, of the GDR cannot be interpreted merely in terms of the *general* contradictions *common* to all East European societies. The most significant incisions in its political history have, in fact, not been the stages in the domestic socioeconomic transformation of East German society, but the turning points in its relationship with the outside world, in particular West Germany and the Soviet Union: Moscow's decision to unequivocally back the GDR's full integration into the "socialist camp" in 1955, the building of the Berlin Wall in 1961, and the "normalization" of relations between the two German states in 1971.

The Years of Uncertainty: 1945–55
The division of Germany was never a declared aim of any of the powers united in the anti-Hitler wartime coalition. At the Potsdam Conference, over two months after the German capitulation, the Allies agreed on a joint administration for all of Germany (except the territories east of the Oder–Neisse line which were to come under Polish administration) in an "antifascist-democratic spirit." It is clear today that Soviet policy toward Germany in the late 1940s was by no means committed to the creation of a "satellite" state out of the Red Army's occupation zone. East Germany was to be a bargaining counter in the negotiations with the Western powers—the key to Soviet influence over the whole of Germany (particularly the heavy industry of the Ruhr region) at best, a fallback position at worst. The prime responsibility for the division

113

of Germany lies clearly with the Western allies under the leadership of the U.S., whose insistence on creating a strong West German bulwark state to spearhead President Truman's anticommunist crusade in Europe forced Stalin's hand at every stage from 1946 onwards.[2]

Even after the formal proclamation of the German Democratic Republic in October 1949, a month after that of the FRG, the survival of the "first German workers' and peasants' state" remained negotiable. The strategic interests of the Soviet Union, as conceived by Stalin and his immediate successors Beria-Malenkov-Molotov, demanded above all the prevention of a remilitarized West Germany joining the NATO alliance, and abandoning the GDR would have been a small price to pay for the strategic neutralization of the Rhine-Ruhr military-industrial complex within a nonaligned, united Germany. In March 1952 Stalin proposed immediate negotiations with the three Western powers with a view to concluding a peace treaty with Germany and followed up this offer in April with an acceptance of free elections under four-power supervision. Again after Stalin's death in May 1953, contacts between Churchill and the new Soviet leadership led to "rumors within the SED that the party had to be prepared to return to opposition or even illegality."[3] It was only the failure of the 1954 Berlin and 1955 Geneva four-power conferences to agree on a solution to the German question and the eventual admission of the Federal Republic to NATO in 1955—after the collapse of the European Defense Community project—that caused Moscow to end its equivocation on the future of the GDR: on his return from the Geneva Conference, Khrushchev declared in East Berlin that a "mechanical reunification of the two German states" was now impossible and that the GDR's "socialist achievements" were irreversible. The GDR was admitted as a full member of the Warsaw Pact, granted "full sovereignty," and a mutual friendship and assistance pact was signed in Moscow.

The prolonged uncertainty as to Moscow's policy on the German question could not, of course, fail to affect the internal politics of the young republic. On the part of the Ulbricht leadership of the

2. Cf. Hans-Peter Schwarz, *Vom Reich zur Bundesrepublik: Deutschland im Widerstreit der aussenpolitischen Konzeptionen in den Jahren der Besatzungsherrschaft, 1945–1949* (Neuwied, 1966).
3. Hermann Weber, *Von der SBZ zur DDR* (Hannover, 1968), vol. 1, p. 77.

SED, the obvious need was to create—as far as the obligatory loyalty to the official Soviet line permitted—a social, economic, and political fait accompli. The existence of a latent conflict of interests between Ulbricht and Stalin was highlighted by the Second Party Conference in April 1952, which proclaimed the "construction of socialism" as official policy; it was not attended by the usual CPSU delegation nor was its new strategic line publicly endorsed by the Soviet press.[4]

Matters came to a head after Stalin's death, when there were signs that the new CPSU leadership supported the replacement of Ulbricht by Rudolf Herrnstadt, editor of the SED central organ *Neues Deutschland*. A Moscow-inspired "new course" made concessions to the farmers, churches, and middle class, but failed to rescind the recently increased industrial work norms. Over 300,000 workers struck and demonstrated on the 16, 17, 18, and 19 June 1953 in the major industrial centers of the GDR, initially against the work norms but increasingly against the regime as such. The "17th June," as the movement is now commonly known, was not only the first mass working-class uprising against Stalinism in Eastern Europe, but was also a movement led by socialist and communist activists who felt their hopes had been betrayed by the Ulbricht regime.

Ironically, it was this revolt that saved Ulbricht's position as Moscow now considered it imprudent to destabilize the situation any further by toppling the party leader. The restoration of order by Soviet tanks was followed by purges: 71 percent of all local party secretaries were fired, and a very large proportion of the expelled and disciplined party members belonged to the pre-1933 communist generation.[5]

From De-Stalinization to the Berlin Wall: 1956–61

The nature of the Ulbricht regime was strikingly illustrated by its reaction to Khrushchev's secret speech against Stalin at the Twentieth Congress of the CPSU in February 1956 and the way it weathered the storm that shook Eastern Europe during that year. Ulbricht had been second to none in his fostering of the personality cult around "our wise teacher, the standard-bearer of peace and

4. Cf. Dietrich Staritz, *Geschichte der DDR, 1949–1985* (Frankfurt/Main, 1985), pp. 74–76.
5. Weber, p. 89.

progress in the whole world, the great Stalin,"[6] and he had, of course, more to fear from any thorough "de-Stalinisation" than most, but he survived politically with a minimum of concessions. "Stalin cannot be counted among the classics of Marxism," he admitted in an article in *Neues Deutschland*,[7] as over 20,000 prisoners were released and a number of purged party leaders rehabilitated without regaining their former positions. There simply was no alternative to Ulbricht in the SED, no German Gomulka or Nagy. Although an opposition grouping around Politburo member Karl Schirdewan and the Minister for State Security Ernst Wollweber did seek to take the opportunity to get rid of Ulbricht and appeared to enjoy Khrushchev's tacit sympathies in the immediate aftermath of the Twentieth Congress and while there was considerable unrest among the intelligentsia, the working class remained passive. Certainly the demoralizing effects of the 1953 defeat were partly to blame for this and the concessions made by the party leadership may have contributed,[8] but the decisive factor was the lack of popular support for, or even knowledge of, any "reformist" faction in the SED leadership. The Politburo opposition could not break out of the bureaucratic cage it had itself helped to build—it was as dependent on Moscow and as devoid of any real roots in the East German working class as the leader it wanted to topple. The shock of the "Polish October" and the Hungarian revolution led Khrushchev to decide that it was best to play safe in Germany and again back Ulbricht, who got a free hand to eliminate all remaining pockets of dissent in 1957 and 1958.[9]

The greatest remaining threat to the internal stability of the political regime in the GDR arose from the national question. The attractions of West Germany's *Wirtschaftswunder* prosperity and parliamentary democracy lured hundreds of thousands into the Federal Republic every year: between 1949 and August 1961 over

---

6. Ulbricht at the Second Party Conference of the SED in 1952; quoted in Weber, p. 143 (Document 26).
7. 4 March 1956; see Document 1 in Weber, vol. 2, p. 149.
8. In June 1956 consumer prices were lowered by 20 to 50 percent, pensions raised, and a substantial housing construction program announced. There was even short-lived talk of establishing factory committees on the Polish model; cf. Weber, vol. 2, pp. 15–16, and Martin Jaenicke, *Der dritte Weg: Die antistalinistische Opposition gegen Ulbricht, seit 1953* (Cologne, 1964).
9. See Karl Wilhelm Fricke, *Politik und Justiz in der DDR* (Cologne, 1979), pp. 352–70, on the "revisionist trials" of the period.

2.6 million people left the GDR for West Germany, the majority of them young people under twenty-five. Although the exodus of many bourgeois and other political opponents of the regime cannot have been unwelcome to the SED, the continuous stream of refugees represented an intolerable strain on the economic resources of a state with a population of around 17 million and a chronic labor shortage. Ulbricht's first response to this problem was, at the Fifth Party Congress in 1958, to promise that by 1961 the GDR would "reach and exceed West Germany's per capita consumption in foodstuffs and the main industrial consumer goods."[10] An ambitious seven-year plan and the collectivization of agriculture were to be the means of achieving this utopian target and "the completion of socialism." The seven-year plan was abruptly shelved in 1962; the collectivization of agriculture, however, was carried out in 1960 at great social and political expense.

The land reform of 1945 had redistributed the Prussian Junker estates and created a smallholding peasantry of about 500,000 former agricultural laborers and resettled workers. Agricultural co-operatives (LPGs, Landwirtschaftliche Produktionsgenossenschaften) were created throughout the 1950s out of the least viable of these, but by the end of 1958 these covered only 37 percent of all agricultural land. By the end of 1960, however, over 84 percent of all land was now organized in more than 19,000 such LPGs.[11] Considerable force and intimidation were applied in most cases, with the result of widespread shortages in food supplies and a new increase in the number of refugees (which was further swelled by the nationalizations of small industrial and commercial enterprises and the rumors about an impending closure of the border); in July 1961 alone 30,000 people left the GDR.[12] On 13 August 1961 East Berlin was sealed off and a wall built between the Soviet and the Western sectors of the city.[13]

10. Quoted by Weber, vol. 2, p. 33.
11. Ibid., p. 51.
12. Ibid., p. 57.
13. From the point of view of the economic and political stabilization of the bureaucratic regime, the wall was arguably an overdue necessity. But it also stands as a monument to the political bankruptcy of the SED, exposing its regular claims to 99 percent support from the East German masses, and the inability of the German workers' movement to solve the national question.

Toward International Recognition: 1962–71

The 1960s were Ulbricht's years: the Berlin Wall had stemmed the flow of refugees and thus forced people on both sides of the border to come to terms with its apparent permanency and impermeability, the socioeconomic "foundations of socialism" had been completed, all opposition to his leadership was silenced, and the Soviet Union unequivocally committed to the division of Germany. Compared to the 1950s, it was to be a decade without dramatic domestic crises, without serious challenges to his leadership, but a decade of significant progress in the GDR's economic development and continuous improvement of its international standing.

Following the adoption of a New Economic System of Planning and Management (NOSPL) in June 1963—which was inspired by the Soviet economic reform discussion initiated by Liberman—the industrial growth crisis of 1959–62 was overcome and, at least until the late 1960s, relatively stable growth rates of around 5–6 percent coincided with a substantial improvement in living standards. East Germany's collectivized agriculture performed well in comparison with those of most other COMECON states. Internationally the economic weight of the GDR led to its increasing prominence in the international organizations of the Soviet bloc and diplomatic recognition by a number of Third World governments.[14] Yet, when Ulbricht resigned "for reasons of age and health" as first secretary of the Central Committee in May 1971 (he remained chairman of the State Council and the titular head of state until his death in August 1973), it was clear that his policies had run into deep problems on three crucial fronts: (1) the economic plans had not been fulfilled in 1969 and 1970 and severe structural disproportions were disrupting the economy; (2) the GDR had been pushed into the defensive on the national question by the *Neue Ostpolitik* of the West German government; and (3) differences with Moscow on both the German question and more general ideological matters had appeared.

During the 1960s the German question had increasingly become an obstacle to the developing détente between the two superpowers and their respective allies. Until the mid-1960s Bonn continued to claim the right to be considered the sole legitimate representative of

14. Especially by Arab countries resenting West Germany's close relations with Israel: Ulbricht's first-ever foreign visit outside the Soviet bloc was to Nasser's Egypt in 1965, and full diplomatic recognition by Egypt and Iraq followed in 1969.

all Germans and refused to recognize the existence of the other German state, whose international diplomatic isolation it attempted to perpetuate through the application of the Hallstein Doctrine (the breaking off of relations with any country recognizing East Germany, except the Soviet Union itself). The SED leadership, on the other hand, had countered this by insisting on Bonn and the Western Allies' responsibility for the division of Germany and seeking to establish themselves as the true standard-bearers of reunification. From about 1967 onwards, however, the roles were suddenly reversed. The "grand coalition" government under the chancellorship of Kiesinger (who, contrary to all previous practice, accepted—and even replied to—a letter from GDR prime minister Stoph) and especially the post-1969 SPD-FDP coalition under Chancellor Willy Brandt abandoned the Cold War stance; it was now Ulbricht, with his insistence on the full recognition of the GDR under international law by Bonn as a precondition for any meaningful negotiations, who represented the chief stumbling block to détente. After the two 1970 meetings between Brandt and Stoph and the beginning of negotiations on the Berlin problem between the four Allies—which he tried unsuccessfully to obstruct—Ulbricht found himself increasingly isolated. In addition, some of Ulbricht's theoretical pronouncements—such as his unorthodox "discovery" that socialism was not merely the transitional phase on the road to communism, but a "relatively independent socioeconomic formation," and his increasing emphasis on the "international significance" of the GDR "model of socialism" as the first to operate in a highly industrialized country[15]—must have irritated the CPSU leaders who, after the Dubcek experience, were particularly sensitive to any hints of "national-communist" deviations in Eastern Europe. For the majority of SED leaders, however, the need to fall in line with Moscow's détente strategy and the prospect of lucrative deals with Bonn outweighed any sympathies for Ulbricht's position.

The GDR after Ulbricht: The Search for Legitimacy
The transition from Ulbricht to Honecker marked the end of the postwar era in the GDR: with the nationalization of most of the

15. On Ulbricht's theoretical divergences from Moscow see Walter Völkel, "Das Problem der ideologischen Integration: Anmerkungen zur Sozialismusdiskussion in der DDR und Sowjetunion," *Deutschland Archiv Sonderheft* (Cologne, 1973): 61.

remaining private and semiprivate industrial enterprises and industrially producing craft cooperatives in July 1972 and the signing of the basic treaty establishing formal relations between the GDR and FRG in December (followed by worldwide diplomatic recognition and membership in the United Nations), both the internal and external consolidation of the regime had been completed. With Ulbricht, the generation of party leaders who had been prominent in prewar KPD politics and had spent the Nazi years in exile in Stalin's Moscow was on the way out, while Honecker—a young Communist youth functionary in 1933, active in the underground antifascist resistance, and liberated from a Nazi prison by the Red Army in 1945—forms a bridge to the rising generation of those who were educated and trained in the postwar years.[16]

The Eighth Party Congress in 1971 initiated (and the Ninth to Eleventh subsequently confirmed) a number of important policy changes. The further raising of the material and cultural living conditions of the masses was declared the "main task for the coming period," and a massive housing construction program, substantial increases in real income, more emphasis on the production of consumer goods, and more social spending were promised.[17] Indeed the largest expenditure increases in the state budget between 1970 and 1975, during which total expenditure increased by 63 percent, were in subsidies for industrial consumer goods (200 percent), culture, sport and recreation (243 percent), public transport (100 percent), and housing and rent subsidies (79 percent).[18] Through a network of Intershops (where Western consumer and luxury goods can be bought for Western currency) and Exquisit shops (where the same goods can be bought for East German marks, but at highly inflated prices) and through increased imports the Honecker leadership attempted to meet rising consumerist expectations and thus broaden its social base, but with only limited success. The Intershops, for example, created social tensions between those with access to Western currency and those

16. Cf. the biographies of the two postwar leaders of the SED/GDR: Carola Stern, *Ulbricht: A Political Biography* (New York, 1965), and Heinz Lippmann, *Honecker and the New Politics of Europe* (London, 1973).
17. See the resolution adopted by the Eighth Party Congress, in Hermann Weber, *Die SED nach Ulbricht* (Hannover, 1974), pp. 29–34.
18. Deutsches Institut für Wirtschaftsforschung (D.I.W.), *Handbuch der DDR-Wirtschaft* (Reinbek, 1977), p. 333.

without, and the gap in real incomes between East and West Germany (estimated at about 40–50 percent)[19] has not narrowed.

Given the impossibility of catching up with the Federal Republic in terms of mass living standards in the near future and the need to counter the potentially dangerous effects of the limited opening to the West after 1971, Honecker's new policy included a new line on the national question. A "two-nations theory" of a West German "capitalist" and a GDR "socialist nation" replaced the old formula of the "two states in one nation," and the 1974 amendments to the 1968 constitution deleted all references to German unity. "The past aim of unifying the two German states and thus eventually arriving at a united German nation has been rendered redundant and unrealistic by the actual historical conditions and the course of the national and international class struggle".[20] The purpose of this turn, and of the new emphasis on the alliance with the Soviet Union and the dropping of Ulbricht's ideological heresies, was clearly to direct mass consciousness in the GDR away from the comparison with West Germany and to orient it toward the COMECON/Warsaw Pact bloc. It is hardly coincidental that tourism to Poland and Czechoslovakia was greatly facilitated and expanded from 1972 onwards, allowing millions of GDR citizens to go and draw the desired favorable comparisons.[21] Official ideologists and historians have also sought to cultivate a more positive identification with the Prussian past, according Frederick the Great and the Prussian Enlightenment an honored position in East German school textbooks. The unique sporting achievements of the GDR have also been mobilized in the cause of fostering a distinctive East German national identity, and not without success.

But the Honecker strategy was built upon the foundations of the economic and political climate of the early 1970s, the twin assumptions of continuing East-West détente and economic growth. The descent of the capitalist West after the 1973 oil crisis into recession—with the concomitant shrinkage of export markets and drying up of cheap credit—and especially the eruption of the "Second Cold War" after 1979 put severe strains on the SED

19. Ibid., p. 233.
20. Alfred Kosing (the leading East German authority on the national question), *Nation in Geschichte und Gegenwart* (East Berlin, 1976), p. 107.
21. In the case of Poland, however, touristic exchanges in both directions were severely restricted again after the explosion of social unrest there in 1980.

strategy. By the early 1980s the GDR's terms of trade had seriously worsened both toward the West and the East, and only two large West German government-guaranteed loans in 1983 and 1984 rescued Honecker's social and economic policy from the potentially devastating effects of huge hard-currency debts of $12 billion— higher, on a per capita basis, than those of troubled Poland. On the diplomatic front Honecker's desire to insulate the economically crucial intra-German détente against the general deterioration of East-West relations provoked an ill-disguised conflict with Moscow over his long-planned official visit to Bonn. Forced to cancel the trip originally scheduled for September 1984 in the wake of West Germany's decision to deploy Cruise and Pershing II missiles, it was not until after the succession of Mikhail Gorbachev to the leadership of the CPSU that Honecker could finally accept the invitation in September 1987.

PARTY AND STATE

> "Would you, just because your neighbor is redecorating his flat, feel obliged to put new paper on your own walls?" (Politburo member and leading ideologue of the SED, Kurt Hager)[22]

The barely disguised hostility shown by the SED leadership toward the concept of *glasnost* is not primarily concerned with the relaxation of rules applying to the literary and artistic intelligentsia or even a greater openness in the media as such. In its cultural policies the SED has for some time now been considerably more tolerant than the CPSU was before Gorbachev, and most East German citizens have always had easy access to the Western press and broadcasting as an alternative source of information. Moreover, a more open discussion of historical matters would hardly be as traumatic for the SED as it is for the CPSU. It is difficult, therefore, at first sight to understand what the SED would have to fear from an adoption of the "new thinking" now proclaimed in the Soviet Union.

The hostility becomes more understandable in the light of the historical experiences of "de-Stalinization." If *glasnost* were possible without a threat to the political-ideological monopoly and the

---

22. In an interview with the popular West German magazine *Der Stern*, reprinted by *Neues Deutschland*, 10 April 1987.

internal homogeneity and discipline of the party, the SED leadership would enthusiastically embrace it as an opportunity to com-
pete more effectively with the Western media: a *Neues Deutschland*
as eagerly read as *Pravda*, a *Junge Welt* or *Sonntag* as lively as
Komsomolskaya Pravda or *Ogonyuk*, an external propaganda organ as
widely sold at West German newsstands as *Moscow News* have for
long been the dream of the professionals in the agitprop departments. But already in 1964, faced with the modest liberalization of
Khrushchev's last years in office and the intellectual excitement
over the Kafka conference in Czechoslovakia, the GDR's minister
of culture Klaus Gysi had warned that "*in our special position*, any
intellectual discussion can all too easily turn into a *political* one."[23]
Next to the old fear of being abandoned by Moscow in a Soviet
deal over Germany with the West, the greatest nightmare for the
GDR leadership has always been that of "social democratism."

In the "special position" of East Germany, "social democratism"
has always been synonymous with any kind of party factionalism
and aspirations toward democratization. Since the SED was
formed in a shotgun marriage between the communists and the
social democrats, the chief concern of the Ulbricht group until well
into the fifties was to break the considerable residual influence,
within the ranks of the united party, of social democracy and those
communists—especially those who had spent the Nazi years in the
underground resistance within Germany—who were deemed to be
susceptible to social-democratic influences. Even after successive
purges at all levels of the organization and the crushing of the
reformist intellectual milieu of the 1956 de-Stalinization phase, the
enormous ideological pressures emanating from the Federal Republic kept the leadership on permanent guard against the slightest
manifestations of "social democratism." For them, the GDR is like
a heavily leaning vessel in turbulent waters, kept afloat only by the
weight of a disciplined crew assembled on one side of the bridge,
which any sudden rushing about on the decks could easily cause to
capsize.

In the eyes of the Honecker leadership, therefore, it may be all
very well for the Poles, the Hungarians, and even the Soviets to
experiment with pluralism in party and state when there is no
immediate threat to the integrity of their states comparable to the

23. Quoted after Staritz, p. 184.

threat to the GDR posed by the Federal Republic and its large social-democratic party. This is as true today as it was in 1964, and this is why *glasnost* is so bitterly resisted.

A Dictatorship of the Politburo?

Today the SED presents itself as a powerful force. With 2,304,121 members (in April 1986) it is one of the largest parties in Eastern Europe and seemingly the most monolithic, as there have been no public faction struggles within the leadership since the 1950s. The party's leading role was written into the constitutions of 1968 and 1974, and an estimated corps of 60,000 full-time functionaries and 300,000 unpaid cadres[24] enable it to keep a tight grip on the East German state apparatus, economy, and society. The other, "nonsocialist" parties in the National Front are organizationally controlled by SED-trained cadres, their only remaining purpose being the integration of Christians, nationalists, farmers, and residual bourgeois elements into the political system.[25] The mass organizations—above all the Free German Trade Union Federation (FDGB) with 8.4 million, the Free German Youth (FDJ) with 2.2 million, and the Democratic Women's League with 1.4 million members— are, as one would expect, firmly under the tutelage of the "leading party."

To speak of the "leading party," however, is in itself a mystification of the real power relations. Political power in the GDR does not simply lie with "the party." The internal regime within the party deprives the vast majority of SED members of any democratic participation in the exercise of political power: party congresses and conferences, even the Central Committee, are little more than acclamatory bodies and vehicles for the downward transmission of information from the real decision-making center, the Politburo of twenty-five (seventeen full and eight candidate) members.

The state apparatus, by official definition "the chief instru-

---

24. Weber, *Die SED* . . . , p. 16; cf. also his *Von der SBZ* . . . , p. 213.
25. They are the Christlich-Demokratische Union (115,000 members), the Demokratische Bauernpartei Deutschlands (92,000), the Nationaldemokratische Partei Deutschlands (85,000), and the Liberaldemokratische Partei Deutschlands (75,000). Some of the CDU members of the People's Chamber were allowed to vote against the legalization of abortion in 1972, in accordance with the Catholic beliefs of their constituency.

ment . . . through which the working class under the leadership of its Marxist-Leninist party organizes the entire population,"[26] is politically subordinate to the party leadership and party apparatus. A minister is of lower status than a Central Committee secretary with responsibility for the same area, and at all levels the system of dual responsibility of state functionaries—to their party unit as well as to their immediate superiors in the state apparatus—and the right of party bodies to issue direct instructions to state agencies are intended to secure the "primacy of politics." The inevitable "statification" of a party that has imposed its absolute political monopoly on society and the increasing importance and complexity of the state's social and economic activity have made the distinction between the specific roles of the two apparatuses increasingly difficult to maintain, however. In the 1960s, when the Ulbricht leadership gambled everything on a quick economic breakthrough under the aegis of the "scientific-technical revolution," the adoption of the New Economic System (NES) was followed by the reorganization of the party according to the "production principle." The horizontal ties of cooperation between the parallel party and state bodies were strengthened at all levels at the expense of the vertical (party) chain of command, and the whole trend was exemplified by the growing role of the recently created (1960) State Council, which "constituted itself as a kind of supreme decision-making and control organ, thus threatening to push back the political leadership proper,. . . the Politburo."[27] Although the succession of Honecker to the party leadership led to a new emphasis on the "leading role of the party and the working class" (whose specific weight had, on the ideological plane, been downgraded by Ulbricht's concept of the "socialist community of man") and, significantly, the restriction of the State Council to an essentially ceremonial role in the revised 1974 constitution, the underlying trend seems irreversible. "The party remains dependent . . . on the cooperation of the state organs in its decision making and thus offers them a vehicle for the transport of *specific interests* into its decision-making process."[28]

26. *Marxistisch-Leninistische Staats- und Rechtslehre: Lehrbuch* (East Berlin, 1975), p. 199; quoted by Gero Neugebauer, *Partei und Staatsapparat in der DDR* (Opladen, 1978), p. 91.
27. Neugebauer, p. 133.
28. Ibid., p. 192.

THE ECONOMY

At first glance the most powerful argument in support of the Honecker leadership's contention that *perestroika* is a specifically Soviet response to a specifically Soviet problem with little or no relevance to the GDR is a comparison of the performance of the East German economy with that of the Soviet and the other East European economies. Almost alone, it has managed to maintain significant growth rates while containing the foreign-debt problem and keeping up a steady rise in living standards. Labor productivity in the GDR is twice the East European average and 80 percent higher than in the USSR.[29]

It is also, however, 50 percent below that of West Germany, and the gap has not grown narrower since the early 1970s.[30] It is this latter figure that is the more significant politically, for not only does the Western orientation of the GDR's population demand a narrowing of the intra-German economic gap, but in the context of the general Soviet and East European drive for modernization the GDR needs to keep pace with the most advanced capitalist countries even in order to defend its position as the prime supplier of industrial equipment within the Soviet bloc. In a global context the East German economy occupies a unique position in a triangle formed by the high-tech capitalisms of Western Europe, Japan, and North America, the cheap-labor "threshold" industrial capitalisms of Southeast Asia (Korea, Taiwan, Singapore, etc.), and the industrialized but technologically more backward CMEA[31] countries: it can either catch up with the first group or face being pushed out of crucial export markets (including East European ones) by both the first and second and end up losing its special position in the third.

In this situation quantitative growth is not everything, especially when these growth figures are in themselves somewhat suspect[32]

---

29. According to Heinrich Machowski, "Die Rolle der DDR in der gemeinsamen Industriepolitik der RGW-Staaten," in *Das Profil der DDR in der sozialistischen Staatengemeinschaft: Zwanzigste Tagung zum Stand der DDR-Forschung in der Bundesrepublik Deutschland* (Cologne, 1987), p. 144.

30. Ibid. Other sources, however, including the SED leadership itself, estimate the productivity gap between the two German states at about 30 percent. Cf. *DDR-Handbuch*, (Cologne, 1985), vol. 1 p. 71.

31. Council for Mutual Economic Aid. The abbreviation CMEA is preferred here to the more familiar COMECON because it is the one used in official translations by the organization itself and is also increasingly used in Western texts.

32. On some of the reasons for treating the category of "net production" as used in

and show a gradual decline.[33] The production of ever more units of certain goods does not improve the relative standing of a national economy either in relation to the capitalist world or to the "socialist camp" if these goods are increasingly difficult to sell on the world markets because they are inferior in quality. This, however, is precisely what has happened to the GDR over the last two decades: in the key technological sectors (electronics, information technology, chemicals) East German industry is today generally reckoned to be further behind world standards than it was in the 1960s.[34] After a few years of expanding trade with the capitalist countries after the signing of the basic treaty in 1971, trade with the Soviet bloc is again growing faster than trade with the West in the 1980s.[35] Moreover, the GDR's exports to the West have increasingly become dominated not by industrial investment goods but raw materials and low-tech consumer goods. The recent surpluses in trade with the capitalist countries were mainly achieved by drastic cutbacks in domestic investment and consumption.[36]

Far from being a model to be emulated by the rest of the CMEA countries, the GDR therefore represents the general contradictions of the bureaucratically centralized state-planning system at their sharpest precisely because it is the most advanced industrially: it has simply exhausted the possibilities of that system to the point where its inherent limits become glaringly obvious. Its problems cannot be explained in terms of cultural backwardness, an underdeveloped work ethic, alcoholism, or corruption, the reasons commonly cited in the Soviet Union under Brezhnev, Andropov, Chernenko, and also, at least initially, Gorbachev. Nor can they be explained, as in Poland, in terms of an adventuristic modernization program

the official statistics with caution, see Doris Cornelsen, "Zur Lage der DDR-Wirtschaft an der Jahreswende 1986/87," *Deutschlandarchiv* 20, no. 3 (March 1987): 292–98.

33. 1985: 5.5%; 1986: 4.3%; 1987: 3.5–3.7%. Source: "Die Entwicklung der DDR-Wirtschaft im Jahr 1987," *Bundesministerium für innerdeutsche Beziehungen: Informationen*, 12 February 1988, p. 16.

34. See, for instance, the examples given by Harry Maier, "Der grosse Bruder ist kein Vorbild," *Die Zeit*, 28 November 1986.

35. Cf. Cornelsen, p. 296.

36. During the first half of the 1980s a particularly lucrative earner for the GDR was found in the reexport to the West of oil purchased at below-world-market prices from the Soviet Union, while increasingly severe energy savings were being imposed on domestic industry. The collapse of oil prices has, however, put an end to this.

(Honecker has always been relatively cautious in this respect), a ruinous foreign debt (against which the GDR, apart from short-term problems in the early 1980s, was cushioned by West Germany) or an inefficient agricultural sector (East Germany's agriculture is, by and large, a success story). Least of all could it be said that the GDR's economy is suffering from educational and scientific backwardness: its labor force is among the best qualified in the world and its academic research capable of highly respectable achievements.

The restraints on the further *qualitative* development of the GDR's economy are imposed by the bureaucratic nature of the centralized planning system: its inability to translate scientific-technological advances into innovative production standards because of the clumsy and arbitrary command structure; its enormous waste of resources through what Bahro called the "system of organized irresponsibility," that is, the discouragement of individual initiative and responsibility on the part of the producers; the low productivity of an alienated work force conditioned to execute orders from above.[37] This is well illustrated by the history of economic reform in the GDR.

The introduction of the New Economic System in 1963 represented the first attempt by any CMEA state to systematically utilize profit, credit, and interest rates as "economic levers" within a more decentralized planning mechanism geared toward intensive rather than extensive growth.[38] The postwar reconstruction of the East German economy had been completed, and all labor reserves had been exhausted: further growth could only come from a more effective utilization of existing resources and, especially, the introduction of new technology to raise labor productivity. The NES was successful in dragging the GDR out of the acute growth crisis of 1960–62 and improving the quality and availability of consumer goods, but the partial introduction of marketlike mechanisms could not bear the expected fruits while the price structure remained distorted by the cumulative effects of decades of arbitrary price-fixing: under these conditions profit and loss accounts did not

---

37. For a discussion of the social obstacles to technological innovation using the example of CAD/CAM, see Wolfgang Stinglwagner, "Die DDR im technologischen Wettbewerb," *Deutschlandarchiv* 20, no. 5 (May 1987): 502–14.
38. For a good summary of the nature of the NES and the main reasons for its eventual failure, see Ian Jeffries and Manfred Melzer, eds., *The East German Economy* (London, 1987).

provide an accurate measurement of economic rationality at either the macro- or the microeconomic level, and the limited entrepreneurial freedom granted to enterprises and banks did little more than create further unmanageable distortions. The introduction of "structure-determining tasks," which amounted to the suspension of the new NES mechanisms in the strategic sectors of industry, only further confused the picture, leading to the eventual abandonment of the NES with Honecker's takeover in 1971.

Compared to the later reforms in Hungary and Poland, the NES was a rather limited attempt at marketization, yet it provided a clear illustration of the basic contradictions of all such reforms: a partial marketization may bring results in particular sectors, but the overall effect is one of disequilibrium and loss of central control without the kind of qualitative advance in productivity and international competitiveness that only a full release of the law of value through the abolition of all effective state controls over investment, prices, and foreign trade could bring about. To do so, however, would entail the loss of not only economic but also *political* and *social* control, thus ending the power monopoly of the party and state apparatus. It would, of course, be tantamount to the restoration of capitalism.

In Yugoslavia, Poland, Hungary, and now increasingly the Soviet Union, the concessions to liberal pluralism demanded by partial economic marketization have produced political regimes that are hybrids between the old Stalinist police states and a new bureaucratic liberalism, albeit in sharply different forms. By contrast the East German leadership has little latitude for such experimentation with a controlled economic and political liberalization in its confrontation with West Germany. It is not accidental that the abandoning of the New Economic System coincided with the "normalization" of relations with the Federal Republic. Rather than deepen the market experiments of the NES, a recentralization of economic decision making was seen as the natural concomitant of the *Abgrenzungspolitik* pursued after 1972 in the ideological sphere: the renewed emphasis on the class nature of the party and the "socialist national identity" of the GDR.

From 1971 onwards the new Honecker leadership developed a strategy of countering the potential destabilization from both West (the closer ties with the FRG) and East (the unrest in Poland) with what the Tenth Party Congress in 1976 was to call "the unity of economic and social policy." When rising energy prices and the Western recession worsened the GDR's terms of trade in the late 1970s, the continuation of the social program was financed largely by increased borrowing in the West, until the shock of the Polish crisis and rising interest rates forced upon the GDR a sharp cutback on imports and a crash loan repayment program to restore its creditworthiness with the international bankers. Since then Honecker's economic policy has largely relied on improvisation and exhortation: in order to sustain the ambitious social program, investment had to be drastically curtailed and continued economic growth almost exclusively derived from squeezing ever more production out of existing resources—chiefly through the extension of shift work, the retention of obsolete machinery, and a further expansion of the environmentally disastrous exploitation of the GDR's large lignite reserves.

In sharp contrast to the prevailing trend in the Soviet bloc, the drift in the GDR has been toward more rather than less centralization, in particular through the creation of large *Kombinate* (combines) out of previously separate enterprises. As the largest of these combines are directly responsible to their respective ministries and comprise all stages of production from research and development to marketing, their creation has undoubtedly eliminated an entire layer of bureaucracy and waste—aspects that attracted some attention elsewhere in Eastern Europe, Gorbachev's included. But the combines are in themselves so large that they have reduced the flexibility of response to unplanned needs and circumstances which the smaller and medium-sized enterprises swallowed up by them used to offer,[39] and it must be doubtful whether they will be able to fulfill the chief task assigned to them by the Eleventh Party Congress in 1986: the accelerated development of the GDR's electronic data processing, robotics, biochemical, and other strategically important technologies.

SOCIAL CONTRADICTIONS AND POLITICAL OPPOSITION

The inability of the ruling bureaucracy to solve its economic problems by recourse to either capitalist solutions—by fully releas-

39. Cf. Harry Maier in ibid.

ing the rationality of the law of value from the shackles of the central plan—or socialist solutions—the release of the creative energies of the producers themselves from the yoke of bureaucratic tutelage—highlights its objective position in East German society: that of a ruling stratum which, far from fulfilling an essential function in the given mode of production, merely administers the status quo. The bureaucracy defends its privileges, its manipulative control over the apparatuses of power, and maintains a strictly hierarchical internal order; but it has no historic mission, no real purpose. It cannot, therefore, establish its hegemony over society by means other than force and bribery—the repression of dissent and the selective rewarding of conformity. In the case of the GDR, it cannot even don the mantle of national leadership: it did not liberate Germany from fascism, it did not lead a revolution against a hated oligarchy, it did not propel a backward country into modernization. Just as the state it rules over owes its existence to the international power constellation arising from Germany's defeat in World War II, the SED owes its political power, in the final analysis, to the bayonets of a foreign army.

This does not mean, however, that the East German bureaucracy is devoid of any national character and national interests of its own. Like the ruling bureaucracies of the other states within the Soviet-led "socialist camp," the East German bureaucracy has on occasion found its own perceived self-interests at odds with those of Moscow and has been quite capable of articulating and pursuing these, albeit with less vigor and openness than those of, say, Poland, Romania, Albania, or Yugoslavia. Generally, as in 1952–53 or in 1969–70, such differences have centered around *Deutschlandpolitik*, but since the succession of Mikhail Gorbachev to the general secretaryship of the CPSU more fundamental divergences over *glasnost* and *perestroika* have emerged. On the whole, however, the ability of the GDR leadership to "go it alone" is severely limited by the weakness of its local roots and its strategic dependence on the Moscow connection.

The Bureaucracy

In contrast to the Soviet Union, where the emerging Stalinist bureaucracy established itself in a symbiosis with all the remaining conservative, petit-bourgeois, and nationalist forces in the country, the rallying of such forces in Germany to the Bundesrepublik meant that a social base for the new regime had to be created "from above," out of the ranks of the Stalinist workers' movement itself and the younger generation of nonparty workers unfamiliar with social-democratic traditions. The "best, most active, most faithful, and most class-conscious segments of the working class" (SED leader Otto Grotewohl, himself a former social democrat) were expected to maintain political control in key positions—in Saxony in 1948, 80.6 percent of factory directors had only an elementary school education[40]—and the new opportunities for upward social mobility were calculated to win the allegiance of broad working-class layers. The latter is particularly true for the campaign to create a "new intelligentsia": tens of thousands of young proletarians were recruited to the Workers' and Peasants' Faculties; a massive expansion took place in the number of university (from 17.2 per 10,000 in 1951 to 41.7 in 1955 and 89.3 in 1971) and technical college students (from 19 per 10,000 in 1951 to 82.6 in 1961);[41] and until 1963 a requirement was imposed that at least 60 percent of all high school and university students should be of working-class origin. The abolition of the latter policy signaled that, by the 1960s, the new upper strata of East German society had begun to consolidate and to show signs of self-recruitment and self-perpetuation: the sons and daughters of white-collar employees (with 25.6 percent) and particularly of the intelligentsia (with 30.1 percent) were by 1967 greatly overrepresented among university students.[42] However the necessity for the bureaucracy to retain its base amongst the direct producers sets limits to this process.

A rough portrait of the East German bureaucracy today can be sketched with the aid of the *Nomenklatur* system. This "instrument for the control of social mobility and the distribution of material privileges"[43] consists of the personnel files kept at the cadre departments of party, state, and the economic organizations, which are graded into four categories ranging from the Politburo to "Category III," local functionaries. The *Nomenklaturkader* form the strictly hierarchical backbone of the bureaucracy, to which the academic, scientific, and artistic cadres, the officers and noncommissioned

40. Thomas A. Baylis, *The Technical Intelligentsia and the East German Elite* (Berkeley, 1974), p. 26, n. 11.
41. Ibid., p. 41.
42. Ibid., p. 50.
43. Neugebauer, p. 207.

officers in the army and police, the 17,000 full-time employees of the State Security, and the leaders of the 350,000-strong factory militias (*Betriebskampfgruppen*) have to be added. One essential qualification for all, but especially for *Nomenklatur* cadres, has of course always been political reliability. Since the late 1950s and early 1960s, however, specialist skills and academic training have become increasingly important: the percentage of central and local state functionaries (including here the economic apparatus) with university or technical college degrees grew from 38 percent in 1958 to 90 percent in 1971.[44] One does not need to go as far as some Western sociologists[45] and speculate about a general tension between a "strategic" (the political apparatchiks) and a "functional" (the academic specialists or "technocrats") elite to realize how the mass production of highly trained specialists committed to efficiency, productivity, and professionalism in a system governed by inefficiency, waste, and bureaucratism is bound to generate conflict and dissent. In contrast to other Eastern bloc countries, however, where the daily frustrations of the specialists with the inefficiency of the bureaucratic-centralist planning process have been at the root of the formation of "reform-communist" currents, the East German bureaucracy has so far retained a politically homogeneous appearance.

Bureaucratic Reform and Political Opposition

Both the apparently monolithic nature of the ruling apparatus and the specific forms and contents of opposition activity in the GDR must be understood against the background of the peculiar historical and geographical position of the East German state. Opposition and "dissent" in the Soviet Union and Eastern Europe cover a variety of political, social, and ideological phenomena. First, there are what one may call *restorationist-conservative* currents, fundamentally opposed not only to the bureaucratic regime but also to socialism in general (although they may not always consider it prudent openly to say so). These are rooted in the remnants of prerevolutionary society (the petite bourgeoisie; the peasantry; the churches; the old bourgeois and, in the case of oppressed minorities,

44. Gert-Joachim Glaessner, *Herrschaft durch Kader: Leitung der Gesellschaft und Kaderpolitik in der DDR am Beispiel des Staatsapparats* (Opladen, 1977), pp. 283–84.
45. Peter C. Ludz's work, *The Changing Party Elite in East Germany* (Cambridge, Mass. and London, 1972), has been the most influential in this respect.

133

nationalist parties; the émigré organizations). Such currents play little or no role *inside* the GDR because the open border of the 1940s and 1950s enabled the regime to rid itself of any bourgeois opposition forces far more thoroughly than was possible elsewhere in Eastern Europe, as there has been no private peasantry since 1960, no large national minority (apart from the small group of Slavic Sorbs), and no German Cardinal Woytila or Mindszenty in Protestant East Germany.[46] But weak as bourgeois-restorationist forces are in terms of their social base inside the GDR, they are strong from the *outside*, through the omnipresent influence of West German capitalism, its bourgeois affluence, and liberal-democratic propaganda.

It is the existence of this external threat that has played a crucial role in helping to close the ranks of the bureaucracy. The typical protagonists of *bureaucratic reformism*, the party intellectuals and the economic and technical intelligentsia, have always found their room for maneuver far more limited than their counterparts in the states with an established national identity. The fact that with the adoption of the NES in 1963 the GDR became an early field of Soviet-approved experimentation with economic reform also contributed to the integration of a number of reform communists of the post-Stalin generation who had earlier had some difficulties with the authorities (professor Fritz Behrens, director of the Institute of Economics, for instance). Others such as the historians Jürgen Kuczynski and Joachim Streisand, the philosopher Georg Klaus, and the social scientist Uwe-Jens Heuer have at times been at variance with the party line, without ever becoming part of a reform-communist current. Only once in the history of the GDR was there a real possibility of the emergence of a cohesive challenge to the leadership: in 1953–57, when widespread discontent in the working class and intelligentsia coincided with the existence of anti-Ulbricht factions in the SED leadership and "de-Stalinization" in the USSR.[47] As we have seen, this historic opportunity was missed by a combination of the early defeat of the workers' rebellion, the hesitancy of the party opposition, and some concessions on the part of Ulbricht. After the crushing of the Hungarian

---

46. But see further below for the role of the Protestant churches in recent years.
47. The best description of the broad ferment of those years and its many different strands and currents remains Jaenicke, *Der dritte Weg*.

revolution and the purging of the Schirdewan faction from the SED leadership, much of the intellectual opposition either left the GDR for West Germany or arranged themselves with Ulbricht.

But the ferment of 1956 also produced those who could not or would not be either intimidated or integrated and were gradually forced to go beyond reform-communist positions. Some were driven out of the GDR, like the Leipzig professor of philosophy, Ernst Bloch; others attempted to organize around reformist platforms and fell victim to repression, like the group around Wolfgang Harich in 1956.[48] The outstanding case, however, is that of Professor Robert Havemann, a member of the German Communist party since 1932 and a veteran of the antifascist resistance (having been imprisoned with Honecker at Brandenburg during the war), who saw his Stalinist worldview collapse with Khrushchev's revelations.[49] After a series of conflicts with the party he was expelled from the SED and the Academy of Sciences in 1964. Never actually arrested and imprisoned, he became the chief spokesman of a left-wing opposition that, precisely because of the nonexistence of a broad reformist current within the bureaucracy, was driven beyond reform-communist positions toward a radical critique of the Stalinist system as such.[50] The radical anti-Stalinism of Havemann, of his close personal friend Biermann, and more recently of a Rudolf Bahro[51] is, in a sense, a *specifically East German kind of "ersatz reform communism,"* the product of the frustration of individual would-be reformers with the monolithic conservatism of the bureaucracy. But Havemann and Biermann also form a bridge between the radical outgrowths of reform communism and a critical literary and artistic intelligentsia, whose chief interest is in

48. On the aims and objectives of the Harich group see Gunther Hillmann, *Selbstkritik des Kommunismus: Texte der Opposition* (Reinbek, 1967), p. 189; Manfred Hertwig, "Deformationen: Die Rebellion der Intellektuellen in der DDR," in R. Medwedew, R. Havemann et al., *Entstalinisierung: Der XX. Parteitag der KPdSU und seine Folgen* (Frankfurt/Main, 1977), p. 477. Harich was released from prison in 1964, recanted his earlier views, and after his legal emigration to Austria in 1979 became an advocate of "communism without growth" and a supporter of the ecology movement.
49. See his self-critical "Ja, ich hatte Unrecht. Warum ich ein Stalinist war und ein Anti-Stalinist wurde," first published in May 1965 and reprinted in *Ein deutscher Kommunist* (Hamburg, 1978), p. 110.
50. See especially his "Die DDR in den zwanzig Jahren nach Stalins Sturz," in Medwedew, Havemann et al., pp. 65–81.
51. Rudolf Bahro, *The Alternative in Eastern Europe*, (London, 1979).

freedom from censorship. The case of Wolf Biermann, stripped of his GDR citizenship while on a concert tour of West Germany in October 1976 and thus prevented from returning to the GDR, triggered off a broad wave of public protest by a large number of prominent writers, actors, and artists and opened an era of public conflicts between the regime and a sector of its cultural intelligentsia which continues to the present day. More recently, at the Tenth Congress of the East German Writers' Union in November 1987, there were signs that *glasnost* is beginning to find an echo among the authors of the GDR: in a series of speeches delegates raised the issue of readmitting those expelled after the Biermann affair into the union, and some of the most prominent East German writers demanded an abolition of state censorship.[52] Further signs of movement in the field of cultural policy can be found in the readmission of the playwright Heiner Müller to the Writers' Union, the publication of several books by writers exiled in the Federal Republic, and the recent praise for Stefan Heym, the veteran novelist and most prominent of the nonconformist authors to have remained in the GDR, in a popular weekly magazine.[53] The publication of his semidocumentary account of the 1953 workers' uprising, *5 Days in June*, may well become as decisive a test for the changing climate as the showing of *Repentance* was for the early days of *glasnost* in the USSR.

The Peace Movement and the Protestant Church

One of Robert Havemann's last political actions before his death in 1982 was the drafting of the Berlin Appeal together with a young Protestant pastor, Rainer Eppelmann.[54] This appeal marked the first spectacular public appearance of a new phenomenon that was to transform the political landscape in the GDR in the 1980s: the emergence of a new generation of political activists in and around the Protestant churches. In contrast to Havemann's own generation, this new activist layer has no roots in the reform–communist movement of the 1950s, and while by no means hostile to social-

52. Cf. Harald Kleinschmid, "Probelauf für Glasnost—Zum X. Schriftstellerkongress der DDR," in *Deutschland Archiv* 21, no. 1 (January 1988): 53–58.
53. Cf. Harald Kleinschmid, "Experimentierfeld für Glasnost? Kulturpolitische Tendenzen in der DDR," in *Deutschland Archiv* 21, no. 5 (May 1988): 473–75.
54. For the text of the Berlin Appeal see W. Büscher et al., *Friedensbewegung in der DDR: Texte, 1978–1982* (Hattingen, 1982), pp. 242–44.

ism, does not generally have Marxism as its main ideological point of reference. In age, social background, values, language, political concerns, and ideological outlook it is closer to the West German Greens than to past "dissident-communist" currents, prompting theoretical speculations about the birth of "new social movements" in Eastern Europe akin to the ecology, feminist, and other "alternative" movements of recent years in the West.[55]

The association of this movement with the Protestant church has its roots in the introduction of conscription in 1962 and the churches' successful pressure for the recognition of conscientious objectors who serve in unarmed (although still uniformed and subject to military discipline) "construction brigades." As religious motivation was the sole recognized reason for conscientious objection, the church became a natural focus for the activities of young pacifists, to whom it also offered an institutional space outside the direct control of the state organs for a wide variety of nonconformist cultural activities. Another key factor was the church's protest against the introduction of compulsory military education in the schools in 1978, which spawned the emergence of pacifist, antimilitarist discussion circles of predominantly young people in their local parishes. Finally, the outspoken criticism of NATO's "dual-track" decision in December 1979 to deploy Cruise and Pershing II nuclear missiles in Western Europe by sections of the West German Protestant churches, culminating in the massive demonstrations at the 1981 Hamburg Kirchentag, encouraged the pacifist currents in the East German church to be more vociferous in their rejection of the militarism on their own side. *Frieden schaffen ohne Waffen* (make peace without weapons) became the common slogan on both sides of the intra-German border for a generation that had entered into adulthood in the climate of détente and was now disturbed to find both sides sliding into a new Cold War for which there appeared to be little justification in the realities of Central Europe.

On the part of the Protestant church these developments

---

55. Cf., for instance, Hubertus Knabe, "Neue soziale Bewegungen als Problem der sozialistischen Gesellschaft: Zur Entstehung und Bedeutung neuartiger Bewusstseinslagen in der DDR und Ungarn," in *Das Profil der DDR in der sozialistischen Staatengemeinschaft: Zwanzigste Tagung zum Stand der DDR-Forschung in der Bundesrepublik Deutschland 9.–12. Juni 1987,* Edition Deutschlandarchiv (Cologne, 1987), pp. 106–19.

coincided with its attempts to redefine its role in East German society. Such a redefinition was long overdúe, given the steady—and accelerating—decline in its traditional following[56] and the breaking of its institutional links with the West German churches in 1968. The state's reward for severing the all-German unity of the Protestant churches had been official pledges of a new tolerance for religious practices, an offer the church was only too eager to accept. By the time the first meeting between an SED general secretary and the head of the church took place in 1978, the Protestant bishops had already come up with the new formula of a "church within socialism"—independent of the state but broadly loyal to it.

In practice, this arrangement meant that the churches increasingly took over the role of looking after those who the state, for one reason or another, could or would not look after. It had, of course, performed a valuable function as an extension of the official health and social security system for some time, with its hospitals, old people's homes, and so on. But now it also increasingly concerned itself with the growing numbers of those who no longer fitted in with official society, among them disaffected youths who resented the regimentation of the FDJ. For a small, but significant minority of young people the churches came to provide a space for a large variety of nonconformist activities and discussions. Given the close links of the churches with the West and the all-pervasive influence of the West German media, it was inevitable that some of the themes of the Western "new social movements" would eventually spill over into these circles—especially as these found a fertile soil in the East German realities.

The "independent peace movement" is a good example of this interaction of domestic issues and Western influences: the concern over the perceived militarization of the GDR (introduction of military education, frequent civil defense exercises, extension of conscription to women, glorification of the armed forces, promotion of war toys, etc.) was compounded by the distress over the new Cold War—fed daily by the official propaganda against the NATO missile deployment plans—and stimulated into unofficial

---

56. The official 1964 census counted 59 percent of the population as Protestants. According to the church's own estimates, this figure was 47 percent in 1978 and 30 percent in 1988. Source: Horst Dähn, *Die Kirchen in der DDR zwischen Krise und Umbruch*, unpublished (as yet) text of paper given at the *DDR-Forschertagung* in Bonn, 1988.

action by the example of the Western peace movements (which again received extensive coverage by the 'official media). Most crucially, however, the East German peace movement was never simply a single-issue campaign to the extent that the Western anti-Cruise/Pershing movement was: its critique of the arms race was closely intertwined with a critique of the social, ideological, cultural, and moral-psychological conditions of militarism, as well as its connections with the industrial destruction of the ecological balance and the exploitation of the Third World. Beyond the explicitly political, however, the influx of young people into the Protestant church groups also reflected a growing *moral* crisis in the relationship between the regime and its youth: if, in the 1950s at least, the rhetoric of socialist revolution had exerted a certain attraction for an activist minority, the increasingly bureaucratic consumerism of the Honecker era left a gaping void for those who were still committed to building a better world. To some considerable extent Christian values have begun to fill this void.

This broad definition of "peace" combined with the role of the church as a "refuge" for all kinds of unorthodox concerns, often indifferent or even hostile toward orthodox religion, could not but give rise to groups and activities that the Protestant hierarchy found increasingly difficult to reconcile with its new role in the state and the petit-bourgeois conservatism of its traditional, especially rural, flock. This conflict came to a head in the small provincial town of Jena, where a particularly conservative bishop openly distanced himself from the local peace movement, thus forcing it into open street actions outside the protection of the church. But elsewhere, too, anxious church functionaries came under pressure from the authorities to exert stricter control over the activists on the fringe of their parishes. As a representative of its progressive wing put it: "The state expects from the church that it either integrates these groups into its institutions, thereby rendering them manageable, or that it distances itself from them; but not to cooperate with those groups critical of society which would jeopardize the stabilization of the status quo. The church, therefore, is being required to act as a stabilizing factor with regard to these critical spirits."[57]

The cancellation of the East Berlin Peace Workshop—an annual showcase for a variety of independent groups and activities—in

---

57. Quoted in *Kirche im Sozialismus* 3 (1987): 63.

order to avoid antagonizing the SED just before the 1987 *Kirchentag* opened a period of conflict between the yóung activists and the Protestant bureaucracy which eventually gave the state the confidence that a decisive move against the most politicized and radical activists could be made without risking a total collapse of church-state relations. A police raid on the Ecology Library in East Berlin in November 1987 gave notice of whom the State Security regarded as their prime target: the Peace and Human Rights Initiative and its journal *Grenzfall* (Borderline Case). In January 1988 a pretext was finally found for the arrest and expulsion from the GDR of the singer Stephan Krawczyk, his wife Freya Klier, Bärbel Bohley, Werner Fischer, Wolfgang and Regina Templin, Ralf Hirsch, and Vera Wollenberger.[58]

Selective repression is unlikely, however, to solve the problem with which the SED is today confronted. There are dozens of groups in most of the major towns of the GDR with hundreds of participants who can no longer easily be intimidated by such occasional, and limited, shows of force on the part of the *Stasi*. A general roundup on the scale required to eliminate all such activities, however, is unlikely because it would endanger church-state relations and besmirch the carefully nurtured image of the GDR abroad.

All this, of course, does not represent a serious threat to the political power of the bureaucracy. The Protestant church in the GDR is a negligible social force compared to the Catholic church in Poland, and the impact on mass consciousness of a few hundred, even thousands of young people involved in unorthodox discussions, experiments with alternative life-styles, and the occasional public demonstration is negligible compared to that of the West German media with which the regime has learnt to live.

Yet on however small a scale, the existence of a relatively stable organizational network of critical thought and action with its own infrastructure of publications and increasingly experienced and sophisticated activists constitutes a qualitative leap from the situation of the 1960s and 1970s when public dissent was confined to small cliques of prominent artists and intellectuals. Rather than a direct mass-mobilizing effect, the more significant impact may well

58. Cf. Kevin Ball, "Re-affirming the Limits," *Labour Focus on Eastern Europe* 10, no.1 (April 1988): 34–35.

be on developments within the party itself: the continuous confrontation of party cadres at all levels with a small but vociferous critical element forces upon them difficult tactical choices in how to deal with this phenomenon and thus can only help accelerate the internal differentiation of the party apparatus into "conservatives" and "reformers." Given the external pressures emanating from the Soviet drive toward *glasnost* and *perestroika*, such domestic stirrings may well prove an important catalyst.

The Working Class

As has been proved time and again in the history of Eastern Europe, the working class is the decisive factor in the political and economic development of "actually existing socialism." The authentic Stalinist model of the Soviet Union in the era of forced industrialization, which relied on the total atomization and superexploitation of a first-generation industrial work force freshly recruited from the peasantry, using slave labor on a large scale, could no longer be operated even in the USSR of the 1950s, let alone in Poland, Czechoslovakia, Hungary, and of course East Germany with their longer and deep-rooted traditions of trade unionism and organized working-class politics. The "de-Stalinization" of the 1950s was therefore more than an ideological, "superstructure" phenomenon confined to the ranks of the party and the intelligentsia: it marked, above all, the introduction of a new relationship between the regimes and their working classes which is best understood in terms of an implicit "social contract."[59]

The terms of this social contract essentially involved the surrender of trade-union and political rights on the part of the workers in exchange for social security and steadily rising living standards, as well as some relaxation in party and police control of their daily lives. Western observers often fail to appreciate the real improvement this "social contract" brought to the lives of ordinary workers in the Soviet Union and Eastern Europe because they remain unimpressed by the advances made in the consumer goods sector, where the gap between West and East has indeed remained a yawning one. But this comparison is in many ways irrelevant;

---

59. For a broader, and in its anticipation of Gorbachev's *perestroika* quite prophetic, analysis of this see the essay on the Soviet Union in Daniel Singer's *The Road to Gdansk: Poland and the USSR* (New York and London, 1981).

partly because the improvements even in this field were substantial enough when compared to the forced austerity of the previous period, but mostly because many of the benefits enjoyed by East European workers do not figure in earnings and consumption statistics—the absence of any real threat of redundancy and umemployment, the much lower intensity of the labor process, the free and easy access to essential social and medical services, the opportunities for upward social mobility for many individual workers. As long as the regime delivered the material goods with some regularity and did not put ordinary workers under excessive political pressure, there was little cause for involvement in political opposition for the overwhelming majority of working people.

The repeated reluctance of workers, first in Czechoslovakia in 1968, then in Poland after 1980, and now in Gorbachev's Soviet Union, to show enthusiasm for marketizing economic reforms that appear to threaten the cosy predictability of long-established practices and privileges confirmed the real substance of this arrangement.

If in the GDR the terms of the social contract tended to be undermined on the one hand by the more immediate comparison of its "socialist achievements" with the living standards of the most prosperous West European capitalism, this was, on the other hand, neutralized by the very steady upward movement of the East German economy and, crucially, by the conviction that there was no realistic alternative to an accommodation with the existing order at the frontline of the East-West conflict—neither collectively nor, after the building of the Berlin Wall, individually.

The repeated clashes between the working class and the government in Poland during the 1970s, culminating in the rise of Solidarnosc in 1980–81, heralded the beginning of the end of this social contract and thus a new era of generalized political crisis in the entire Soviet bloc. The economic basis for this political crisis is the need of the ruling bureaucracies to release sufficient investment funds for the modernization of their stagnant industries—funds which, for a time, they attempted to obtain through hard-currency loans from the West and increased exports to the capitalist world market, but which the recession in the capitalist world now forces them to extract from a tightening of belts at home: through the reduction of price subsidies for consumer goods and social services, closer links between pay and productivity, the intensification of production, and the elimination of unproductive industries.

For the working classes of Eastern Europe this has increasingly tended to mean inflationary pressures on their living standards, a deterioration of working and living conditions, and a perceived threat to their cherished social security through the ever more frequent references to redundancies in the public debates between the reformers as well as the pressures for greater geographical mobility. Only in Poland—and, under different political conditions, Yugoslavia—has the point of open revolt been reached so far, but everywhere else the storm clouds are gathering. The more farsighted elements in the bureaucracy are, of course, aware of the dangers to political stability and are seeking to forestall a general confrontation with the working class by courting potential allies in the intelligentsia, the farmers, and those sections of the working class employed in the key growth industries by a policy of controlled political, ideological, and economic liberalization: more creative freedom in science and the arts, extension of the private sector in agriculture, and social differentiation through market competition. In other words, it is now possible to discern the contours of a new social contract at the expense of both the conservative, centralist wing of the bureaucracy and the manual workers in the traditional and now declining industries (steel, coal, shipbuilding, etc.).

In this respect the GDR enjoys a special position in comparison with its West European neighbors. Its historic developmental advantages over the rest of the "socialist camp" have by and large been maintained by its privileged role as the chief provider of high-technology industrial equipment within the CMEA, and its close relationship with the Federal Republic, especially its access to large amounts of hard West German currency at easy conditions, has largely cushioned it against the debt repayment crisis suffered by the Poles, Hungarians, and Yugoslavs. The pressures on the East German working class have therefore been considerably weaker than those elsewhere: price rises have been modest and have usually taken the form of "hidden rises" through repackaging, and acute shortages in essential foodstuffs and consumer goods have been comparatively rare and episodic. And, as we have seen, the Honecker leadership has pursued a conscious policy of prioritizing its social program even at the expense of the social investment fund, in sharp contrast to the austerity policies applied almost everywhere else in Eastern Europe.

Nonetheless, there are signs that the rapid improvement of working and living conditions under the slogan of the "unity of economic and social policy" is coming to a halt in the 1980s. The rise in real wages has slowed,[60] there have been no further cuts in the average working week,[61] and the rapid proliferation of shift work has made deep inroads into the quality of life enjoyed by East German production workers.[62].

What the reaction of the GDR's working class to any sharper assaults on its social and economic position would be is difficult to predict. The working class is the overwhelmingly dominant class in East German society,[63] but it has no recent tradition of militancy or independent organization. Short of a catastrophic collapse of the GDR economy, therefore, it is extremely unlikely that there would be a spontaneous eruption of protest from below. It can be assumed that, especially after the Polish experiences, the SED leadership is acutely aware of the dangers of stirring this sleeping giant and will therefore be extremely reluctant to take measures that seriously and provocatively encroach on workers' living standards. In its anxiety to avoid such a course it may well be driven into an even closer economic symbiosis with the Federal Republic, and it is perhaps against such a background that a resurgence of the strong trade-union and social-democratic traditions of the workers east of the Elbe will occur.

What form that might take is anybody's guess. But the strong sympathies of most East German workers for the SPD and their continuing desire for a reunification of Germany remain potent ingredients in the political make up of the GDR today and in the foreseeable future.

THE FUTURE OF THE GDR

No other East European state has had the same continuity of political leadership and stability of political development (at least

---

60. Cf. Gernot Schneider, "Arbeitsbedingungen und Einkommen,in der DDR, 1981–85," *Deutschland Archiv* 20, no. 4 (April 1987). 402–8.
61. Ibid. The average working week (excluding overtime, etc.) is still forty-three hours, the same as in 1967.
62. Ibid.
63. According to official statistics the working class comprises 72.4 percent of the population. Cf. Günter Erbe et al., *Politik, Wirtschaft, und Gesellschaft in der DDR*, 2d ed. (Opladen, 1980), p. 405.

since the 1953 crisis) as the GDR, and none (except perhaps Bulgaria) has been as reliable an ally of the USSR. This apparent stability would seem all the more surprising in the light of the unique difficulties that the regime has had to contend with: its creation under foreign occupation; its restriction to a fragment of prewar Germany; an uprooted economy; over twenty years of international isolation. No other East European member of the "socialist camp" has suffered from a comparable lack of established national identity or experienced similarly direct pressure from the strongest imperialist power in Europe. The direct confrontation with West Germany has tended to neutralize even the one advantage the GDR did enjoy in relation to most of the rest of Eastern Europe: both internally—where living standards have always been directly compared with the glittering model of the West German "consumer society"—and externally—where the Bundesrepublik could employ its superior industrial and financial muscle in order to maintain the international diplomatic quarantine imposed on the GDR—it has failed to translate its growing economic weight into commensurate political strength.

Yet it has been precisely the precarious position of the GDR as the westernmost outpost of the East European bloc that has underpinned its stability. Since the immediate postwar years the division of Germany has been the linchpin of the European status quo, and despite the continuation of Bonn's aggressive irredentist noises (somewhat muted, although by no means silenced, after 1969) the two German states have been securely locked into the recognized spheres of interest of their respective power blocs since at least the mid-1950s. For the last four decades both German states have been bulwark states, essential strategic positions of the U.S. and the Soviet Union which could not be surrendered by either side without risking the collapse of the entire postwar settlement between imperialism and Stalinism in Europe. As has already been pointed out, this fundamental determinant of the GDR's existence has been largely responsible for the homogeneity of the East German bureaucracy. The interests of the SED leadership as a whole are far more directly tied to those of the Soviet Union than is the case with any other East European party: without the Soviet guarantee it simply could not withstand the West German pressure. If it is possible to speak of a "bureaucratic nationalism" elsewhere in Eastern Europe (Romania being the outstanding example, but

Poland and Hungary are also cases in point), the SED's stance is characterized instead by a kind of "bureaucratic internationalism" which, rather than downplaying the political, economic, and military dependence on Moscow, positively celebrates it.[64] This is why the emergence of a reformist general secretary of the CPSU poses such a tricky problem for the SED leadership: unable, for reasons of its own self-preservation, to cut the umbilical cord linking it with the Kremlin, it nonetheless clearly disapproves of Gorbachev's policies and perceives them as a threat to its own position in East German society.

Its response to this dilemma has so far consisted of delicate maneuvers designed, at one and the same time, to disguise the extent of its differences with Moscow from the East German public and to support the antireform opposition in the Soviet Union.[65] At the same time, however, it would be an oversimplification to reduce the problems in Soviet-GDR relations simply to the questions of *glasnost* and *perestroika*. Before Gorbachev even came to power, there were clear signs of a growing self-confidence in the SED leadership in the pursuit of its own interests where these differed from Moscow's: as, for instance, in Honecker's lukewarm reaction to Soviet retaliation for the deployment of Cruise and Pershing missiles in Western Europe, his attempts to preserve intra-German détente throughout the new Cold War, and, subtly but unmistakably, his resistance to any closer supranational integration of the COMECON economies that would run counter to the needs of the GDR economy.[66]

In the field of foreign policy, therefore, Gorbachev's disarmament initiatives and his break with the adventurism of the Brezhnev era are finding a warm welcome in East Berlin. And insofar as

---

64. Article 6, Clause 2 of the GDR's constitution reads: "The German Democratic Republic is irrevocably and forever allied with the Union of Socialist Soviet Republics. The close and fraternal alliance with it is a guarantee to the people of the German Democratic Republic of its further advance on the road to socialism and peace."

65. Cf. the prominent place given in the SED daily *Neues Deutschland* to the notorious anti-*perestroika* letter published by *Sovyetskaya Rossiya* in March 1988. When *Pravda* eventually published a sharp retort in April, *Neues Deutschland* accompanied its reprint of the reply with a polemic by a Czech Stalinist against the Prague Spring. See *Neues Deutschland*, 2 March 1988 and 9 April 1988.

66. Cf. Siegfried Kupper, "Absichtserklärungen—kein konkretes Programm: Zur Diskussion über die Reform der Wirtschaftsbeziehungen im RGW," *Deutschland Archiv* 21, no. 1 (January 1988): 59–64.

perestroika promises to raise the efficiency and productivity of the Soviet economy, of course, this also can be hardly unwelcome. The misgivings concern the links between economic reform and *glasnost*, the effects that the *political* liberalization is beginning to have on party, state, and society in the USSR, and the galvanizing effects of the Soviet changes on Eastern Europe as a whole: given the permanent crisis in Poland, the acceleration of economic and political reform in Hungary, and the first signs of imminent change even in Czechoslovakia, the East German leadership faces the prospect of international isolation in the "socialist camp." Already human rights activists, Protestant churchmen, leading writers and artists, and even party functionaries[67] are invoking Gorbachev's speeches against the official SED line and find a powerful sounding board in the omnipresent West German media and their obsession with the reformist general secretary.

Why then does the SED leadership not join in the spirit of the "new thinking"? And what will happen if it does not? The answer to the first question is to be found in the SED's fundamental lack of confidence in its own ability to survive politically a period of public debate even as limited as the one under the first three years of the Gorbachev regime. This is not simply a matter of an aging generation of functionaries hanging on grimly to their offices, but of the very foundations of the GDR's polity that set it apart from the rest of Eastern Europe: its extreme vulnerability to the pressures emanating from West Germany. This vulnerability does not necessarily preclude change—and given the GDR's high degree of dependence on the Soviet Union it is in any event inconceivable that it could resist some adaptation to the new course from Moscow in the long run—but it imposes certain conditions on the management of any such change which not only the present Honecker leadership, but any likely successors, are bound to observe: above all, the maintenance of the unity of the party and of its political monopoly and the avoidance of any confrontation with the sleeping giant of East Germany, the working class.

This leaves the SED with little room for maneuver. It can make some limited concessions to the spirit of *glasnost* by granting more leeway to its artists and intellectuals, it can build on the new

---

67. Cf. Karl Wilhelm Fricke, "Zur inneren Situation der SED," *DDR Report*, 5 (1988): 257–60.

relationship with the Protestant church, it can further relax the restrictions on travel to and contact with West Germany, but it cannot permit the open articulation of different ideological currents within the party of centers of independent political activism outside it. On the economic front, it cannot engage in experiments with internal marketization which would threaten to accentuate social conflicts and thus risk the politicization of the working class, even though the huge demands placed on the state's budget by the continuation of the social program[68] seriously hamper its ability to make available the investment funds needed to achieve the ambitious high-technology targets set by the Eleventh Party Congress.

Much will depend on the outcome of the momentous struggles unfolding in the Soviet Union. It is now clear[69] that the project pursued by Gorbachev goes far beyond anything predicted three years ago: even if the CPSU leadership manages to retain control over the process of reconstruction and democratization—a rather uncertain assumption indeed—it is difficult to see the SED practicing the kind of new relationship between party, state, and society implicit in the Soviet reform program.

In the final reckoning, the only possible resolution to this contradiction lies beyond the sphere of domestic East German politics. Just as the present regime in the GDR required the Cold War for its creation and the East-West détente of the 1970s for its consolidation, its democratization may be inseparable from yet another change in the European political context: a new deal between the Soviet Union and Western Europe, above all West Germany, which transcends the postwar settlement and irrevocably alters the external conditions upon which the stability of the political order in the GDR has always rested. The weakening of American hegemony over the Western world, the emergence of Western Europe as an independent factor in East-West relations, and above all the Soviet interest in the sort of close economic, technological, and security partnership with the West which only Europe can offer make such a new deal more conceivable now than at any time since

68. Cf. Hannsjörg F. Buck, "Zur Struktur der Staatsausgaben des öffentlichen Gesamthaushalts der DDR," *Deutschland Archiv* 20, no. 12 (December 1987): 1274–86.
69. These lines are written while the delegates are assembling in Moscow for the crucial Nineteenth Conference of the CPSU in June 1988.

the end of the Second World War.

We have argued elsewhere[70] that this constellation offers a historic opportunity for the Western Left to emancipate itself from the U.S., to promote the democratization of the Soviet Union and Eastern Europe, and to solve the German question within the framework of a united, socialist Europe. But it is also important to be alert to the dangers of the situation: apart from the possibility of a decisive defeat for the reformers in Moscow, which would plunge Europe back into Cold War, there is also the possibility of the West European, and especially the West German, Right seizing the initiative and making its own offers of a new cooperation, attracted by vast potential markets and cheap, disciplined labor. The causes of democracy and socialism would be unlikely to benefit.

For the SED leadership this latter option, translated into the terms of intra-German relations, may hold considerable attraction as a response to the pressures of *perestroika*. If adaptation to the new realities is needed, it is most likely to prefer the dangers of a closer symbiosis with the Federal Republic to the risks of internal democratization. As we have seen, it already has some experience in using the West German connection to stave off reforms: this tactic may be elevated to a survival strategy on an unprecedented scale, involving huge injections of West German capital through direct investment and joint ventures.

At this point the speculation must stop. Honecker, now seventy-six, is still firmly in charge, while Gorbachev's *perestroika* has not yet reached the point where firm predictions can be made as to its eventual outcome. Equally, Western Europe is only just beginning to suspect that there may be life beyond Atlanticism, with the Left in particular finding it hard to break with old habits formed in a bipolar world. It is quite possible, even likely, therefore that Europe may continue to stumble on along the old paths for quite a while yet, the breakup of the postwar settlement taking a more contorted and muddled form than suggested above. As to the immediate future of the GDR, this would give Krenz, Felfe, Schabowski, or whoever else will be the next general secretary of the SED considerable room for maneuver and adaptation. But in the long run, it is difficult to see the GDR cast off the bonds tying it

70. Cf. Peter Brandt and Günter Minnerup, "Eastern Europe and the German Question," *Labour Focus on Eastern Europe* 9, no. 2 (July-October 1987): 4–9.

to a Europe locked in Cold War confrontation and settling as an equal partner in anything like its present form into the new European order that surely must be on the horizon now. Much the same applies, of course, to the Federal Republic: in this sense the German question still holds the key to the future of Europe.

7 ELITES AND POLITICS IN THE GERMAN DEMOCRATIC REPUBLIC

Mary Fulbrook

What sort of a political system is the German Democratic Republic? For the first decade after its foundation in 1949, Western scholars tended to portray the "Soviet zone" of Germany as a simple instance of "totalitarianism." However, changes began to be observed in the course of the 1960s, after the building of the Berlin Wall in 1961. Phenomena such as the New Economic System—a partial decentralization of the economy, introduced in 1963—and the fostering of a career-oriented society, in which people had to make the best of a now inescapable situation, led scholars to reconceptualize the nature of the GDR. A major Western authority, P. C. Ludz, now argued that the GDR represented a case, not of totalitarianism, but rather of "consultative authoritarianism." Associated with discussions of the type of political system have been debates over the question of the structure of elites and their relations to politics. Does the GDR have a "unitary" elite, in contrast to the supposedly "pluralistic" societies of the West with their multiplicities of elites, as suggested by Dahrendorf and Krejci, or does the GDR provide further evidence rather of the inevitable bureaucratization and arguable convergence of all advanced industrial societies?[1] Despite wide-ranging discussions, both theoretical

1. See, for example, P. C. Ludz, *The German Democratic Republic from the Sixties to the Seventies* (Harvard Center for International Affairs: Occasional Papers in International Affairs, no. 26, November 1970); R. Dahrendorf, *Society and Democracy in Germany* (London: Weidenfeld and Nicolson, 1968), chaps. 17, 26, 27; J. Krejci, *Social Structure in Divided Germany* (London: Croom Helm, 1976), chap. 4.

and substantive, these questions are still open. Recently the notion of "totalitarianism" has even been resurrected as applicable to the GDR.[2] On one point, however, scholars are prepared to agree: in comparison with many of its Eastern bloc neighbors, the GDR has—at least until the end of 1987, although there are signs of change in early 1988—evinced a notable domestic stability since the suppression of the GDR's only serious uprising in 1953, showing little of the internal unrest experienced in Poland and Czechoslovakia.

A complete explanation of the relative political stability of the GDR would require reference to a range of factors.[3] One clue would however have to do with the structure of elites in the GDR and, in particular, their relative cohesion in contrast to those of neighboring states. This article seeks to develop an anatomy of the structure and relations of different elite groups in the GDR that diverges from the interpretations presented in either the "totalitarian/ unitary elite" or the "convergence/technocracy" approaches and leads to a reformulation of the political system departing from the notion of "consultative authoritarianism."

There are obvious difficulties in a study of elites in the GDR, both conceptual and empirical. While the abolition of private ownership of the means of production has entailed the abolition of antagonistic classes in the traditional Marxist sense, even GDR sociologists recognize that social distinctions remain and that there are "nonantagonistic" classes in "actually existing socialist society" (which is now conceived to be a relatively long-term transitional stage). GDR social analysts are however themselves not in agreement as to how best to define and interpret the social distinctions that persist in their society; but they argue against Western attempts to assert that social inequalities intrinsically nullify claims to being a socialist society and Western suggestions that the "scientific-technical revolution" actually necessitates the leading role of specialist elites.[4] East German sociologists until recently even denied the

2. S. Thielbeer, "Ist die DDR ein totalitärer Staat?" in E. Jesse, ed., *Bundesrepublik Deutschland und Deutsche Demokratische Republik: Die beiden deutschen Staaten im Vergleich*, 3d ed., (Berlin: Colloquium Verlag, 1982).
3. Cf. M. Fulbrook, "Solutions to German History? East and West Germany Compared," *Parliamentary Affairs* 40, no. 1, (January 1987): 113–29; M. Fulbrook, "The State and the Transformation of Political Legitimacy in East and West Germany since 1945," *Comparative Studies in Society and History* 29, no. 2 (April 1987), for some suggestions.
4. Manfred Lötsch, "Annäherung von Arbeiterklasse und Intelligenz: Gesetz-

existence of elites in their society, despite the admission of systematic social differences. "Elite theory," in the 1978 edition of the *Kleines politisches Wörterbuch*, is promptly denounced as a "bourgeois theory" which denigrates the creative historical role of the working masses.[5] The conceptualization and interpretation of the role of elites in Western social theory is even more diverse, and there is no simple, generally accepted definition. There are moreover empirical problems concerning access to relevant data, inconsistencies in official statistics (the category "intelligentsia" is included in some tables in the *Statistisches Jahrbuch der DDR* but not in others, for example, with no indication of how recategorization has been performed), and lack of reliable insider knowledge of political processes. In the face of such problems, what follows can hardly be presented as a definitive analysis of elites and politics in the GDR. It represents, rather, a preliminary anatomy of the structure and relationships of key elite groups which may contribute to the development of a more adequate characterization and interpretation of the GDR political system than is implied by the older approaches mentioned above.

Before presenting such an anatomy of elites, it will be helpful to give a brief characterization of the ways in which East German society has changed since the destruction of the Third Reich. The socioeconomic structure of East Germany has undergone two sorts of transformation since 1945: a radical transformation of the social relations of production and a more gradual transformation of the technological division of labor, a shift in the proportions of people employed in different areas of the economy. It has also experienced considerable changes in patterns and avenues of social mobility.

Among the first measures of the Soviet occupation following the defeat of the Nazis in 1945 were land reform and the expropriation of key industrial and financial concerns. The redistribution of large estates in September 1945 abolished the historically significant Prussian Junker class at one stroke; the subsequent waves of collec-

mässigkeiten der Reduzierung sozialer Unterschiede zwischen körperlicher und geistiger Arbeit," and "Zur Dialektik der Annäherung von Arbeiterklasse und Intelligenz" in *Lebensweise und Sozialstruktur: 3. Kongress der Marxistisch-Leninistischen Soziologie* (East Berlin: Dietz Verlag, 1981), p. 220, pp. 82–83.
5. *Kleines politisches Wörterbuch* (East Berlin: Dietz Verlag, 1987), p. 197.

tivization of agriculture in 1952–53 and in 1959–60 radically transformed the structure of East German agriculture. Similarly,
following early expropriations of Nazi-owned factories, subsequent measures reduced the proportion of industrial production
by the private sector to about 15 percent in 1955 and as little as 2
percent in 1970.[6] According to the 1984 *Statistisches Jahrbuch der
DDR*, in 1983 only 397,100 out of 8,445,300 economically active
individuals were engaged in privately owned concerns, although
there have been some signs of a return to private ownership of
small shops and businesses—on a very inconsequential scale—since
then.[7]

The transformation from a capitalist economy to one with state
ownership (in the name of the people) of the means of production
has been accompanied by changes in the planning and direction of
the economy and the organization of labor. There have also been
less notable, although still important, changes in the division of
labor. East Germany has participated in the general trend of
advanced industrial societies away from manual labor toward white-
collar occupations, giving rise to a considerable amount of structurally induced social mobility. There have been changes too in the
proportions employed in industry relative to agriculture, with the
latter declining from 27.9 percent of the work force in 1959 to 10.7
percent in 1983.[8]

Along with the politically induced transformations of the social
structure, as well as the less intentional, although partly planned,
shifts in the occupational structure, have gone changes in patterns
and avenues of social mobility. A key ideological aim of the first
decade and a half of the GDR was the sponsorship, through
education, of children from working-class backgrounds. In the
1960s, with the New Economic System, the goal of fostering
talent, from whatever background it might spring, began to pre-
dominate over that of positive discrimination and equality of
opportunity. Despite the fact that the reproduction of social status
across the generations is now a factor giving GDR sociologists

6. See Karl Hardach, *The Political Economy of Germany in the Twentieth Century*
(Berkeley: University of California Press, 1980), pp. 116–20.
7. Staatliche Zentralverwaltung für Statistik, ed., *Statistisches Jahrbuch 1984 der
DDR* (East Berlin: Staatsverlag der Deutschen Demokratischen Republik, 1984),
p. 111.
8. Ibid., p. 109. See also Krejci, *Social Structure*, pp. 81, 83.

some cause for concern, the GDR nevertheless remains a society in which class background is a less important factor in determining social mobility via the education system than is the case in West Germany.[9] Political conformity is however a key factor which must be combined with appropriate educational qualifications if social mobility is to be achieved.

What of the actual turnover of personnel in East Germany since 1945? Certainly the Soviet zone of occupation experienced a far more radical denazification process in the early years than did the zones in the west. The communists (first in the KPD and then, after 1946, in the new Socialist Unity Party, the SED) were keen to assert their political control in all areas of administration, the economy, and the educational system, as well as, obviously, politics proper. With the transformation of Nazi Germany into a new, Soviet-style state over the years, the old German Junker, industrial, military, and Nazi elites disappeared. Elites in the GDR are the product of a new society and not the transformed vestiges of "traditional" elites in new colors.

Who, then, are the elites in this new society which the GDR has become? As mentioned above, many Western observers suggest that, in contrast to Western "pluralist" societies, the GDR has a single unitary elite: the party. Undoubtedly there is some truth in this: the party is the repository of supreme power (if ultimately subordinate to the Communist Party of the Soviet Union, the CPSU); but the picture of a single, uniform political elite is too simple. The Socialist Unity Party (SED) has sought to attain, maintain, and use power in a complex society and through complex instruments. It has had to deal with, co-opt, or neutralize other important groups; it has had to shape, sponsor, and control powerful organizations; it has had to balance competing and conflicting interests. Additionally, the SED has had to deal with

9. See A. Hearndon, *Education in the Two Germanies* (Oxford: Basil Blackwell, 1974); John Page, "Education under the Honeckers," in D. Childs, ed., *Honecker's Germany* (London: George Allen and Unwin, 1985); G.-J. Glaessner, "The Education System and Society," in K. von Beyme and H. Zimmermann, eds., *Policymaking in the GDR* (Aldershot: Gower, 1984); also G.-J. Glaessner, "Universitäten und Hochschulen," in *DDR Handbuch*, 2d ed. (Cologne: Verlag Wissenschaft und Politik, 1979); Lötsch, "Annäherung," p. 214.

155

tensions and differences within its midst: between hard-liners, humanists, and revisionists; dogmatists and pragmatists; ideologists and technical experts. The ruling Communist party of the GDR has been notable—particularly in comparison with its closest neighbors, Poland and Czechoslovakia—in having achieved an apparently stable balance, such that it has been able to present a relatively monolithic face to the outside world. But the details of this balance—which must be continually fought for and renewed—have to be explored and explained, not simply asserted away with a blanket label about a "unitary elite." It is necessary to explore the strengths, positions, and interrelations of different important groups within the GDR as they relate to the party.

The higher reaches of the SED do undoubtedly constitute the key elite group, at least in terms of power: the Politburo, the Secretariat, and the Central Committee (or at least some members of it). The SED is a mass as well as a cadre party—about one-fifth of the working population belong to it—and, based as it is on principles of democratic centralism, members at the lower levels have very little claim to be included in an elite. The party elite itself is notable for the relatively cohesive face it presents to the outside world. Since the late 1950s there has been little evidence of serious factionalism within its ranks, although much may go on behind the scenes of which Western observers are unaware.

The relative uniformity was hard won in the early years and has required perpetual reassertion. The Ulbricht group of communists who flew in from Moscow at the end of the war had very different views on many matters of policy and political practice from those German communists who had remained in Hitler's Germany, underground or imprisoned, or who had been exiled in the West. Additionally, after the forced merger of the German Communist party (KPD) with the Social Democratic Party of Germany (SPD) in 1946 to form the SED, there was the question of the former Social Democrats in the party, who were unused to notions of democratic centralism. Some had already fled to the West, prompted by prior misgivings over unification (such as Gustav Dahrendorf); others may have had initial fears partially allayed by the official line, represented by Anton Ackermann, of a specifically "German road to socialism." Nevertheless, former KDP members controlled appointments and ensured that social democrats were subordinated in practice to communists in party administration. In

1948 the "German road" was abandoned as a "nationalist deviation," and the party was "cleansed" of former Social Democrats, ex-members of the NSDAP ("small Nazis" who had suffered a change of heart had been allowed to join), and "careerists." By the time of the First Party Conference in January 1949 the parity principle between ex-KPD and ex-SPD members had been dropped. In October 1950 there was an exchange of party cards, involving an interview with all members and candidates. The GDR also participated in the general East European movement to expel "Western agents," "Zionists," and those who had had connections with Noel Field, although not as severely as in the show trials elsewhere.[10]

Despite all these cleansing measures, however, there were still considerable differences of opinion within the party by the summer of 1953. Walter Ulbricht's position was by no means secure, and support existed in Moscow for an alternative group associated with Rudolf Herrnstadt and Wilhelm Zaisser. It was these internal differences which played a major role in the origins of the only large-scale popular uprising in East Germany's history, that of June 1953. Following the "new course" in the Soviet Union after Stalin's death, contradictory changes of policy were made in the GDR: concessionary measures toward certain groups on the one hand, while at the same time retaining the increased work norms for industrial workers on the other. These measures were announced suddenly, without prior discussion and preparation of party functionaries. Different views appeared in the press: an article in *Neues Deutschland* (of which Herrnstadt was the editor) on 14 June criticized the SED's hard-line policies, while an article in the FDGB newspaper *Tribüne* on 16 June supported the raised work norms. These uncertainties provided the context and opportunity for the confused course of developments of protest on 16 June which eventuated into the more widespread uprising of 17 June. Although one immediate effect of the uprising was the withdrawal of the raised work norms, ironically the main political consequence was the confirmation in power of Ulbricht and the hard-liners.

10. W. Leonhard, *Die Revolution entlässt ihre Kinder* (München: Wilhelm Heyne Verlag, 1981); D. Staritz, *Geschichte der DDR, 1949–1985* (Frankfurt/Main: Suhrkamp, 1985), chap. 2, sec. 3; M. McCauley, *Marxism-Leninism in the GDR* (London: MacMillan, 1979), chap. 2; H. Weber, "The Socialist Unity Party," in Childs, ed., *Honecker's Germany*.

Herrnstadt and Zaisser (who had been minister for state security) were removed from their positions in the Politburo, and in January 1954 they were expelled from the SED for "factionalism." (Their downfall was made easier by the fall of their supporter in Moscow, Beria.) Max Fechner, the justice minister, who had argued for lenience toward the strikers on the basis of a constitutional right to strike, was ousted from his position on 16 July, and harsh sentences were imposed on many "ringleaders" on the basis of political charges. In the months following the uprising further purges took place throughout the ranks of the SED: approximately 20,000 functionaries and 50,000 ordinary members were denounced as "provocateurs," and some were arrested while many others resigned. Former SPD members were particularly affected, and party organizations which were strongholds of former Social Democrats were thoroughly purged.[11]

In the course of the 1950s there were two further major purges of the SED. In 1956 a group of critical Marxists associated with Wolfgang Harich published a program which included demands for "the abolition of the hegemony of the bureaucratic apparatus over party members, expulsion of the Stalinists from the SED, the restoration of absolute legal guarantees, the abolition of the state security agency and the secret court, workers' shares in the profits in factories, and an end to collectivization in agriculture," as well as for elections with several candidates and, in the context of possible reunification with West Germany, the need to respect a possible majority for the Western SPD in free elections.[12] Needless to say, this eclectic program did not find favor with Ulbricht; nor did the fact that Harich was in active contact with the West German SPD and with Polish reform communists. Harich was sentenced to ten years' imprisonment, but released in 1964 after an apparent change

11. A. Baring, ed., *Der 17. Juni 1953* (Stuttgart: Deutsche Verlags-Anstalt, 1983), passim.; K. W. Fricke, "Der Arbeiteraufstand: Vorgeschichte, Verlauf, Folgen," in Ilse Spittmann and K. W. Fricke, eds., *17. Juni 1953: Arbeiter-Aufstand in der DDR* Edition Deutschland Archiv (Cologne: Verlag Wissenschaft und Politik, 1982), pp. 18–19.

12. H. Weber, "The Third Way: Bahro's Place in the Tradition of Anti-Stalinist Opposition," in U. Wolter, ed., *Rudolf Bahro: Critical Responses* (New York: M. E. Sharpe, 1980), p. 15. For this and the rest of this paragraph, see also Staritz, *Geschichte*, pp. 113–15; K. Reyman, "The Special Case of East Germany," in F. Silnitsky et al., eds., *Communism and Eastern Europe* (Brighton: Harvester Press, 1979); W. Volkmer, "East Germany: Dissenting Views during the Last Decade," in R. Tökes, ed., *Opposition in Eastern Europe* (London: MacMillan, 1979).

of heart. His associates had lesser sentences. Also in 1956 an unrelated group of revisionist economists were dealt with: Fritz Behrens, Arne Benary, and others who had advocated economic reforms involving decentralization were attacked. In 1958 there was a further attempt to remove any internal opposition to Ulbricht and his policies. Ulbricht's rivals in the Central Committee and Politburo, Karl Schirdewan, Ernst Wollweber, Gerhart Ziller, Fritz Selbmann, Paul Wandel, and Fred Oelssner, were removed. This effectively ended the presence of "Third Way," anti-Stalinist Marxists in the higher ranks of the SED, and Ulbricht did not have to face further serious challenges to his leadership until his own final removal from power—when it suited the Soviet Union—in 1971. The tradition of the so-called "Third Way" of humanistic Marxism has since the end of the 1950s been represented only by isolated intellectuals who have failed to gain mass followings or to secure an institutional foothold in party organization. Thinkers such as Robert Havemann, and later Rudolf Bahro, were relatively easily removed from influence, whether by internal or external arrest or exile. There are signs that there may be a ground swell of change in this respect, partly encouraged by the new processes of *glasnost* in Gorbachev's Soviet Union. But the fact remains that the SED's success until the late 1980s was based to some considerable degree on the isolation and exclusion of dissenters.

A more subtle threat to the position of the orthodox party elite has arguably been the putative rise of the technical intelligentsia in East Germany. P. C. Ludz even went so far as to write of an "institutionalized counterelite." In contrast to the splits between the hard-liners and humanists of the 1950s, the major distinction in the changed political and economic context of the 1960s was one between dogmatists and technocrats. After the closure of the last escape route to the West with the erection of the Berlin Wall in 1961 and the introduction of the more decentralized New Economic System in 1963, economic and technical experts gained in strategic importance, status, and material rewards in East Germany—and arguably also in political influence. Ludz, who presents the strongest thesis, argues that the pressures of industrialization produce the rise of institutionalized counterelites who effectively set limits to the totalitarian aspirations of the traditional political

159

"strategic clique." In Ludz's view: "Economic progress encourages a functional differentiation within the political leadership and gives rise to new, competing elite groupings. Consequently, the total interpenetration of a society by the ideological will of one party is substantially decreased."[13] There is undoubtedly evidence to show that technical experts were able to attain positions in the higher echelons of the party organization in the 1960s and after and that the advice of economic and other experts has been consistently sought by party leaders. There have also been clear improvements in the level of educational qualifications of active party members in local and central government. What is less clear, however, is the interpretation of the political implications of these phenomena.

In the first place, the technical intelligentsia as a whole can only with some difficulty be identified as a self-conscious group actor; and within this group there exists a broad range of diverse political orientations and values. Thomas Baylis's study of the technical intelligentsia (published in 1974) suggested that while the predominant political orientation was one of accommodation to or acquiescence in the regime, political attitudes ranged from conviction through apathy to routine dissatisfaction, reformism or revisionism, and finally outright dissent and opposition. The most common stance was one of pragmatism and the separation of "professional" and "political" concerns. Only those technical experts who also conformed to the official party line and who had a long and acceptable record of party membership and participation in party activities and organizations were recruited into the party leadership.[14]

Moreover, even when in top party organizations, members of the technical intelligentsia were generally kept to positions of an advisory character rather than gaining places of real power. In Baylis's view, "economic specialists have been given hardly more than token representation, sufficient to provide an input of needed technical expertise but of little direct significance as a power factor."[15] Not only were technicians outweighed by "apparatchiks" at the centers of policy making, but also "those 'representatives' of the

13. P. C. Ludz, *The Changing Party Elite in East Germany* (Cambridge, Mass.: MIT Press, 1972), pp. 6–7.
14. T. Baylis, *The Technical Intelligentsia and the East German Elite* (Berkeley: University of California Press, 1974), chap. 6, also pp. 81–82, 179–80.
15. Ibid., p. 213.

technical strategic elite in the Politburo and Secretariat are subject to continuing pressures not to be genuine representatives of group interests at all, but men who share with their apparatchik counterparts a commitment to a conservative vision of the party's leading role and a loyalty to collective leadership decisions."[16] Baylis ultimately agreed with those critics of Ludz who argued that "the technical strategic elite and the apparatchiki are partners in power rather than rivals for it."[17]

This view is borne out by the record of economic policy in the 1960s. Economic specialists were brought in to advise on the functioning of the New Economic System (NES), and there were greater powers of managerial decision making devolved down to intermediate levels of economic organization.[18] But a main concern of Ulbricht was to avoid the concomitant decentralization of political power and decision making—in contrast to the aims of the economic revisionists of the 1950s. Moreover, certain key decisions were made which had little or nothing to do with economic rationality and a lot to do with pressures brought to bear by the Soviet Union. The very introduction of the NES was influenced by critical and perhaps decisive pressure from the USSR; the intervention of the Soviets produced the economically unfavorable Soviet trade agreement for 1966–67, probably linked to Erich Apel's suicide in December 1965; and the ultimate demise of the NES, before initial problems had been allowed the time for sorting out, was much influenced by Soviet concerns about the political implications of comparable experiments in Czechoslovakia, such that East German reforms were quietly abandoned after 1968. Thus the "rise" of the technical intelligentsia in the course of the 1960s was very much a state-sponsored one, nurtured and fostered by Ulbricht in the pursuit of politically defined goals and within the limits set by the Soviet Union.

Economic and other experts have retained a certain set of political positions under Erich Honecker, but the emphasis has been on the leading role of the party of the working class. Hermann Weber suggests that since 1971 ideology has again gained ground over

16. Ibid., p. 218.
17. Ibid., p. 267.
18. On the New Economic System see, for example, G. Leptin and M. Melzer, *Economic Reform in East German Industry* (London: Oxford University Press, 1978).

technocracy.[19] According to David Childs, since 1981 there has been a rise in what he calls "dogmatic conservatives" rather than "pragmatists."[20] Günter Minnerup's analysis of the social composition of the 1981 Politburo produces the comment that "it is striking . . . that chief responsibility for security matters lies with the older members, while the 'third generation' holds all the key economic posts."[21] In noneconomic intelligentsia occupations, such as medicine, a certain political conformity is a prerequisite for gaining a place as a student to begin with; subsequent political conformity is nurtured through compulsory political schooling at intervals. Although there may be a considerable range of political attitudes in the medical profession—helped not least by the contribution made to the health service by church hospitals and by the importance attached by the state to the maintenance and improvement of public health as part of its general social program—individuals in medical and other scientific and technical professions lead largely private lives as far as political influence is concerned. Baylis's interpretation of the position and treatment of the technical intelligentsia in East Germany, although written some time ago, is perhaps still the most perceptive: discussing the alternation between "hard" and "soft" policies toward the technical intelligentsia, he suggests that the fluctuations can only be explained in terms of "rival insecurities: the fear of the loss of the indispensable services of the intelligentsia against the fear of the corrosive effects of political diversity."[22] The technical intelligentsia, it must be concluded, whatever their centrality to the efficiency of society and economy in East Germany (and hence to a certain legitimation of the party's claim to leadership), remains firmly under the control of the SED and, curiously—in distinction to neighboring East European countries—without firm allies among the cultural intelligentsia.

Equally important to the regime, but in a rather different way, is the cultural intelligentsia. Here a similar lack of effective political influence can be observed. On the one hand, the regime wishes prominent writers and artists to articulate and propagate official

19. Weber, "Socialist Unity Party," pp. 2–3.
20. D. Childs, *The GDR: Moscow's German Ally* (London: George Allen and Unwin, 1983), pp. 98–102.
21. G. Minnerup, "The DDR's Frozen Revolution", *New Left Review* 132 (1982): 5–32, p. 16.
22. Baylis, *Technical Intelligentsia*, p. 124.

values as part of the drive toward social, cultural, and psychological transformation; on the other hand, the development of independent critical thinking as a possible basis of opposition to the regime must be inhibited. By and large, the East German regime has been more successful in the latter part of this dual set of tasks than in the former.

There have been various shifts in cultural policy during the history of the GDR. An early policy in the immediate postwar years of a broad antifascist democratic front shortly gave way to socialist realism in the 1950s. A certain thaw after the death of Stalin in 1953 did not go very far or last very long. The "new course" in culture ended with the arrest of the Harich group in 1956. A new beginning was supposedly found in 1958, when the Bitterfeld Conference supported an integration of creative writing and work experience: workers were supposed to "grasp the pen" while writers were urged to gain some practical experience of manual labor. An important text which reflected this emphasis, but which transcended simplistic attempts at the optimistic portrayal of socialist society, was Christa Wolf's novel *Der geteilte Himmel* (Divided Heaven).[23] Its publication coincided with the introduction of the New Economic System and a general rethinking of socio-political relationships. Christa Wolf herself became a candidate member of the Central Committee, a position she held until 1967. The publication of her more pessimistic *Nachdenken über Christa T.* (Reflections on Christa T.) in that year found moderate criticism in the regime. Ulbricht's final years were—from the silencing of Wolf Biermann in 1965 onwards—characterized by renewed repression in cultural policy.

Honecker's era opened with the promising statement that there would be "no taboos" in relation to culture—so long as one started from the position of socialism (as officially interpreted, although he did not add this explicitly). A certain latitude of experimentation was indeed possible in the early 1970s, with publications such as Ulrich Plenzdorf's *Die neuen Leiden des jungen W.*, (The New

23. For Western, "bourgeois" readers, the ending of *Der geteilte Himmel*—when the heroine chooses to stay and work in the East rather than follow her lover who has left for the West—is perhaps surprising. Individual love would probably have triumphed over the rather arduous building of socialism had this been written in the West. But the stress on the difficulties of socialist society and the personal growth which is developed in the novel render *Der geteilte Himmel* a book with universal appeal as well as a product of a particular time, place, and cultural policy.

Sufferings of Young W.), a portrayal of a drop-out youth style hardly complimentary to the picture of satisfied workers over-fulfilling their work norms in the enthusiastic building of socialism so desired by the regime. Christa Wolf's masterly *Kindheitsmuster* (published in English under the somewhat misleading title *A Model Childhood*, perhaps better rendered as A Pattern of Childhood), an exploration both of questions of individual identity and memory and of the distant and recent historical past and present, vindicated the policy of permitting a space for the development of critical creativity in the GDR. But 1976 saw the onset of renewed repression in cultural policy. Wolf Biermann, who had not been permitted to perform in the GDR since 1965, was involuntarily exiled during one of his trips to the West. A protest letter signed by a number of prominent artists and writers, and supported by many more, brought penalties to those who had dared to criticize Biermann's exclusion. Christa Wolf and others lost their positions in cultural organizations, and many also lost their party membership. In the late 1970s, a number of prominent writers who had worked for many years in the GDR decided they could stand the constraints and pressures no longer and left for the West. For others, as Hanke has pointed out, "keeping silent" has become a major theme in their writings.[24]

There are of course other members of the cultural intelligentsia: teachers and writers in the humanities, journalists, and others. Many of these have found acceptable ways of living with the regime, and indeed certain of them do the business required of a supportive cultural intelligentsia: write and rewrite the history books, produce acceptable journalistic reports, either on developments in the GDR or, if they are foreign correspondents, a range of reporting from abroad, not all of which has to be directly political. English literature specialists attend conferences on Shakespeare in the West as well as the East; Reformation historians debate with British colleagues over various interpretations of the role of Luther. One should not give too simplistic a view of the role and position of the cultural intelligentsia in East Germany. It is a diverse group, and many of its members enjoy privileged life-styles and experience few unacceptable restrictions on their practice.

24. Irma Hanke, "Continuity and Change: Cultural Policy in the German Democratic Republic since the VIIIth SED Party Congress in 1971," in von Beyme and Zimmermann, eds., *Policymaking*.

Nevertheless, it is arguable that the cultural intelligentsia is not so easily co-opted as the technical intelligentsia. It is easier to separate professional, technical concerns from politics than it is to separate the creative perception and representation of social relationships and contexts from political ideals and values. It is also less of a loss to the regime—on the contrary, it is highly desirable —if productive, articulate, and critical members of the cultural intelligentsia emigrate to the West than if top scientists, engineers, or economists leave. What is also interesting about East Germany is that the two sets of intelligentsias have failed to form any sort of alliance and have failed to make a joint bid for the representation of an alternative society or an alternative elite. If the technical intelligentsia, through its material rewards, status, and privileges, has become a co-opted elite, then it is the cultural intelligentsia who might have made a claim to become a genuine "counterelite"; but this they have not done. In effect, they have permitted themselves to be silenced, isolated, exiled, or tamed into some form of conformity. The proximity of the other Germany, a common language community where they can also publish and have an audience, has of course aided this process.

A comparable position of compromise and partial co-option can be observed if one considers what might be called East Germany's "moral elite," the leaders of the churches. Nominally approximately half the population is Christian, the majority of whom belong to the Protestant churches; in practice, probably about a quarter of the population are active, professing Christians. The churches in the GDR are in a relatively strong institutional and financial position. They retained their property intact across the socioeconomic revolution of the postwar period; and they are heavily supported in a range of endeavors by the West German churches. They perform a variety of very useful, quite tangible functions in GDR society: they run hospitals, in which expensive equipment such as X-ray machines may be bought with West German money; they have old people's homes, homes for the handicapped and disabled, nursery places for children. They cooperate with the state in the renovation of historically important church buildings, such as the Berlin Dom, which helps the state's current policy of latching on to national traditions and the German

MARY FULBROOK

cultural heritage. There was also major cooperation between church
and state in the Luther quincentenary celebrations of 1983, serving
both in the attraction of foreign currency through tourism and the
building of a national identity. Church leaders, after many false
starts and difficulties in the 1950s and 1960s, have now become
respected discussion partners with the state, since the "summit
discussion" with Honecker in 1978 which regularized and furthered
recent more harmonious church-state relations.[25]

The political implications of this situation are interesting. At least
in the case of the Protestant churches it can be argued that the
relatively tolerant church-state relations since 1978 have predominantly served to incorporate potentially radical dissent, particularly
among youth, while at the same time creating the conditions that
foster the discussion and development of dissenting views. Whatever the precise balance—and it is a developing, dynamic situation
—the general aim of the SED is to persuade Christians that they can
work in partnership with the state in pursuit of common, humanistic goals, in the building of a more just and equal society.
Whether or not this is realized in quite the way portrayed in official
propaganda, there can be little doubt that some of the probing and
searching discussions currently going on among certain Protestant
circles do seem to have contributed to the development of means of
creatively living with the regime.[26] At the same time, church
leaders have frequently acted to moderate and restrain the more
extreme activities of radical dissenters. And for many more East
Germans, particularly among the older generation, church activities certainly continue to provide a focus for a meaningful life, quite
irrespective of current political issues. When the various aspects of
religious life in East Germany are viewed together, a case may be
made that, although church leaders might hardly be the moral elite
the SED would like to have chosen as the most effective for actually
existing socialism, they have nevertheless fulfilled a range of stabilizing and integrating functions for large numbers of the populace.

25. For further details and full references, see M. Fulbrook, "Co-option and
Commitment: Aspects of Relations between Church and State in the GDR," *Social
History* 12, no. 1 (Jan. 1987): 1–19.
26. For official views see, for example, the Panorama DDR "first-hand informa-
tion" pamphlets on *Christians and Churches in the GDR* (Dresden: Verlag Zeit im
Bild, 1980, 1983); for indications of Christian thinking see, for example, the
unpublished manuscript produced by the Department of Theological Studies of the
Federation of Protestant Churches in the GDR, "Leben und Bleiben in der DDR."

The concomitant risk of nurturing and provoking explicit dissent —which can be relatively easily dealt with by security measures at home or export to West Germany (helpfully strengthening Western antinuclear movements, for example!)—is a price the regime has seemed willing to pay.[27] There are however recent signs of changes in the balance: in late 1987 and early 1988 the regime has reacted with greater shows of force (arresting numerous demonstrators on a number of occasions, for example), and there are signs of splits within the church between leaders, individual radical pastors, and grass-roots members. Further developments may be in a direction quite different from that of the period 1978–88.

What of bureaucracy and brute force? The roles of the state and the military and their relations with the party and society are of relevance to any discussion of elites and politics in the GDR.

Over the years the SED has obviously attempted to transform, shape, and control the state and state apparatus in pursuit of its own political ends. Thus for example the *Länder* were abolished in 1952, being replaced by smaller *Bezirke*, which allowed a greater centralization of power; in December 1958 the second chamber of Parliament, the Länderkammer, was abolished. In 1960, with the death of President Wilhelm Pieck, the Staatsrat was formed as a collective body under the chairmanship of Walter Ulbricht, who thus united in his person leadership of the party and the state. With the displacement of Ulbricht by Honecker in 1971, the Staatsrat was demoted in favor of the Ministerrat. In 1973, after the death of Ulbricht, Willi Stoph for a time became chairman of the Staatsrat, but in 1976 Honecker took on this position as well as chairmanship of the National Defense Council, thus again uniting the headship of party and state and controlling military policy at the same time.

The state apparatus, like the SED, is organized according to principles of democratic centralism and cadre politics. The party attempts to control and monitor the execution and effects of politically determined decisions. This has led to the use of terms such as "party state" or even the assumption of the identity or fusing of party and state by some Western commentators. K. Sontheimer and W. Bleek, for example, speak of the extent to which "party and state have fused together in the GDR and how much the GDR is

27. For a fuller exploration of these arguments, cf. Fulbrook, "Co-option and Commitment," and Fulbrook, "The State and the Transformation of Political Legitimacy."

the state of the SED."[28] It is true that at the top levels there are many overlaps of personnel between state and party. A conscious policy has been adopted, for example, of having leading party officials (such as the Central Committee secretaries) also be members of the Staatsrat so that they can officially represent the GDR state, and not just the party, when traveling abroad.[29] The 1984 Politburo included ten members (one of whom was a candidate member) who were also members of the Staatsrat.[30] But to point to overlaps in personnel between party and state and to the recent relative lack of visible intervention by the party in state processes, as compared with the 1950s, is not completely to clarify the relations between the two. G. Neugebauer's detailed study of party and state in the GDR elucidates some of the complexities and tensions involved in the relationship. Neugebauer discusses the current tendencies toward, on the one hand, the instrumentaliza-tion of the state by the party and, on the other, the "*Verstaatlichung*" of the party by the state. His conclusion is that while, at the moment, the party appears to retain political dominance, there are many aspects of the role, structure, and functions of the state apparatus which serve to define the sorts of tasks that the party can place on the agenda and, indeed, to form and shape the structure of party organization (such as the specialist committees) as well. Hence the state acts at least to limit the social and economic goals which are seen as realizable by the party, suppressing more far-reaching political goals of total societal transformation and restrict-ing the party's claim to represent total social interests by putting forward the views of partial, local, and sectional interests. It is arguable too that a certain bureaucratic inertia has set in, with an interest in the maintenance and reproduction of the status quo.[31] These developments obviously require further close observation and analysis.

28. K. Sontheimer and W. Bleek, *The Government and Politics of East Germany* (London: Hutchinson, 1975), p. 65.
29. H. Zimmermann, "Power Distribution and Opportunities for Participation: Aspects of the Sociopolitical System of the GDR," in von Beyme and Zimmer-mann, eds., *Policymaking*, p. 51. Zimmermann also points out that the Staatsrat's functions were severely curtailed in the 1974 revision of the constitution.
30. *DDR Handbuch*, 3d ed. (1985), vol. 2, pp. 1006–9.
31. G. Neugebauer, *Partei und Staatsapparat in der DDR* (Opladen: Westdeutscher Verlag, 1978), chap. 3: "Instrumentalisierung des Staatsapparats oder Verstaat-lichung der Partei?"

The role of the military, although exceedingly difficult to evaluate by outside observers, seems not to be so independent of the party as it is, say, in neighboring Poland. A recent émigré from the GDR and erstwhile insider of sorts, Professor Franz Loeser, has in fact suggested that since the Polish crises of 1980–81 preparations are being made in the GDR for a possible military dictatorship.[32] Whatever his own former privileged position in terms of insider knowledge, Loeser's evidence for this surmise in his published work is quite unconvincing. Loeser also suggested that in the mid- and late 1970s there were differences of opinion between the military and civilian leaderships over matters of military policy, such as the question of whether there could be a "just" nuclear war.[33] These differences seem at best a question of tactics and public presentation. The replacement of General Heinz Hoffmann, after his death in December 1985, by General Heinz Kessler indicated a continuity of line on defense matters: Kessler was known as a "200 percenter" on party matters, with a hard line on defense and absolutely loyal to the Soviet Union.[34] According to the author of an article on "militarization" in the 1985 edition of the *DDR Handbuch*, politics retains its primacy over possible military solutions to domestic and foreign policy questions; and although the military is strongly represented in the Politburo, the military men are at the same time strong and orthodox party figures.[35]

The ultimate military sanction or countervailing power is of course the Soviet Union. There is an asymmetrical relationship between the GDR and the USSR, with the latter undoubtedly having considerable influence on politics in the former. This influence varies with circumstances, issues, and individuals, however. (M. McCauley, for example, suggests that "during the late Brezhnev era the GDR enjoyed considerable room for manoeuvre" in comparison to ten years earlier.)[36] The implications of Gorbachev's reforms in the USSR for politics in the GDR are not as yet clear; the SED has officially been somewhat dismissive of the concept of

---

32. F. Loeser, *Die unglaubwürdige Gesellschaft* (Cologne: Bund-Verlag, 1984), pp. 130–31.
33. Loeser, speaking at an ASGP conference in Nottingham, 16 February 1985.
34. K. W. Fricke, "Hoffmann's Nachfolger: Armeegeneral Heinz Kessler," *Deutschland Archiv* 19 (January 1986): 10–13.
35. *DDR Handbuch*, 3d ed. (1985), p. 892.
36. M. McCauley, "The German Democratic Republic and the Soviet Union," in Childs, ed., *Honecker's Germany*, p. 162; see also p. 147.

glasnost, while certain members of the population appear to be taking it more seriously than the regime would like. Here, however, only a general point needs to be made. The whole history of the GDR from its origins in the Soviet zone of occupation to the present curbs and limits on its relations with West Germany testifies in large degree to the changing interests and policies of the USSR, with the latter's influence detectable in all manner of domestic and foreign policy decisions which need not be documented in detail here. These ultimate limits should not be forgotten when discussing elites and politics within the national framework of the GDR.

What conclusions can be drawn from this brief anatomy of the pattern of elites and politics in the GDR? Despite the opacity of certain areas, certain preliminary conclusions seem possible.

First, the overall picture is not one of monolithic party dictatorship, as implied by the conventional model of a totalitarian one-party state. The SED is surrounded by a range of elite groups which are important to it in different ways and with which it has to deal and come to terms. The technical intelligentsia is important if the SED is to achieve its goals of economic productivity and efficiency and maintain a standard of living high enough to ensure at least the acquiescence of a majority of the populace. The cultural intelligentsia in principle is important in attaining the SED's goal of producing "socialist personalities" with appropriate values and attitudes; should this not be possible, then it is at least important to silence or export overcritical voices. The moral elite is a more curious case, over which there have been marked changes of policy since the early persecution of Christians under Ulbricht; but again a compromise has been developed which appears to have represented, at least for a time, a more stable solution than the production of a potentially hostile counterelite. And the nature of the system through which the SED has to operate to achieve its goals serves both in part to define and to limit these goals as well as to affect the solutions found for particular economic and social questions.

But to point to the ways in which the GDR diverges from a unitary model is not to assent to notions either of the convergence of industrial societies or of the rise of counterelites. In many respects the structure of elites in the GDR, as sketched above, differs from that in West Germany.[37] Moreover, the primacy of politics—while exaggerated in the totalitarian model—remains in the GDR in certain respects. The technical intelligentsia, for example, is of course essential to the efficient functioning of the regime; at the same time, it has not been allowed to take overall political control or assert undue influence, and its conditions of livelihood and input into decision-making processes have been very firmly determined by the SED. In some ways it is easier for the technical intelligentsia to come to a form of accommodation with the regime than it is for the cultural intelligentsia, or what I have termed the moral elite. Yet neither of the latter two can be seriously identified as counterelites. The moral elite can in some respects be seen as a form of countervailing power, with an (officially tolerated) alternative worldview and institutional structure; but it is a power which is co-opted by the state in a form of asymmetrical partnership that currently seems the most satisfactory arrangement for both partners. Within the state apparatus there may be tendencies toward the development of special-interest groups; but so far here too the party has remained in apparent ultimate control. No externally visible signs of a split between party and military have yet been seriously detected.

The overall picture is also one of nonalliances of non-Party elite groups in the GDR. No firm alliances seem to be developing between, say, the technical intelligentsia and the cultural intelligentsia. There do not even seem to be very widespread followings for dissenting voices within any one group, with perhaps the exception of unofficial peace initiatives in the church, perhaps due to the proximity of West Germany as a prime place of export for dissidents. Co-option by the party in different ways, depending on the nature of the different groups, appears to be the main integrating factor. These are, after all, elites of a sort under discussion: conditions of life hardly provide a material basis for major dissatisfaction, despite the limits on certain activities and views. Furthermore, certain of the permitted activities are highly valued by the different elites: leaders of the church, for example, certainly see their field of allotted endeavors as being the actually existing

37. See, for example, G. Endruweit, "Elite," in W. Langenbucher et al., eds., *Kulturpolitisches Wörterbuch: Bundesrepublik Deutschland/DDR im Vergleich* (Stuttgart: J. B. Metzler, 1983), pp. 147–51.

socialist society of the GDR and are grateful for every opportunity to exercise their pastoral and other functions; technical specialists of one sort or another may be able to derive considerable satisfaction from their work. The process is also, it should not be forgotten, two-sided: accommodations and compromises of one sort or another are made with the regime (perhaps most irksome when entailing problems of censorship, self-censorship, or being liable to prosecution for "tax offenses" when publishing abroad, in the case of the cultural intelligentsia), but at the same time these groups are able to affect and influence the regime in certain ways and to varying degrees, a fact which may make it worth their while to continue working and living in the GDR. The incorporation of these groups and the consequent relative lack of tensions or sharp fissures and opposing alignments among different elites is an important factor in attempting to explain the relative domestic stability of the GDR.

How can this pattern best be conceptualized? Ludz attempted to replace the notion of totalitarianism with that of consultative authoritarianism. This does not seem to me to be the most appropriate label for the type of system I have attempted to portray here. It is not only a question of the authoritarian party that requires and elicits feedback through a range of monitoring processes and expert advice; it is also a question of conceptualizing the dynamics of the system as a whole, including the spaces for alternative orientations and the effects on political processes of the range of groups (and not only elite ones) with which the party has to deal. The GDR is not characterized by a single unitary elite; nor is it a form of Western pluralism (itself a concept harboring a host of problematic assumptions and questions); how then can the GDR best be characterized? A preliminary suggestion might include reference to multiple co-opted elite groups subordinate to, but acting at least as limiting factors on, a relatively dominant party elite closely linked to a parallel, but not identical, party-influenced state apparatus. Perhaps more briefly: relative party domination with partial co-option of subordinate elites? How then one explains—in all the necessary range of respects—the way in which the GDR was able to develop this dynamic balance, producing on the whole a relatively stable system, must be a question for further, more detailed exploration; as must the monitoring of changes in this delicate balance, which is by no means an enduring achievement exempt from challenge.

8 POP FOUCAULTISM*

Robert Darnton

History has taken an odd turn in the last few years. The professionals cleared it of kings and queens so that they could study the play of structures and conjunctures. But the most recent run of publications suggests a new range of subjects, one stranger than the other. We have had books on the lesbian nun, the anorexic saint, the wild boy, and the pregnant man. We have had dog saints and cat massacres. We possess a whole library of works on madmen, criminals, witches, and beggars. Why this penchant for the offbeat and the marginal?[1]

I see two explanations, one literary and one political. There comes a time in the career of many historians when they yearn for contact with the general reading public. Having won a place in the profession with a dissertation and a string of scholarly publications,

* Reprinted with permission from *The New York Review of Books*. Copyright © 1986 Nyrev, Inc.

1. See, for example, Judith C. Brown, *Immodest Acts: The Life of a Lesbian Nun in Renaissance Italy* (New York: Oxford University Press, 1985); Rudolph M. Bell, *Holy Anorexia* (Chicago: University of Chicago Press, 1985); Roger Shattuck, *The Forbidden Experiment: The Story of the Wild Boy of Aveyron* (New York: Farrar, Straus, and Giroux, 1980); Roberto Zapperi, *L'uomo incito: L'uomo, la donna, e il potere* (Lerici, 1979); Jean-Claude Schmitt, *The Holy Greyhound: Guinefort Healer of Children since the Thirteenth Century* (Cambridge: Cambridge University Press, 1983); Robert Darnton, *The Great Cat Massacre and Other Episodes of French Cultural History* (New York: Basic Books, 1984; Random House/Vintage, 1985); Michel Foucault, *Madness and Civilization: A History of Insanity in the Age of Reason* (New York: Random House/Vintage, 1973); Carlo Ginzburg, *The Night Battles: Witchcraft and Agrarian Cults in the Sixteenth and Seventeenth Centuries* (Baltimore: Johns Hopkins University Press, 1984; Penguin, 1985); and Arlette Farge, *Délinquance et criminalité: Le Vol d'aliments à Paris au XVIIIe siècle* (Paris: Plon, 1974).

they want to break out of the monographic mode. They want to write for someone besides their fellow specialists. But how to reach the general reader?

They need to find the right subject, not merely something sexy like sex itself but something that can qualify as legitimate scholarship. Sheer vulgarization will not do; it must be *haute vulgarisation*, and it must involve a subject that will pass with the professionals—some curious folklore from the Middle Ages, or a strange sect of the Reformation, or a bizarre custom unearthed from the archives of the Inquisition. Best of all, it should combine elements of sexuality and popular mentality drawn from manuscript sources and served up with a dash of anthropology. Le Roy Ladurie worked a miracle with that formula.[2] Every historian who hungers for readers says to himself *in petto*, "Le Roy did it; why can't I?"

Easier said than done; for the dilemma—how to reach readers while clinging to your scholarly legitimacy—is complicated by a further consideration, which for lack of a better word I would call political.

The new subjects bear the mark of the 1960s. Before the student movements, the Vietnam War, and the "events" of May-June 1968 in Paris, historians of the Left took on large subjects—the making of a working class, the rising of a peasantry—and viewed them "from below." Their successors in the next generation favor microhistory, case studies of the deviant and the dispossessed, which they see aslant or from the side. Marginality has emerged as both a subject and a point of view.

It has its prophet, Michel Foucault, whose voice rose over the confusion of May-June to proclaim the importance of understanding the cognitive aspect of power—power as a way of ordering reality or sorting things out so that mental boundaries operate as social constraints and give shape to institutions. The victims of history for Foucault were its displaced persons, those who did not fit squarely on the cognitive map: the mad, the criminal, and the deviant. They fell outside the boundaries of the social order; but by

2. Emmanuel Le Roy Ladurie, *Montaillou: The Promised Land of Error* (New York: Random House/Vintage, 1979).

virtue of their marginality, they made the map stand out. They brought it within the range of perception of historians located in another social space.

The marginal therefore became the principal concern of history as a "discourse," a way of construing a subject on the part of the professionals. This fresh sense of subject matter gave rise to a new style of writing as well as a new way of thinking. Intransitive verbs tended to become transitive. Thus according to Foucault, madness had to be *thought* before madmen could be consigned to a special category of humanity and set apart in cells. The history of insanity took place on epistemological ground, which led from the border areas of society to the heart of its power system.[3]

When other historians looked from the outside in, they too began to rethink the past. Inclusion and exclusion, fitting and misfitting, appeared as a historical process, and the marginal moved to the center of a discipline that began to be called a discourse. The epistemological shuffling about probably would not have had much effect in itself, except that it smelled faintly of flower power; and the generation of the 1960s was quick to catch the scent. When Foucault was still undreamt of in the philosophies of the West Coast, the margins had closed in on Berkeley. Students attempted to seize power by taking over fringe areas (People's Park), approaching taboo sectors of language (the Free Speech Movement), and switching categories ("Make Love Not War"). With this experience behind them and behind their counterparts on the largely symbolic barricades of Paris in 1968, Foucault made sense.

But the sixties are gone, and Foucault is dead. We now have pop-Foucaultism, a celebration of the marginal in and of itself. The pop-Foucaultist (Foucaldien? We still lack a label.) does not pause to consider the epistemological ground of his subject. He races for the fringe or beyond it and rummages about until he comes up with something suitably exotic. So history is becoming cluttered with curiosities. It is losing its shape. Its center will not hold.

Pop-Foucaultism is a dangerous temptation for the professional seeking a public. It offers spurious intellectual legitimacy, a voguish left-wing appeal, and readers. Not that everyone who writes about madmen and criminals can be considered a follower of Foucault or

3. See Foucault, *L'ordre du discourse* (Paris: Gallimard, 1971).

that all of Foucault's followers can be indicted for vulgarization. But vulgarized Foucault, Foucault spiced up in order to be sensational and thinned out in order to be accessible, the Foucault of pop history can serve only to trivialize history in general.

Consider the case of *Damning the Innocent: A History of the Persecution of the Impotent in Pre-Revolutionary France* by Pierre Darmon, a historian who entered the profession in the 1960s and is now a *chargé de recherche* at the French Centre National de la Recherche Scientifique. According to the publishers of the English translation, the book "is intended for the general reader." According to Darmon, it is meant as a study of a neglected kind of marginality: "Among the many groups of people who suffered at the hands of the *Ancien Régime* in France—the insane, the poor, sodomites, alchemists and blasphemers—the impotent have long been forgotten." Foucault and his followers had covered nearly all the marginal areas of early modern society; but somehow they had overlooked one, which Darmon made his own: impotence.

The impotent of early modern France faced a potentially humiliating ordeal. If married and accused by their wives of being unable to fulfill their "conjugal duty," they could be brought before an ecclesiastical court and challenged to prove their virility. Proof took the form of a daunting obstacle course—erection, intromission, ejaculation—which had to be negotiated before witnesses. The most spectacular impotence trials involved "congress," that is, sexual intercourse between the spouses with a collection of midwives and surgeons hovering in the background, ready to provide expert testimony about the erectness of the penis, the dilation of the vagina, and evidence of sperm deposits.

The Catholic church sanctioned these procedures because impotence constituted one of the few grounds for annulling marriage. Some early theologians had looked favorably upon marriages without sexual relations, "fraternal cohabitation" as it was known in one of the more exotic branches of canon law, but by the thirteenth century the church linked marriage to procreation, and by the seventeenth century trial by congress provided one of the few ways for a wife to get rid of an impotent husband.

The husbands would seem to have suffered most from the ordeal. They certainly had most to lose: wife, dowry, and reputation. Yet Darmon sympathizes mainly with the wives. He writes from the viewpoint of a committed feminist and adopts a tone of moral indignation, so that "congress" appears as the cruelest form of domination in a "phallocentric" society.

What is phallocentrism? Darmon does not pause to explain this key idea, but he indicates that it goes deeper than penis envy, phallic worship, or similar afflictions. It is a kind of discourse. The French had always had sex, but from the late sixteenth century to the early nineteenth century—the classical period of Foucaultist research—they had "the putting into discourse of sex." Foucault had discovered this phenomenon and had puzzled out its basic mechanism: the elaboration of "structures of exclusion," which defined certain groups as deviant and relegated them to the margins of society.

Darmon recognized that the impotent and their wives became marginal in precisely this manner. If they did not suffer in the same way as some of their contemporaries—Protestants hanged for heresy, food rioters broken on the wheel, salt smugglers worked to death in the galleys—they deserved a prominent place among the victims of the old regime and on the agenda of Foucaultist history.

Darmon therefore set about the rehabilitation of the impotent. To Foucault he added Freud: "Deep in the shadowy unconscious of every man lurks a terrible fear of castration. The myth of virility can be seen as the sublimation of this anxiety." Behind the myth of virility, manipulating the unconscious and "damning the innocent," Darmon detected the principal power of darkness at work in the early modern world: the Catholic church. By investing all of its authority in the impotence trials, the church created an uncompromising standard of masculinity: no undersized penises, no flabby erections, no seed spilled outside the divinely ordained orifice.

According to Darmon, this policy promoted the interest of the clergy in two ways. It defended them against the imputation that they lacked virility themselves, and it provided an outlet for their "confused and murky libido" by giving them an opportunity to interfere in the sex lives of their parishioners. "In these circumstances, the [impotence] trial assumes the form of a sacrifice in the pagan sense of the term, in which the high-priest or judge unburdens himself of his neuroses by transferring them to his victim."

177

We therefore have a Voltairean gloss on a Freudian gloss on Foucault. From one end of the book to the other, Darmon vents moral outrage against the Catholic church—its "openly misogynistic philosophy," "intellectual onanism," "exacerbated voyeurism," "sadistic" delight in imposing "mental torture," and so on. The impotence trials appear as the most evil variety of priestcraft. By causing the impotent to become marginal, they created a system of sexual enslavement.

How important were they? Darmon assures us that a "tidal wave" of impotence trials hit France in the sixteenth century, yet he found evidence of only a "few dozen" cases in the archives. That did not prevent him from attempting some quantitative analysis. Upon closer inspection the few dozen cases came down to sixteen, all of them from the period 1730–88, in the papers of the ecclesiastical court of Paris. After working them over statistically, Darmon offers some conclusions about the average age and the socio-occupational position of the litigants. His main finding, an "astonishing predominance" (20 percent) of the nobility, seems to rest on three cases.

Normally, however, Darmon relies on a literary reading of the sources—a more effective technique than quantification because he is gifted with the ability to see through a text to the motivation of the person described in it. Thus his account of ecclesiastical cross-examining: "Admission did not put an end to the torture, for the ecclesiastical judge wanted to know everything about the evil afflicting the impotent husband. Relentlessly, and impelled by a kind of sadistic relish, he would ponder the smallest details."

This effect is heightened in the American edition because the translator also plays tricks with the text. On page 134 the same "learned theologian" presses five prurient questions on a hapless defendant, whereas in the French edition, page 149, the questions come from different prosecutors in five different cases. The elimination of all footnotes and of most other references makes it impossible for the reader of the English text to know the sources of the quotations—a serious problem since some passages come from court archives, some from legal treatises, and some from quasi-pornographic pamphlets, all of them scattered over several centuries and often crammed into the same paragraph. Moreover, the translation frequently deviates from the original, nearly always in a way that distorts or dramatizes. Thus *"procès et justification de la visite féminine"* becomes "the science of misogyny." But why fuss over niceties? History "intended for the general reader" can accommodate some hype.

And the general reader can regale himself with the anecdotes scattered liberally through the text. We are treated to theological inquiries on holy copulation: "'Did the Virgin Mary emit semen in the course of her relations with the Holy Spirit?'"; papal pronouncements on erêctions: "'It is necessary,' advised the Holy Father [Pius IX in 1858], 'to verify whether the penis is capable of a prompt erection which can last the time necessary for the achievement of coitus'"; and all manner of details on struggles in the marriage bed: "Hubigneau asserted that his wife, Anne Gabrielle de La Motte, 'had refused to perform her conjugal duty time after time, by adopting postures which did make it impossible for him to advance upon her.'" We follow the great debate about the testicles of the Baron d'Argenton, "which did withdraw inside his person when he turned over." We learn about narrow vaginas and elephantine penises, about hermaphrodites and eunuchs, and about the effects of horseriding on pubic hair. We read recipes for faking virginity and for casting sexual spells. We take detours through the literature on the hymen (Darmon calls it a "more or less hypothetical film" but can't seem to decide whether it exists), on the mating habits of elephants (they were believed to have such natural modesty that they copulated in private and always washed before returning to the herd), and on the cruel deflowerings of Fez (the wedding feast could not begin until the newlyweds produced a bloodstained sheet).

Some of this seems rather peripheral to the subject but then the subject belongs to the periphery. Once he makes it to the margin, the pop-Foucaultist cannot go wrong. For that is where he locates the new historical frontier, where he finds his richest lodes of material, where he feels ideologically at ease, and where he hopes to entice his readers. Caveat emptor.

9 POP FOUCAULTISM REVISITED
The Foul and the Fragrant

Simon Schama

Hold on to your homburg, Leopold von Ranke. *Scheissgeschichte* has arrived. Ten years ago, a slim volume entitled *Histoire de la Merde* was published by one Dominique Laporte; it is typical of the kind of source that Alain Corbin cites repeatedly and reverently in his own alternately brilliant and infuriating book.[1] In the self-consciously choric manner made fashionable by Foucault, Laporte called his cloacal rumination a "prologue," threatening us with a heavier outpouring. He has proved mercifully retentive. Others, however, have stepped into the, er, breach. Once there were too many books on the French Revolution. Now there are too many books on the history of sewage. Instead of histories of the body politic, we have histories of the politics of the body. Instead of the history of ideas, we have the history of emotions (of *angoisse*, of *chagrin*, and so on). Recently a history of eighteenth-century crying appeared. Whatever else its significance, its publication means that, according to the ranking list of twenty bodily secretions compiled by the authors of *End Product: The First Taboo* (1977), there are only eighteen types of effluvia still available for distribution as topics of doctoral theses to students of the Ecole des Hautes Etudes en Sciences Sociales.

This is probably not what was meant when, in the heroic days of social history (long since passed), historians were commanded to write "from the bottom up." But the history of shit is, in some

---

1. Alain Corbin, *The Foul and the Fragrant: Odor and the French Social Imagination* (Oxford: Berg and Cambridge, Mass: Harvard University Press, 1986).

sense, the terminal outcome of the injunction to practice "*histoire totale*"—that is, the history of absolutely everything. In founding the *Annales*, the vanguard of a "new" social history, in 1929, Lucien Febvre and Marc Bloch stigmatized the history of political elites and institutions as blinkered and partial. But their counterinjunction to embrace the totality of past experience has, in the end, led to an equally callow positivism: the positivism of the historically indiscriminate.

Social historians for whom Everything is fair subject matter are alarmed by the notion that not Everything may be historically constructed. More seriously, not Everything may show sufficiently striking variations over time to be worth historical discussion. One need not be a sociobiologist to speculate about whether there are not some human and social arrangements (important ones at that) in which perennial constraints and impulses prevail over cultural variations and differences. Consider family affection, now a favorite topic of the new generation of social historians. From the prodigious quantity of research expended on the subject of parent-child relations, it now appears that in any given period of Western European history there are likely to have been children who were treated (a) affectionately; (b) instrumentally; (c) brutally; or (d) any permutation of the above. Whether the dominant culture's institutional sanctions affected the prevalence of cruelty or tenderness in any particular period is virtually impossible to say.

Shrugging off the awful possibility that many of our everyday affairs might not have changed over time, at least in any way that makes good history and interesting reading, historians have rushed in the opposite direction. They are now eager to invest any and every alteration of sensibility with immense significance. To ward off the banality of the continuum, "revolution," that jackpot of the historical measurement of magnitude, is awarded to phenomena that might otherwise not seem to qualify. So that we now have cultural revolutions in nose blowing, and shopping, and, in Corbin's case, cesspool clearing. The history of the senses has been peculiarly (and aptly) prone to this kind of sensationalism. It was Febvre who asserted, in the best work of history ever written on a nonproblem (the imputation of atheism to Rabelais), that sixteenth-century European culture was blinkered by an underdeveloped sense of sight. Albrecht Dürer would have been interested to hear this. Yet the poetic allusiveness with which the observation was delivered masked its empirical silliness.

"Revolutions" appear with gratuitous regularity to dull the brilliance of Corbin's book. He, too, is bent on rescuing the history of the senses from the dead hands of relativism and perennialism, by giving the history of olfactory thresholds in France its own peculiar and dramatically marked out chronology. Corbin argues that an indiscriminate tolerance of filth and stench (especially of human waste) was suddenly transformed, by scientific fears that putrid vapors were life-threatening, into the feeling that these conditions were unbearably obnoxious. Around the third quarter of the eighteenth century, sensibilities that had coped with the pungent ooze of the human cheese started to gag and to heave. One result, richly documented in the book, was the brief ascendancy of a science devoted to the classification of dangerous odors. It created the working data for the more enduring reign of social sanitation.

Corbin's book departs from this relatively well-known history, however, to make a much more ambitious claim. The threat posed by the unsavory aromas of the urban masses was so great that it made all animal essences repellent, especially those extracted—like civet, musk, and ambergris—from the mammals' meatier regions. In their place, as a kind of social pomander to distance the elite from the sweating poor they feared, bouquets of floral scents were produced. Their purpose was to effect an idyllic transformation of the urban dunghill into a perpetually vernal garden. The perfumes of Paris were born, then, from the same knee-knocking bourgeois trepidations that are now said to have produced most of the consumer diversions we associate with the nineteenth-century city: the department store, the *grand boulevard*, the public park, the *café-concert*, and so on.

If this kind of argument sounds vaguely familiar, it should. In most of its essentials, the scenario was written by Michel Foucault, whose great and ominous shade looms darkly over this book and whose theory of modernization is rapidly taking on the status of an unexamined dogma. According to this received wisdom, bourgeois culture is always neurotically defensive. Pleasures that we might suppose to be casually adopted to gratify the epicurean hunger of the senses are said instead to be marshaled like an army against the oncoming hosts of class panic. And by the same token, the notion of a value-free empirical science is seen as another mystification, manufactured in the service of social domination.

For knowledge, we are to read power; for liberty, confinement; for therapy, control; for sanitation, segregation.

While Corbin obediently toes the line on urban bourgeois culture, it would be unjust to classify his book as merely a variation on the Foucauldean theme (played ever more relentlessly by urban historians). His argument is too subtle, his material too complex, his syntheses of the history of science with the history of cultural practice too elegant to be shunted into some little league of Foucault epigones. In his account, for example, the manipulative and self-serving aspects of the scientific inquiry into contamination and bad air are more gently treated. And it is very much to the credit of the book that his astonishing (and often hilarious) account of the culture of social cleansing—from learned calculations of the height and weight of excremental vapor columns produced by the average person's diet to the deodorization of the formidable carcass of Louis XVIII with lime chloride—never descends to sneering. Much of this history, especially that of the experiments with captive populations in prisons, hospitals, and naval stations, is well-known, particularly from the English sources on which Corbin more or less exclusively relies when he strays beyond France. But the story has never been told so brilliantly, nor with such verve and perceptiveness. That alone would make Corbin's book worth reading, but one may read it as well for a deeper understanding of the roots of modern urban anxieties about the unwholesome.

Yet if *The Foul and the Fragrant* surpasses Foucault in its eye for historically telling evidence and much improves on Foucault in its polemical reticence, its thesis suffers from some of the same blemishes. For a historian so finely attuned to the guile of language, Corbin is often very naughty with it. (Poststructuralists, as a crowd, are exasperatingly oblivious to the way in which their resort to items of trade vocabulary like "strategies" and that fatuous buzzword "discourse" instantly loads their descriptions with self-importance.) In Corbin's history, for example, the word "obsession" is used insistently to describe what, by the standards of the day, were perfectly rational preoccupations with the relationship between bad air, foul water, and death. His use of the term persuades by sheer accumulation that it is the protagonists, and not the historian, who are obsessed.

Occasionally the lure of hyperbole takes over completely. Not only, we are told, were "the ruling classes . . . obsessed with excretion," but "excrement now *determined* [my emphasis] social perceptions." And to prove this point Corbin wheels out the "dung man," "impregnated with excrement," as though the term were commonly used by contemporaries to describe the threat of the filthy poor. In fact the "dung man" seems to be a coinage of the author's. And there are other problems. When Corbin claims about the end of the fashion of wearing musk-scented gloves that "there is a vast amount of evidence on this subject," we must take him on trust, since he cites only one contemporary source. Havelock Ellis is cited on this and other similar matters (such as the sexuality of floral scent) as though he were a dependable historical witness. Sometimes, in the manner of Febvre, a cultural judgment is delivered with a kind of airy panache in inverse proportion to its sense, as with the observation that "the interiors of Tiepolo's paintings corresponded to the inarticulate expression of a new sensitivity to smell." Which Tiepolo can possibly be meant here, since the *interiors* of neither of the contenders (Gian-Domenico is the likelier) exactly spring to mind to support the analogy? And can one really trust a book on the history of smell that seems to think buttercups are scented?

All this would be trifling, except that the slips here and there build into a serious doubt about the entire chronology of Corbin's argument. For, as with all of Foucault's followers, Corbin shares the assumption that in some decisive way the modern world came into being in the century between 1750 and 1850. Foucault himself was weakest in his characterization of the early modern world, which he thought of as some sort of primordial historical soup in which there floated the bits and pieces of modern culture, waiting for the Enlightenment to systematize them into a cultural alphabet. It is typical of this reinvention of time that Corbin should imply that it was only when the thresholds of tolerance for dirt were lowered that Jews were regarded as "filthy individuals" with an "unpleasant odor." In fact, the *foetor judaicus* was one of the most ancient and persistent of all anti-Semitic demonologies in Western Europe. But perennialism is the enemy of "revolutions."

In other respects too Corbin's chronology is muddled enough to jeopardize his entire argument. The cult of nature was, of course, both the product and the cause of the Romantic discovery of sensibility in the 1760s and 1770s, predating the great onslaught on urban filth that began in the 1780s and continued for at least a century. No doubt the two phenomena were linked in their rejection of modern urbanity. But cause and effect are not as certainly connected as Corbin believes. More seriously, the distinction between a premodern nose savoring heavy animal scents and a modern nose inhaling the delights of the *jardin fleuri* is very much less clear-cut than Corbin suggests. In fact, the evidence for the disuse of civet, musk, and ambergris in the nineteenth century is very thin. If they were used more sparingly in commercially produced perfume, it was at least as obviously due to their considerably greater expense in comparison with the more prolific floral essences.

These perfumes, moreover, far from suddenly coming into their own in the nineteenth century, had been a staple since the Renaissance, when amateur alchemists and virtuosi experimented with combinations of attar of rose, jasmine, lavender, orange blossom, and violets. Far from being an invention of the modern world, the exquisite scent of spring narcissus was brought to Europe by Islam (along with many of its other sensuous pleasures). It was widely known and used in the early modern world. For example, Constantijn Huygens, the great Baconian scientist, poet statesman, and composer of Holland, used it in his experiments with scenting leather, paper, and delicate cloth in the 1630s and 1640s.

To say as much is not to play the dreary game, practiced by too many historians, of trumping the century. ("You imagine *your* century invented this! Poor dear, *my* century was there long, long before.") But it is to raise serious questions about a necessary chronology according to which modern scents exuding their vernal blossoms are the inexorable consequence of urban sanitary defenses against fecal waste. Oddly enough, the much more evocative French title of Corbin's book, *Le Miasme et la jonquille*,[2] echoes those famous structuralist oxymorons of Lévi-Strauss: *The Raw and the Cooked, Honey and Ashes* and, most wonderfully, *La Pensée sauvage* (Wild Pansy as well as Savage Mind). Structuralism—the bugbear of Foucault's historicism—presupposed a kind of partnership be-

---

2. Originally published in Paris by Editions Aubier Montaigne, 1982.

tween value systems and codes of behavior, which appeared to contradict each other but actually were symbiotically interdependent. Against this, a kind of dialectical hegemonism has become the established norm of recent sociocultural history, in which the inchoate early modern world is subjected to merciless Enlightenment social controls and then presented as the cultural ideology of bourgeois supremacy. One world is obliterated by the other.

But flowers and shit have always had a more ambiguous relationship. That oldest of intensely scented roses, the musk rose (which is, by the way, a conceptual impossibility under Corbin's scheme), is, by designation, both animal and floral at the same time. Saint-Simon complained of the ghastly reek of urine and feces at Versailles, but he understood that it was the prelude, as it were, to stepping outside to the parterre and inhaling the blossoms arrayed in Mansart's monumental Orangerie. "Night soil" as a source of profit was also not an invention of the bourgeois nineteenth century. In most European cities it passed to the hands of contractors, who in turn took it to the market gardens of the Dutch countryside or the Kentish weald, where it was turned into blooms and vegetables to nourish the burgeoning city population, which in digesting the food in turn produced more manure.

If it ultimately fails as argument, however, Corbin's book is a tour de force as chronicle. This is not faint praise, for the axiom that history is "an argument without end" has become miserably stale in the mechanical countersuggestibilities of the learned journals. Though he may well be horrified by the idea, Corbin's special brilliance lies in his narration, a gift never more stunningly demonstrated than in the opening passages of the book, where the reader accompanies the first professor of public hygiene in Paris on an olfactory tour of the most gruesome city cesspools. But when the professorial voice takes over, after this coloratura passage, and we are told that "it is also necessary to relate divergent modes of perception to social structures" and that "abhorrence of smells produces its own form of social power," the stale aroma of the academy begins to form above the bright prose like a scholarly smog.

If Corbin's book is slightly less than it means to be, Patrick Süskind's novel *Perfume* is more than it seems.[3] And the two books do, it turns out, share more than the (admittedly amazing) accident of their shared subject matter of the history of smell. If Corbin's book is a tract on social power, in the pleasing form of a chronicle about olfactory perception, Süskind's novel is a fable about the Enlightenment in the guise of a gothic fantasy. Both are histories. Süskind, who studied history in Munich, has provided one of the very best accounts of the topography, the social flavor, and the material life of eighteenth-century Paris to be found anywhere, inside or outside historical scholarship. He has quite obviously assimilated not only the great contemporary accounts—by Sébastien Mercier, Réstif de la Bretonne, and the like—but also a great deal of recent scholarship on a great variety of topics from wet nursing to the postal system of the ancien régime. He gets straight A's for his social history. More important, he does so without the footnotes swarming over the narrative like a plague of flies.

Süskind the novelist, moreover, is happily free of the obligations of Foucault-decreed cultural chronology. But he is no historical innocent. In place of Corbin's repulsive stinks, he gives us a repulsive stinker. Or rather, a nonstinker, since Grenouille, the monster of the story, gives off no odor himself, though he was born with the most finely tuned nostrils in the world. This formidable apparatus serves, in effect, as his esprit—as his wits and his senses combined; it is his only means of navigation through a world he innately despises. Able to tolerate only disembodied smells, he fortuitously discovers a perfume so heady that its essence, if captured, would provide the base for a scent of overwhelming potency and sweetness. So he disembodies it—from the freshly murdered corpse of a young virgin. After a spell of mystical self-annunciation, Grenouille ends up in Grasse, where he stocks up overliberally with this hot property, after which the story and its antihero go over the top and then steeply downhill.

Süskind's book is much more ambitious than its gripping gothic plot suggests. Grenouille is invented in the double image of the cultural world into which he is summarily deposited. He is the

3. Patrick Süskind, *Perfume: The Story of a Murderer* (London: Hamish Hamilton and New York: Alfred A. Knopf, 1986). Originally published as *Das Parfum: Die Geschichte eines Mörders*, (Zürich: Diogenes Verlag, 1985).

perfect acolyte of the Enlightenment's belief in the world as a machine, of humanity as a bundle of sensory and chemical matter (*l'homme machine*) that could be made to react in predictable ways through the administration of organized knowledge. The deists have demoted God to the status of the Great Clockmaker, and Grenouille becomes a little god, a Supreme Mechanic of the Nose. Through the Ultimate Olfactory Filing System he comes to believe that he too can create a disembodied essence of Humanity. Unlike the materialist and mechanist philosophes, however, Grenouille is a misogynist rather than a benefactor—an extreme case of scientific dispassion.

And yet there also stirs within him the budding counter-Enlightenment urge to become some sort of human "I." Without the Romantic suspension of disbelief and without the innate gifts of Nature, he is obliged to manufacture a synthetic nature from the materials of his accumulated expertise. In the end he is a victim of his own success at supplying an olfactory version of the sublime. In the admittedly rather overstretched climax, Grenouille surrenders himself contemptuously to the crowd, which has been deceived by his perfume into imagining a humanity that might be fragrant.

The eccentrically beautiful prose of *Perfume* is itself an alchemical shop of images of the Enlightenment—its fixation with process (set out, for example, in the engravings of the *Encyclopédie*) and the codification of acquired knowledge and its relentless search for an improved version of Homo sapiens. Among the novel's most memorable creations is the Master Perfumer (working, as Süskind accurately represents, with *both* floral and animal essences), depressed by his inability to keep pace with the speed of changing fashion. In a very important passage, Grenouille as *sauvage* becomes the protégé of a crackpot marquis philosophe. His conviction that air breathed from close to the rotting earth was the source of modern ills is much less bizarre than a great deal of what actually passed for scientific speculation at the end of the eighteenth century. (It is close, too, to many of the working theories of "miasma" reviewed by Corbin.)

Perfume, then, is argument by narrative insinuation and historical parable. Leading us by the nose through a highly specified time and place, it manages to engage with matters of universal significance:

essence and existence, sense and spirit. That it should do so in the form of a stunningly imagined chronicle is of great importance, since it adds to a growing list of profound works of fiction and brilliantly executed works of imagination that use history in ways wholly compatible with what "professionals" suppose to be the recovery of an authentic past.

The great historical novels of our time are not to be found in the ponderous costume epics that fall off the airport book racks. (These merely mirror the pathetic fallacies of the twentieth century.) They are to be found, rather, in works like Carlos Fuentes's *Terra Nostra*, Graham Swift's *Waterland*, Umberto Eco's *The Name of the Rose*, Salman Rushdie's *Midnight's Children*, and now Patrick Süskind's *Perfume*. These books go beyond historical decor to grapple with the elusive poignancies of time, memory, and persistence. Historians sometimes imagine fondly that the indeterminate boundaries between fantasy, historical narrative, and authorial argument in all these works set them sharply aside from their own "scientific" endeavors to recover the past *wie ist eigentlich gewesen*. But if the rise of a new kind of historical novel does nothing else than dispose of these childish relics of a collapsed positivism, they will have been worth the writing. Meanwhile they stand as an urgent reminder that in a present where the past has a dauntingly short shelf life, history is becoming too important to leave to the historians.

SELECT BIBLIOGRAPHY
AND SCHOLARLY RESOURCES

FRANCE AND GERMANY: HISTORICAL
BACKGROUND AND GENERAL

For France, the eight-volume Cambridge History of Modern France provides detailed and authoritative coverage of the past two centuries. For a single volume that provides a good bibliographical discussion, see Gordon Wright, *France in Modern Times, 1760 to the Present* (New York: Norton Books, 1978). The late Alfred Cobban's three-volume *A History of Modern France* is lively, but it ventures few conclusions about the Fifth Republic.

For the political structure and institutions of France, see Henry Ehrmann, *Politics in France* (Boston: Little Brown, and Co., 1983) and Vincent Wright, *The Government and Politics of France* (London: Hutchinson, 1983). Rightly described as "a mine of information," D. L. Hanley, A. P. Kerr, and H. N. Waites in *Contemporary France: Politics and Society since 1945* (London: Routledge and Kegan Paul, 1984) also provides a superb bibliography. For social and economic issues, see M. Parodi, *L'Economie et la société française depuis 1945* (Paris: Colin, 1981).

For the 1980s, John Ardagh has updated his wide-ranging *France in the 1980s* (1982) to *France Today* (New York: Penguin, 1987). Daniel Singer, *Is Socialism Doomed? The Meaning of Mitterrand* (New York: Oxford University Press, 1988), is an informed survey, as well as an indictment, of recent Socialist policies. For a succinct overview of France in the 1980s and previous postwar political developments, see Jane Jensen and George Ross, "The Tragedy of the French Left," *New Left Review* 171 (September/October 1988), 5–44. Consult the bibliographies below for specific topics in the 1980s. For the French character, Theodore Zeldin, well known for his *France, 1848–1945*, takes up contemporary French mores and culture in *The French* (New York: Pantheon, 1983). It also has an outstanding bibliography.

On German history, the modern period is well covered by combining Gordon Craig's *Germany, 1866–1945* (New York: Oxford University Press, 1978) with his broader sweeping survey *The Germans* (New York: Putnam, 1982). Hajo Holborn's three-volume *History of Modern Germany* (New York: Alfred Knopf, 1970) covers the period from the Reformation to the end of World War II.

For a concise treatment of twentieth-century Germany, with useful statistical tables and chronologies, see V. R. Berghahn, *Modern Germany* (Cambridge: Cambridge University Press, 1987). For the postwar Germanies, see Henry A. Turner, *The Two Germanies since 1945* (New Haven: Yale University Press, 1987). John Ardagh's *Germany and the Germans* (New York: Harper & Row, 1987) imitates the freewheeling style of his books on contemporary French civilization.

For bibliographies on recent Germany, see Gisela Hersch, *A Bibliography of German Studies, 1945–1971* (Bloomington: University of Indiana Press, 1972); Dietrich Thranhardt, *Bibliographie Bundesrepublik Deutschland* (Göttingen: Vandenhoeck und Ruprecht, 1980); and the periodical *Bibliographie zur Zeitgeschichte*, which covers Germany East and West. H.-U. Wehler has produced three useful bibliographies in a series for Vandenhoeck und Ruprecht, *Bibliographie zur Imperialismus* (1977), *Bibliographie zur modernen deutschen Sozialgeschichte* (1976), and *Bibliographie zur modernen deutschen Wirtschaftsgeschichte* (1976). See below for more listings on the GDR.

CHAPT. 1   MUNICH

For the most comprehensive bibliography, consult the standard account of the Munich accords, Telford Taylor, *Munich: The Price of Peace* (New York: Vintage, 1980 [1979]).

For additional background and other perspectives, see Keith Middlemas, *The Strategy of Appeasement* (1972) and Gerhard Weinberg, *The Foreign Policy of Hitler's Germany*, 2 vols. (1970 and 1980);

volume 2 has chapters on the Czech crisis and the undoing of Munich. Among the early pack of writings on Munich, the most authoritative remains John Wheeler-Bennett, *Munich: Prologue to Tragedy* (1948).

Gordon Martel, ed., *The Origins of the Second World War—The AJP Taylor Debate after 25 Years* (Boston: Allen & Unwin, 1986) ignites controversy over interwar diplomacy; see especially Paul Kennedy's reflections on appeasement.

For a recent essay that challenges the meaning of Munich from another perspective of the American Left, see Gene H. Bell-Villada, "No More Munichs," *Monthly Review* (April 1988): 9–21. Johnstone in her essay makes ample reference to *Telos* (Spring 1982), which sides with the conventional wisdom in France on Munich.

From a more mainstream perspective Ernest R. May, *"Lessons" of the Past* (New York: Oxford University Press, 1973), explores the misuse of the Munich analogy in the postwar world (chapter 2). His account does not discuss the conference itself.

For an early discussion of the rise of a "revisionist" school on Munich, see D. C. Watt, "Appeasement: The Rise of a Revisionist School?" *Political Quarterly* 36, no. 2 (April 1965). For a recent article on the "lessons" of Munich that rejects revisionism, consult Gerhard Weinberg's reflections in the Fall 1988 edition of *Foreign Affairs*.

CHAPT. 2 MAY '68

For France, Daniel Singer has provided the following selective bibliography:

For the student side of the crisis see *La Sorbonne par elle-même* (Paris: Les Éditions Ouvrières, 1968) and the major documentary source: Alain Schnapp and Pierre Vidal-Naquet, eds., *Journal de la commune étudiante* (Paris: Éditions du Seuil, 1969) translated into English as *The French Student Uprising* (Boston: Beacon Press, 1971).

There is nothing comparable for the strikes. One must consult the newspapers and journals of the period, notably the useful work carried immediately after by the *Cahiers de Mai*. In book form, there is *La grève à Flins*; *Notre Arme c'est la grève (la grève chez Renault-Cléon)*; and Yannick Guin, *La Commune de Nantes*, all three published as *cahiers libres* by François Maspero in Paris, the first two in 1968, the third in 1969. (In the same series, *Ce n'est qu'un début continuons le combat* [Paris, 1968], on the 22d of March Movement.)

For views of participants see Jacques Sauvageot, Alain Geismar, Daniel Cohn-Bendit, and Jean-Pierre Duteuil, *La Revolte étudiante* (Paris: Seuil, 1968) and Cohn-Bendit, *Le Gauchisme remède à la maladie sénile du communisme* (Paris: Seuil, 1968).

For the trotskyist view, see Daniel Bensaid and Henri Weber, *Mai 1968: Une répétition générale* (Paris: François Maspero, 1968).

For the CP view see René Andrieu, *Les Communistes et la révolution* (Paris: Julliard, 1968) and Georges Séguy, *"Le Mai" de la CGT* (Paris: Julliard, 1972).

For (sympathetic) comments see Edgar Morin, Claude Lefort, and Jean-Marie Coudray, *Mai 1968—la brèche* (Paris: Fayard, 1968); Epistemon, *Ces idées qui ont ebranlé la France* (Paris: Fayard, 1968); Henri Lefebvre, *L'irruption de Nanterre au sommet* (Paris: Editions Anthropos, 1968), translated into English as *The Explosion, Marxism, and the French Upheaval,* (New York: Monthly Review Press, 1969); Alain Touraine, *Le Mouvement de Mai ou le communisme utopique* (Paris: Seuil, 1968).

For a hostile assessment see Raymond Aron, *La révolution introuvable* (Paris: Fayard, 1968). For fun, for the view of a new philosopher at the time, see André Glucksmann, *Strategie et revolution en France, 1968* (Paris: Christian Bourgois, 1968).

For cultural background consult *Internationale situationiste, 1958–69* (Paris: Editions Champ Libre, 1975).

For confirmation of the events from the other side see Maurice Grimaud, *En Mai fais ce qu'il te plait* (Paris: Stock, 1977). (The author was prefect of police in May.)

Amid the books published for commemoration see Herve Hamon and Patrick Rotman, *Génération*, 2 vols. (Paris: Seuil, 1987–88). The first volume provides background for leaders of the movement; the second deals with the years after 1968, particularly with the Maoists. Based on interviews with leaders, gossipy, lively, it has the defects of its quality. It is history from above, through personalities, as reliable as the interviews themselves and their selection. The second volume, in particular, reveals the biases of the authors.

For general works covering 1968 not only in France, but also throughout Western Europe and beyond: David Caute, *1968: Year of the Barricades* (New York: Harper & Row, 1988); Ronald Fraser, et al., *1968: A Student Generation in Revolt* (New York: Pantheon, 1988), a superb oral history, by arguably the best contemporary practitioner of this genre, it also provides insightful analysis and a useful chronology; George Katsiaficas, *The Imagination of the New Left: A Global Analysis of 1968* (Boston: South End Press, 1987).

For Germany see Jürgen Miermeister and Joachim Staadt, *Provoka-tionen: Die Studenten-und-Jugende-Revolte in ihren Flugblattern* (1980) and Miermeister's biographical *Rudi Dutschke* (1986). For the best account of the long-term significance of these movements for contemporary German politics, see Werner Hulsberg, *The German Greens* (London: Verso, 1988).

CHAPT. 3 THE *HISTORIKERSTREIT*

Readers are urged to turn to Charles S. Maier's *The Unmasterable Past: History, Holocaust, and German National Identity* (Cambridge, Mass.: Harvard University Press, 1988).

The literature on the *Historikerstreit* is growing rapidly, but the following are the standard volumes on the subject: Dan Diner, ed., *Ist der Nationalsocialismus Geschichte? Zu Historisierung und Histori-kerstreit* (Frankfurt/Main: Fischer Verlag, 1987); Hilmar Hoffmann, ed., *Gegen den Versuch: Vergangenheit zu verbiegen* (Frankfurt/Main: Athenaeum Verlag, 1987); Reinhard Kuehnl, ed., *Vergangenheit, die nicht vergeht: Die "Historiker-Debatte" Dokumentationen, Darstellung, und Kritik* (Cologne: Pahl-Rugenstein Verlag, 1987); and Ernst Reinhard Piper, ed., *"Historikerstreit": Die Dokumentationen der Kontroverse um die Einzigartigkeit der nationalsozialistischen Judenver-nichtung* (Munich: Piper Verlag, 1987).

Maier's work in this issue, as well as that of Saul Friedländer, Jürgen Kocka, David Schoenbaum, and Andrei Markovits, can be found in the February 1988 issue of *German Politics and Society*, available from the Center for European Studies, Harvard Univer-sity. Particularly noteworthy in this collection is Markovits's ex-cellent survey of the literature on the *Historikerstreit*, marred only by his zeal to equate critics of Zionism on the German Left with the anti-Semites of the traditional Right.

Among the more valuable of recent interventions is Geoff Eley, "Nazism, Politics, and the Image of the Past," *Past and Present*

(November 1988): 171–208, which provides a wealth of biblio-graphic resources, despite the author's apology that his footnotes were chopped in half by the editors.

CHAPT. 4   FRENCH AND GERMAN SOCIAL THEORY

Consult Mark Poster's footnotes and scholarly apparatus for a survey of the important texts on poststructuralism and Habermas.

Three books cited by Professor Poster are particularly worthy of commentary. Peter Dews's *Logics of Disintegration* (1987), a work that in its early stages informed Perry Anderson's critique of poststructuralism, favors the Frankfurt currents over Foucault and Derrida, contrary to Poster. A Poster-Dews debate might be shaping up, the lines finely drawn in *Logics of Disintegration* and in Poster's contribution above.

For background on Habermas, the most authoritative study is Thomas McCarthy's *The Critical Theory of Jürgen Habermas* (1978); the interviews with Habermas assembled by Dews in *Autonomy and Solidarity* (1986) are helpful in providing further context.

For general background on critical theory, see David Held, *Introduction to Critical Theory: Horkheimer to Habermas* (Berkeley: University of California Press, 1980). Martin Jay in *Marxism and Totality* (Berkeley: University of California Press, 1985), especially in chapter 15 and the epilogue, takes up Habermas and his relation-ship to Marxism and poststructuralism. For a sampling of Jay's recent interventions on Habermas, Gadamer, and other seminal figures of European intellectual life, see his latest collection, *Fin de Siecle Socialism and Other Essays* (New York: Routledge, 1988).

Those readers having little acquaintance with French poststruc-turalist thought should probably be cautious about consulting the earlier masterworks of traditional intellectual historians; that is, even the best practitioner of this genre, H. Stuart Hughes, in his excellent trilogy on European and American intellectual thought, *Consciousness and Society* (1958), *The Obstructed Path* (1968), and *The Sea Change* (1975), concluded in the middle work that poststructur-alism would have little or no influence beyond France. Previously Colin Smith, in his *Contemporary French Philosophy* (1964), failed even to mention Saussure in his tracing of influences on French thought. Much more satisfying in this regard is Vincent Descombes' *Modern French Philosophy* (Cambridge: Cambridge University Press, 1980), obviously benefiting from the additional decade of historical hindsight.

For both the novice and the expert, two books that give valuable background and perspective include John Sturrock, ed., *Structuralism and Since* (Oxford: Oxford University Press, 1979) and Terry Eagleton, *Literary Theory: An Introduction* (Minneapolis: University of Minnesota Press, 1983). Both of these are helpful in unpacking the relationship between earlier structuralisms and poststructuralisms. A forewarning: Eagleton has become especially combative contra Derrida, though he expresses a grudging admiration for Foucault. There is a burgeoning literature on Foucault, including Poster's own insightful study. In the 1980s Deleuze, Dreyfus and Rabinow, Lemert and Gillan, Smart, Rajchman, and Sheridan have each contributed books on this thinker.

For a book that grapples with the transition from modernism to postmodernism, identifying the salience of aestheticism in the latter, see Alan Megill, *Prophets of Extremity: Nietzsche, Heidegger, Foucault, Derrida* (Berkeley: University of California Press, 1985). A complex but forceful commentator on recent intellectual history is Dominick LaCapra; see his *Rethinking Intellectual History: Texts, Contexts, Language* (Ithaca: Cornell University Press, 1983).

CHAPT. 5 FRENCH FOREIGN POLICY

Consult Jolyon Howorth's footnotes.

Among the contributors to this book, see Singer's chapters on Mitterrand's foreign policy in *Is Socialism Doomed?* (1988) and especially Diana Johnstone's *The Politics of Euromissiles* (1984). For recent French foreign-policy developments elsewhere, see Johnstone, "What's Playing in the Mediterranean Theatre: French Scenarios," *Zeta Magazine* (January 1988): 37–42.

Among the most important commentators on French foreign policy is Stanley Hoffmann; his most recent meditations can be found in George Ross, Stanley Hoffmann, and Sylvia Malzacher, eds., *The Mitterrand Experiment* (Oxford: Polity Press, 1987).

Howorth's essay is predicated on the decline of "consensus" among the contending parties in France. For an essay written close to the heyday of the "achievement" of "consensus," see Edward Kolodziej, "Socialist France Faces the World," *Contemporary French*

Civilization 8, nos. 1 & 2 (Fall/Winter 1983–84). Kolodziej's conclusion: "There appears to be no marked departure from the policy paths of preceding Rightist regimes."

CHAPT. 6 AND 7 THE GDR AND *PERESTROIKA*; ELITES AND POLITICS IN THE GDR

For ongoing developments in the GDR, consult the journals *Labour Focus on Eastern Europe* (3 issues per year; enquiries to Berg Publishers Ltd, 77 Morrell Avenue, Oxford OX4 1NQ, England) and *Across Frontiers* ($10 for 4 issues, PO Box 2382, Berkeley, CA 94702). *Labour Focus* provides intellectual commentary on Central and Eastern Europe (the Medvedevs, the Hallidays, Minnerup, et al.) and some primary documentation. *Across Frontiers* is valuable for its recovery and translation of primary documents from critical and dissident currents.

Books of note on the GDR include Jonathan Steele's slightly dated *Socialism with a German Face* (1977). Steele, Moscow correspondent for *The Guardian* (UK), is among the premier commentators on Eastern Europe. David Childs, *The GDR: Moscow's German Ally* (1983; rev. edn 1988), Günter Minnerup, *DDR: Vor und hinter der Mauer* (1982), and Martin McCauley, *The German Democratic Republic since 1945* (1983) cover developments till the end of the Brezhnev era. See also Childs, ed., *Honecker's Germany* (1985) and A. James McAdams, *East Germany and Detente* (1985).

On the question of the class and power structure in the Eastern bloc, readers are urged to turn to Part 8 of Anthony Giddens and David Held, *Classes, Power, and Conflict: Classical and Contemporary Debates* (Berkeley: University of California Press, 1982). While most of the selections (Parkin, Nove, Yanowitch, and Garnsey) are preoccupied with Soviet society, the conceptual issues are germane to GDR society. Also provides a valuable bibliographical listing of the most important works on class and power in the East: i.e., Bahro, Konrad, Szelenyi, Bettleheim, and Brus.

CHAPT. 8 AND 9 POP FOUCAULTISM; POP FOUCAULTISM REVISITED

Darnton's and Schama's essays are not designed to do justice to Foucault's contribution to historiography, but rather to call attention to abuses by some of its practitioners. For readers seeking a wider context on historical trends in the postwar world, see Georg Iggers, *New Directions in European Historiography* (Middletown: Wesleyan University Press, 1983). For a specific critique of the historical trajectory of Foucault's thought, with reflections on Chomsky's and Said's differences with the French philosophe, consult the often inelegant but perceptive analysis of Jim Merod, *The Political Responsibility of the Critic* (Ithaca: Cornell University Press, 1987).

LIST OF CONTRIBUTORS

ROBERT DARNTON, a graduate of Harvard and Oxford, is Professor of History at Princeton University. He has written numerous books, including *Mesmerism and the End of the Enlightenment in France*, *The Business of Enlightenment: A Publishing History of the Encyclopedie*, *The Literary Underground of the Old Regime*, and *The Great Cat Massacre and Other Episodes of French Cultural History*. He is a frequent contributor to *The New York Review of Books*.

MARY FULBROOK teaches at the Department of German, University College, London. She is author of *Piety and Politics: Religion and the Rise of Absolutism in England, Württemberg, and Prussia*, and she recently contributed an essay on Perry Anderson to Theda Skocpol's *Vision and Method in Historical Sociology*.

JOLYON HOWORTH is Professor of French at the University of Bath. He has contributed several books and articles on French defense and foreign affairs, including essays that have appeared in *Foreign Policy* and the *Journal of European Nuclear Disarmament*.

DIANA JOHNSTONE is European correspondent for the American weekly *In These Times* and the monthly *Zeta Magazine*. Her articles have been published in *Le Monde Diplomatique* and *The New Statesman*. In 1984 she wrote *The Politics of Euromissiles*. Based in Paris, she is a respected commentator on such diverse topics as defense issues, European integration, the history of

Eurocommunism, and the politics of the New Left.

CHARLES S. MAIER is Professor of History at Harvard University. He is the author of *Recasting Bourgeois Europe*, a study of the interwar years, and is currently researching the postwar reconstruction of Europe. His latest work is *The Unmasterable Past*.

GÜNTER MINNERUP is Senior Lecturer in German Studies, Portsmouth Polytechnic. His articles and books have appeared in several European languages, and he serves as editor of the journal, *Labour Focus on Eastern Europe*.

MARK POSTER is Professor of History at the University of California/Irvine. His prolific output on European intellectual history includes books on existential Marxism in France, Foucault, and the family. He has recently edited a collection of the writings of Jean Baudrillard.

SIMON SCHAMA is Professor of History at Harvard University. He is author of two studies of Dutch history, *Patriots and Liberators* and *The Embarrassment of Riches*. His latest book is a narrative of the French Revolution, *Citizens*.

DANIEL SINGER is European correspondent for *The Nation* and a frequent contributor to *Monthly Review*. He is an expert not only on France, but also on Eastern Europe. His books include *Prelude to Revolution*, *The Road to Gdansk*, and *Is Socialism Doomed? The Meaning of Mitterrand*.

INDEX